Designing Family Support Programs

To my husband Roger who provided so much support in our years together. You were the wind beneath my wings.

Designing Family Support Programs

Building Children, Family
and Community Resilience

Margaret Sims

COMMON
GROUND

This book is published at theLearner.com
a series imprint of theUniversityPress.com

First published in Australia in 2002
by Common Ground Publishing Pty Ltd
PO Box 463
Altona VIC 3018
ABN 66 074 822 629
www.theLearner.com

National Library of Australia Cataloguing-in-Publication data:

Sims, Margaret C.
Designing family support programs : building children,
family and community resilience.

ISBN 1 86335 105 1.

ISBN 1 86335 106 X (PDF).

1. Family social work. 2. Family services. 3. Family. I.
Title.

362.828

Cover designed by Diana Kalantzis.
Typeset in Australia by Common Ground Publishing.
Printed in Australia by Mercury Printeam on 80gsm White Bond.

Contents

Introduction

Around the world, family support programs are thriving. In America, it is now possible to obtain credentialed family support training. In the developing world, parent and child support programs are used to address a range of community needs (Evans & Stansbery, 1998). International Aid agencies, Government Departments and professional groups are all calling for increased investment in family support programs. Australia, too, has responded to the call for family support. For example, the 1999–2000 Family and Community Services budget includes a plan to work with State and Territories, community organisations and business to build a national framework to strengthen and support families (the National Family Strategy). 'Social immunisation' is considered a strategy to reform social welfare for disadvantaged children. New Zealand has attempted to define family responsibilities in order to provide a framework for family support (New Zealand Government, 1998). A vision for children and young people has also recently been released in the United Kingdom which seeks to identify appropriate measures of 'social health and wellbeing' for children and families, with the aim of more effectively targeting intervention and support programs (see http://www.cypu.gov.uk/).

Such a growth in interest in family support comes from an attempt to address many of the problems faced today. The problems we face are such that Keating and Hertzman (1999) claim modern society is breaking down. We confront poverty, and violence, people no longer feel safe in their houses or in their communities. Something is wrong with our world when increasing advances in technology and material improvements in standards of living have not been mirrored in our feelings of connection with others and the social world and the wellbeing of our communities. Existing services, whilst they may meet some crisis needs, do not seem to be altering the underlying causes of the problems we face as a society. The downward trend does not seem to be arrested. Family support is seen by many to offer a hope; a hope that, in the long term, we can change this pattern and turn around the decay we are seeing in our communities.

However, there are dangers in seeing family support as the cure-all. Firstly, family support programs will only work effectively when they are developed appropriately and operate in an effective and supportive environment. Short-cuts, whilst less costly in the short-term (and therefore attractive to policy-makers and politicians who need to show immediate gains), have significant impacts on the long-term effectiveness of programs. Secondly, family support needs to be understood in its entirety in order to operate effectively. There are no simple answers to the problems we face today, and no simple formulae that can be used to develop family support programs. Solutions to complex issues are, themselves, complex and require a broad understanding of all the necessary components.

This book aims to provide a framework for understanding family support programs. It does not provide formulae for the development of programs in specific contexts to meet specific needs. Rather, it provides a framework that can be applied in crafting programs at policy and procedural levels. It is hoped that the material in this book will help provide information to facilitate a society-wide change in the way services are conceptualised and delivered in our communities. As Leon (1999) suggests, such a change will enhance the quality of services offered to our children, families and communities.

A brief history of family support

The first family support programs developed in America in the 1970s, evolving out of the early work undertaken as part of President Johnson's war on poverty (Family Resource Coalition of America, no date). In 1981 the Family Resource Coalition was formed. This group have acted as information brokers ever since, disseminating information and establishing an international network of individuals and agencies working in family support. By 1986 the Family Resource Coalition had published their first documents outlining the principles and practices appropriate for family support work, and the first training in family support was offered in 1987. The movement continued to grow through the nineties, with landmark publications identifying best practice in family support. Funding gradually became more available throughout America for the operation of family support programs and small, local initiatives began to be trialed nationwide.

Professionals in Australia and New Zealand followed the development of the movement in America with much interest. Within existing agencies and programs, people began to attempt to enact some of the family support principles and practices. In 1978 the Australian federal Government introduced a pilot Family Support Services Scheme aimed at encouraging the development of services which supported families. In 1986, the Family Support Programme was developed and was responsible for the growth in childcare services, neighbourhood centres, marriage counselling, mediation services, child protection services and for home and community care for people with disability and for people who were frail and elderly (Gledhill, 1994). In the nineties, these community based services have faced ongoing funding cuts which impacted significantly on the support they were able to offer families. Towards the mid-nineties, Gledhill (1994) called for a re-evaluation of family support, and advocated for a co-ordinated national approach in building family support.

This call has been answered at government level with the support of a number of key projects, one of which was the commissioning of the project aimed at measuring social and family functioning (Zubrick, Williams, Silburn, & Vimpani, 2000). Also in the year 2000, the Australian government announced their aim to encourage a national approach to parenting and early childhood intervention, firstly, through making funds available for discrete parenting projects. In addition, the Good Beginnings National Parenting Programme aimed to provide family support to parents. Playgroups and indigenous childcare services were also seen as having a key role in a national family support strategy (Department of Family and Community Services, 2000). The year 2001 saw the introduction of the term 'social immunisation' and a suggested focus on thinking about ways to reform social welfare in order to best support disadvantaged children and families.

Family support is an area currently generating considerable interest both at professional service delivery and government/policy levels. It is crucial that, as programs are developed, they are informed by the best knowledge and expertise available. This book can be used by policy makers and service delivery staff as they grapple with the most effective way in which to deliver their programs and services. It provides guidance which will aid in the conceptualisation of programs and with their implementation.

Chapter 1

Why do we need family support programs?

Introduction

There are a number of concerns in our society today relating to children and families. It seems that children and families are under increased pressure and outcomes are worsening (Stanley, 2001). Current service delivery models do not appear to be effective in making the broad-based changes necessary to improve their lives. What appears to be needed is a new approach to service delivery; one founded on a different set of underpinning assumptions about the world and the way it operates.

Children and families' entitlements

Maslow's Hierarchy of Needs (Maslow, 1970) can be reframed as a hierarchy of rights. At the most basic level, children and families have a right to adequate nutrition and housing. Unfortunately, there are families in our communities who do not get adequate food, and families who are homeless. Children and families have a right to safety. Some children do not feel safe within their homes, which are characterised by abuse and violence. Others do not feel safe within the communities in which they live. There are now well-publicised cases of children who are not safe when they are at school. Safety is an increasing concern in our society.

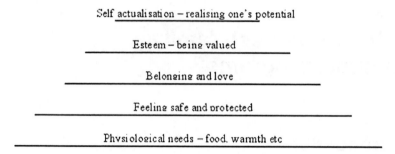

Self actualisation – realising one's potential

Esteem – being valued

Belonging and love

Feeling safe and protected

Physiological needs – food, warmth etc

Figure 1: Maslow's Hierarchy of Needs

Children and families who are not safe will be less likely to feel they belong and to establish loving relationships. Children need to feel loved and cared for in order to feel good about themselves. Developing caring relationships is a crucial indicator of children's mental health. A positive self-esteem, a feeling that one is of value, allows children to approach learning opportunities effectively. Where society does not provide opportunities for all children and families to maintain their rights, long-term outcomes for children are adversely effected.

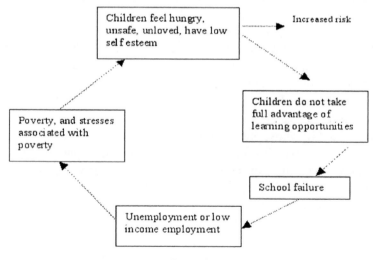

Figure 2

Children who have not experienced warm and caring relationships are less likely to feel connected to others, and their community. They are more likely to be aggressive, perhaps develop violent offending behaviours, and to re-enact the violence with their own children, perpetuating the cycle of violence and lack of caring.

Our changing world

The world around us is constantly changing, which impacts, not only on the needs of children and families in our communities, but on the way our communities attempt to meet those needs (National Research Council and Institute of Medicine, 2000). When children and families do not have their needs met appropriately, they are more at risk for poor outcomes.

Child outcomes

More children tan ever before are demonstrating behaviour problems: approximately 10 to 15% of preschool aged children have moderate to severe behaviour problems (Marshall & Watt, 1999). In New Zealand, 5% of children were reported difficult to manage by age 3, and 2% to be very difficult to manage (McGee, Partridge, Williams, & Silva, 1991).

Incidence of behaviour problems

- 68% of children with *severe* behaviour problems have more than 1 diagnosis. Conduct disorder[1] plus ADHD[2]—most common combination (Marshall & Watt, 1999).

- 21% children with mental health diagnoses have 2 diagnosed conditions, 47% have 3 or more (Zubrick et al., 1995)

- boys CD plus ADHD—more aggressive than boys with ADHD alone (McGee et al., 1991)

- 5% school children engage in ongoing bullying (Rigby, 1996)

- 20% primary school children and 10% secondary school children - victims of bullying (Rigby, 1996)

---

[1] Conduct disorder (CD) is the largest group of psychiatric disorders in older children and adolescents and is typified by severe and ongoing antisocial behaviour including aggression, destruction of property, deceit, theft, running away, fire setting, vandalism and serious violation of rules (Marshall & Watt, 1999).

[2] Attention Deficit Hyperactivity Disorder (ADHD) includes inattentive, hyperactive and impulsive behaviours. Marshall and Watt (1999) include American Psychiatry Association Criteria for diagnosing ADHD in an Appendix to their book.

- 83% bullies—mental health problems (Zubrick et al., 1997)

Aggression in childhood is related to aggression in adolescence, which, in turn, is related to aggression, violence, alcohol and other substance abuse, and chronic offending in adulthood (Hawkins et al., 2000). Other long-term outcomes include higher risk of school failure, unemployment, marital difficulties and interpersonal problems. Approximately 50% of adolescents with diagnosed CD demonstrate ongoing antisocial behaviours in adulthood including significant psychiatric and social impairments. Social isolation increases the risks for delinquent and violent behaviour (Chaiken, 2000). Children with severe CD are likely, in adulthood, to have children of their own who are aggressive. Only 16% of children diagnosed with CD are likely to become 'well-functioning' adults (Marshall & Watt, 1999).

CD poses significant costs to the community. Although only 2% of children with significant behaviour problems in Western Australia actually received treatment (Zubrick et al., 1995), the costs to the health system in 1992 amounted to over five million dollars (Health Department of Western Australia, 1993), suggesting that the cost of universally available programs would be enormous.

Children with behaviour problems also incur additional costs to the education system. They require additional support to maintain academic progress and to manage their behaviour. Indirect costs are involved when children do not achieve to their potential. Costs to the justice system are also incurred: the cost of all crime is estimated to be over 4% of gross domestic product (about $1000 per person per year), and the costs of juvenile crime alone is estimated to be around $40 million (Walker, 1997).

Violence

There is growing concern world wide about increasing levels of juvenile violence, with rates of violent offences committed by juveniles rising across the United Kingdom, Europe and the United States (Cavadino & Allen, 2000, Howell & Bilchik, 1995).

Growth in crime and violence

- UK—28% of males and 10% of females, aged between 14 and 25, admitted committing an act of violence against a person (3x more than the early 1990s (Graham and Bowling, 1995, cited in (Cavadino & Allen, 2000, p4)

- USA—homicide second leading cause of death among 15–24 year olds (Osofsky, 1997)

- 16–19 year olds—more likely to be victims of violent crime than any other group in American society, followed by children aged 12–15 years (Jenkins & Bell, 1997), (Wilson, 2000)

- 1 in 8 young people report carrying a weapon for protection—violent neighbourhoods 2 in 5 (Osofsky, 1997)

These figures are mirrored in Australia (National Crime Prevention, 1999). Although Australia is a much less violent society than it was a hundred years ago (Graycar, 2001), the fear of violence impacts significantly on our communities. Fear of violence is almost as significant as the crime itself, with women on low incomes, older women, and women living without partners reporting the greatest fear of violence (Carcach & Mukherjee, 1999).

Indigenous communities in Australia experience particularly high rates of violence. Injury and homicide rates in Aboriginal communities are as much as 12 times higher than in non-Aboriginal communities (National Crime Prevention, 2001b). The four areas with the worst incidence rates of violent crime are those which all have a history of being mission centres. Violence in traditional indigenous societies played an important, ritualised role in the maintenance of social order. Colonisation has impacted on the expression of that violence, whilst the traditional acceptance of violence remains. The use of alcohol as a coping strategy also exacerbates the expression and impact of violence in indigenous communities.

Violence in the home is also of growing concern (Laing, 2000). Family forms valued in the western world are inherently violent, with cultural norms that tolerate, or actually endorse, violence (Ghate, 2000).

Violence in the home

- 38% women who experienced domestic violence said that their children had witnessed the violence (Australian Bureau of Statistics, 1996b)

- 30–60% of domestic violence cases also include child abuse (Laing, 2000).

- Aboriginal women 45 times more likely to be victims of domestic violence than non-Aboriginal women

- Aboriginal children experience higher rates of abuse and neglect than non-Aboriginal children (National Crime Prevention, 2001a).

Research suggests that children who have experienced severe violence, are more likely to show delayed or impaired physical and neurological development, emotional problems, CD, poor educational attainment, lower IQ, psychopathology, depression, antisocial behaviour, substance abuse and offending behaviours (Ghate, 2000, Gayla & Gordis, 2000).

Children who do not have secure attachments are more at risk for social isolation, impaired cognitive development and development of low self-esteem (Hutchins & Sims, 1999, Bronfenbrenner & Neville, 1994, Mardell, 1992, Howes, Rodning, Galluzzo, & Myers, 1988). Violent behaviour, and child murder, are also traced to attachment relationships children have developed in their early years (Karr-Morse & Wiley, 1997). Violent communities create conditions leading to violent children.

Garbarino (1992; Garbarino & Kostelny, 1997) compares living in some American communities with living in a war zone. Children living in violent communities, are, by nature of their youth, particularly at risk. Not only are they physically and cognitively incapable of ensuring their own safety, their immature cognition makes it difficult for them to create realistic understandings of the risks to which they are exposed. In coping with the trauma of violence, young children develop patterns of behaviour which compare unfavourably with those shown by their peers who are not exposed to violence. Children exposed to violence are more likely to join gangs. They are more likely to carry weapons. They demonstrate extreme startle responses, sleep disturbances, emotional numbing, and recreate the trauma in their play. They may develop fear of benign objects or people. They may develop aggressive patterns of behaviour, or alternatively, may demonstrate extreme withdrawal. Ultimately they may develop Post Traumatic Stress Disorder (PTSD). One study identified that children exposed to trauma before they were 10 years of age were three times more likely to develop PTSD than were children whose exposure occurred after 12 years of age.

Constant exposure to violence impacts on the biochemical balance in children's brains. Perry (1997) uses the recent neurobiological research (for example Bremner & Narayan, 1998, Metcalfe & Jacobs, 1998, Shore, 1997) to develop a model explaining the link between violent experiences and children's brain development. He argues that stimuli from the environment prompt neurons in the brain to connect up with other neurons, forming pathways to process incoming stimuli. Stimuli received repeatedly by the brain will develop well-established, strong pathways. As children grow through late childhood, adolescence and, ultimately adulthood, a pruning takes place in the brain, where neurons not part of well-established pathways are removed. A 'healthy' cortex develops when children receive a range of stimuli, ensuring a balance between cognitive, affiliation and rational components of the brain, with the lower brain areas which control basic functions (such as heart rate, sleep, motor regulation and arousal). In an ideal situation, the upper brain areas of cortex and limbic system receive sufficient stimulation (through nurturing and loving care-giving) to become complexly wired. They thus have sufficient 'strength' to over-ride impulses which arise out of the lower brain (for example the fight-flight response). However, when children grow up in a violent environment, the complexity of the wiring in the lower parts of the brain decreases the ratio between upper and lower brain. This impacts on the ability of the upper brain to over-ride lower brain impulses, and predisposes children to violent behaviour. If children's exposure to violence is coupled with an environment in which they do not develop attachments, nor receive appropriate schooling opportunities, the complexity of the upper brain areas is decreased, further impacting on its ability to over-ride lower brain impulses.

Neurobiological research examining the relationship between environmental stimuli and brain development is in its early years and there is considerable argument in the literature relating to the degree to which early animal studies, and limited human research, can be applied. McCain and Mustard (1999) strongly support the speculative use of this research to justify the development of appropriate services for children and families. In contrast Bruer (1999) signals caution in applying the research too widely.

Children growing up in an ideal environment

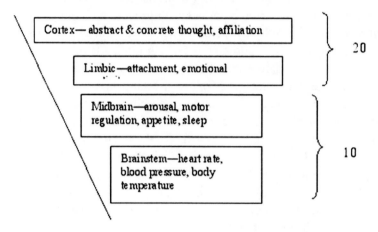

Children growing up in a violent environment coupled with lack of secure attachments and positive learning opportunities

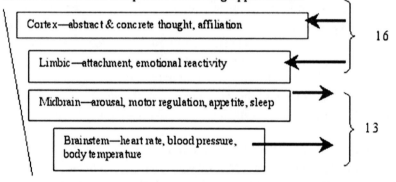

Figure 3: A summary of Perry's model of cortical impact of violence

Child Abuse and neglect

Child abuse and neglect went virtually unrecognised until the 1960's (Besharov, 1990) as many behaviours were not recognised as maltreatment (Tomison, 2001). It is unclear if the incidence of abuse and neglect is growing, as it appears to be in many countries around the world (Sarantakos, 1996), or if increasing numbers of cases are due to improvements in reporting systems. What is clear is that there is growing concern about the long-term costs to society of abuse and neglect (Karr-Morse & Wiley, 1997).

Figures for child abuse and neglect

- 6/1000 children subjected to substantiated abuse & neglect
- more substantiations for children 0–4
- greatest substantiations in girls 10–14 years
- girls are more likely to experience emotional & sexual abuse, boys physical abuse & neglect

(Moon, Rahman, & Bhatia, 1998)

Parents who abuse their children are likely, themselves, to have been abused (Sarantakos, 1996). They are likely to be experiencing stress (family or personal problems, financial stress), may be involved in drug or alcohol abuse and demonstrate anger and lack of support. Factors leading to increased stress such as single parenting, young parental age, illness, social isolation, immaturity, an unwanted or unplanned pregnancy, low socioeconomic status and low self-esteem are also implicated in increased risk of child abuse and neglect.

Crime

High rates of crime tend to be concentrated in areas of socioeconomic disadvantage where there are high rates of unemployment and low household income figures (Weatherburn & Lind, 1998). Low income parents tend to rear their children using harsher and more inconsistent discipline strategies, are less likely to be nurturing and less likely to supervise their children closely. These strategies tend to weaken attachment between parents and children, which increase the risk of children behaving in a criminal manner. Economic stress thus seems to be related to child outcomes, particularly in terms of criminal behaviour. This link is further supported by research in Australia and New Zealand demonstrating that members of minority groups are both victims and convicted as perpetrators of crime at a disproportionately higher rate than other members of the community (Mukherjee, 1999). People from minority groups tend to be clustered in the lower socioeconomic groups in both countries.

Wilkinson (1999b) further explores the link between violence and income levels, suggesting that peoples' perceptions of income inequality leaves them feeling powerless, and lacking in respect from the community around them. Homicide rates support this, being strongly related to income inequalities. Gilligan (1996) argues that violence is provoked by feelings of shame, disrespect and humiliation which results in actions aimed at ameliorating the 'loss of face'.

Child criminal behaviour

- children arrested before 14 years are more likely to re-offend
- 75% with 3 or more arrests before 18 were arrested at least once before 14
- violent boys more likely to have violent fathers
- shop lifting starts 11–12 years, peaks at 15 then declines

(National Crime Prevention, 1999).

Many people now call for harsher penalties and greater police powers in an attempt to curb crime (Graycar & Nelson, 1999). However, it is generally agreed that addressing rising crime rates is not a simple as this. Changes in families, neighbourhoods, schools and employment are all linked to crime (Graycar & Nelson, 1999) and must be addressed in any crime prevention programme. Indeed, in analysing the literature on crime prevention, the National Crime Prevention team (1999) concluded that multi-method approaches to crime prevention were the only way to address the diversity of risk factors leading to criminal behaviour.

Family stability

Because families are so central to our social organisation, some people argue that the problems we see in children's behaviour is due to changes in families: both changes in family structure and changes in the ways families operate.

Family Structure

Families are getting smaller as the birthrate declines. Children are less likely to grow to maturity with both biological parents.

Family figures

- Australian women bear 1.78 children compared with 1.84 10 years ago (Australian Bureau of Statistics, 1999a). New Zealand women 1.97 children (Statistics New Zealand: Te Tari Tatua, 1999)
- average household sizes: 1996—NZ 2.7, Australia 2.6

- 2001–NZ 2.7, Australia 2.4, US 2.5, England 2.3 (Australian Bureau of Statistics, 1999a)

- median age of mothers at birth of 1st child—Australia 27.1 years, NZ 29.1

- more couples in Australia without children (2.15 million couple families), than with children (2 million couple families) (Swan, 1999)

- 60% all children in Australia have combined family income of <$50,000. 50% of these were living in families with an income <$20,000, 20% in families whose members were unemployed (Swan, 1999)

Australian families

- one parent with dependents 1976—6.5%, 1991—8.8%

- couple with dependent children 1976—48.4%, 1991—44.4% (Sarantakos, 1996).

- living with biological parents 1992 /3—75% (Weston & Hughes, 1999)

- living with step-parent 1992/3 and 1997—8% (Australian Bureau of Statistics, 1998c)

- Almost 1/3 of all 0–4 year old children will be living with one parent by 2021 (Australian Bureau of Statistics, 1999a)

- 75% Aboriginal families dependent children—25% one parent, 11% >2 parents (National Council for the International Year of the Family, 1994)

- 22% Aboriginal households include other adult relatives compared with 7% for total WA population (Australia, 1995)

New Zealand families

- one parent families—lowest income of all family types—$16,000 compared with $50,200 for 2-parent families with children (Statistics New Zealand. Te Tari Tatau, 1996a).

- 17% European children, 41% Maori children, 37% Pacific Island children, 31% Asian children—families with incomes <$20,000 (Statistics New Zealand. Te Tari Tatau, 1996b).

- families with children under 18, parent receiving a benefit—13% in 1986, 25% in 1991 (Ministry of Social Policy, 1999).

- 2 parent families: 1986 53.2%, 1996—44.9% (Statistics New Zealand. Te Tari Tatau, 1996a)

- one parent families: 1986—14.3%, 1996—17.7%—mostly headed by women

- one parent families mainly European—82.3%

- two family households mainly Pacific Islander—18.3%

- extended families: 1996—7.1%; 49.2% included 3 or more generations: Europeans 5.9%, Pacific Islander 40.9%

Divorce is changing family structures and is widely considered to increase the risk for children developing problem behaviours (Marshall & Watt, 1999). Some of the many negative impacts of divorce include health problems, poor academic performance, aggression, low self-esteem, interpersonal problems, and long-term emotional distress. Boys generally tend to be more affected than girls, although girls may have more difficulties in adjusting to a step-father. However, divorce results in a range of changing circumstances, of which relative economic deprivation is one. It is suggested that many, if not most, of the negative consequences of divorce observed in children derive from the economic impact of divorce (Weston & Smyth, 2000). In addition to economic hardship, sole parents may also experience a range of other stressors which influence their ability to parent effectively post-divorce. Increasing household responsibilities, loneliness, social isolation and depression all impact on children and contribute towards the negative outcomes observed in much of the divorce literature.

Divorce

- 46% marriages likely to end in divorce—highest divorce rates those who marry before they are 20 years of age (Australian Bureau of Statistics, 2000a)

- nearly 66% divorces involve at least one child under 10

- 28% men and 23% women estimated to never marry in the future

- 15% all marriages 1999 involved children (under 16 years of age) from previous marriages, of these marriages, 43% involved only one child

- number of children involved in divorce: 1989 0.95 per 100 children under 18, 1999 1.13

- 50% cohabiting relationships likely to break down (Kilmartin, 1997)

- births to cohabiting women represent approximately 27% of all births (Australian Bureau of Statistics, 1996a)

For some women, re-partnering offers an opportunity to move from the low income levels characteristic of sole parenting (Weston & Smyth, 2000), (Parker, 1999). Re-marriage also offers opportunities to share household responsibilities, lessen social isolation and lessen stress levels. Child behavioural outcomes improve with re-partnering (Marshall & Watt, 1999), with greater improvements noted when re-partnering occurs early in children's lives. Some re-partnering relationships involve same sex couples with children from previous marriages. Sarantakos (1996) argues that the resultant step-families demonstrate the same benefits and tensions as do step-families with heterosexual parents.

Family functions

Some see that child rearing is the most important role a family undertakes, and argue that, without children, a couple should not be defined as a family. Where this view is taken, changes to family structure, impacting on parental ability to offer the best environment for the well-being of children, (such as divorce) are perceived as harmful and undesirable.

Families ensure security of all family members. In the western world during the 1950's, the ideal family met its needs by having father in the workplace providing economic security, and mother in the home providing emotional security (Gittens, 1993). Since that time there have been major changes, both in roles of men and women, and in the economic structure of society. Employment patterns have changed, with increasing demands for skilled employees resulting in high unemployment levels for unskilled workers (Danziger & Waldfogel, 2000). Feminism challenged the role of women as the major nurturers and carers of children. At the turn of the century men are now perceived to be as able as women in providing nurturance and care for their children. Despite these changing views, women in the late nineties still spend more time in direct care of children (Australian Bureau of Statistics, 1998b).

Parental time with children (Australian Bureau of Statistics, 1999b)

- 1992—mothers 2 times more time with children than fathers
- 1999—mothers 2 times more time in caring tasks
- 1999—fathers increased playing time by 8 minutes per day on weekdays and 18 minutes per day at the weekend

Where both parents work, 70% of mothers often or always they feel rushed and pushed for time compared with 52% of women with no dependent children, and 56% of fathers (Australian Bureau of Statistics, 1999b). Baxter (2001) found that cohabiting couples tend to have less traditional divisions of labour in the home with men taking on more childcare and indoor tasks than married men.

In addition to changing perspectives of the mothers' role in the home, many mothers are now engaged in the workforce—a changing role outside of the home.

Women in the workforce in 2000 (Australian Bureau of Statistics, 2000b)

- women were employed in 61% of couple families with dependent children
- full-time employment with dependent children: early 1980s—20%, 2000—26%
- 70% parents with children aged 15–24 years were employed, compared to 30% parents with children aged 0–4 years

In New Zealand (Statistics New Zealand. Te Tari Tatau, 1998)

- 84% fathers and 54% mothers with children 0–13 years were in employment
- 28% mothers working part-time and 26% working full-time.

There is intense social and political debate about the rights of mothers (as primary caregivers of children in western society) to work. Many perceive that maternal employment is selfish; a sacrifice of quality for children in order to meet the needs of mothers. Patriarchy, in particular, emphasises the role of women in the home, subordinate to men, as unquestionably the 'right' way for families to operate (Gittens, 1993). Changes from this 'right' way are seen as an explanation for the problems seen in our communities today. Others argue that maternal employment is an economic necessity, as increasingly difficult economic times require most households to have more than one income in order to meet their needs.

The role of childcare in supporting maternal employment is often either castigated as a poor substitute for loving, maternal care, or viewed as a necessary evil. Early research suggested that non-maternal care for young children had long-term negative effects (for example (Bowlby, 1969). For many years, practitioners in childcare have argued that it is the quality of the alternative care that impacts on child outcomes, rather than the fact that children are not at home with their mothers (Hutchins & Sims, 1999). Recent research has supported that view, suggesting that children of working mothers are not negatively affected by their parents' employment: rather it is both the quality of alternative care and the quality of family life that are the determinant of child outcomes (Harvey, 1999). Not only are children not negatively affected by parental employment, this research indicated that children may, in fact, benefit from early parental employment because of the increase in family income.

Childcare

Australia (Australian Bureau of Statistics, 1999b)

- 1995—51% children 0–12 years used childcare of some kind

- 23% used formal care

- informal care 57% of children: sibling care—6%, other relatives—19%, unrelated people—25%

- parental employment the reason for care in 85% of children in before and after school programs, 67% in family day care programs, 55% in long day care programs and 45% in informal care

New Zealand (Statistics New Zealand. Te Tari Tatau, 1998)

- 60% preschool aged children and 20% school aged children involved in education and care programs

- childcare centres—17% preschool aged children, kindergartens—19%

- care by relatives—10% of children

- school holiday care—49%

Value of parenthood

Changing family forms are sometimes seen as signs that society no longer values the role of child rearing (Stacey, 1996, Gittens, 1993). In the middle of the twentieth century, becoming a parent was seen as an indicator of adult status. It was action adults took to cement their status in the community as contributing citizens (Whitehead, 1998). By the 1970's this view began to change and parenthood no longer represented the only choice available to adult couples. People felt they could contribute to society in many ways (through employment, community participation etc) other than raising children. Parenting has become devalued (Sanson & Wise, 2001) because it does not bring with it economic benefits (Westman, 1994).

Parents who have children today are expected to raise their children in an environment which does not value their needs. Working mothers are blamed for neglecting their children in an economic environment where most families need two incomes to survive. Childcare workers, who make their living caring for children other than their own, criticise mothers for not spending enough time meeting their children's needs (Whitehead, 1998). Parents, doing the best they can in often less than ideal circumstances, receive approbation for not being more successful at child rearing. More and more parents are experiencing difficulties and many parents are failing to provide optimum environments for their children. Whitehead (1998, p78) argues that even middle class parents, those traditionally perceived to reflect the parenting ideal, are thought to be failing.

Poverty

Extreme poverty is becoming more common for children worldwide (Rice, 2001).

Poverty rates (Redmond, 2000)

- Australia, Canada, US 15.8–27.1% of all children
- Norway, Sweden and Finland 6.2–8.5%
- UK—3x increase in past 20 years—34% in 1997/8 (Bradshaw, 2000)

Poverty in Australia

- Henderson measure: 1995 20.6% Australians, 1998—30.4% (Head, 1998)

- Henderson measure 1998: <$452 week for a family of two adults and two children

- unemployed two-parent family with two children received, in 1998, benefits amounting to 98% of poverty line. A single parent with two children—91% of the poverty line (World Socialist Web Site, 1998).

- 8.6% families with at least one person working fell into the category of 'working poor' in 1998, as did 93.7% of families with no family member in employment (World Socialist Web Site, 1998)

- children in poverty: under 15 years—9 to 26%, aged 15–18—7 to 21% (depending on which measure used)

- 4 or more children in a family, 2x risk of poverty (Redmond, 2000)

- lack parental education 2x risk of poverty (Harding & Szukalska, 1998).

- immigrant families: South and Central America, the Middle East and North Africa poverty rates almost 25%

- Aboriginal family income in 1996—64% of non-indigenous Australians (Australian Bureau of Statistics, 1998a)

- Aboriginal unemployment—18%, non-Aboriginal 9%

- post secondary qualification—10% Aboriginal, 35% non-Aboriginal

- poverty rates: 1990—11.3%, 2001—13% (WACOSS, 2001)

- poverty rate unemployed people: 1990—52.6%, 2001—57.5%

- poverty rate no educational qualifications: 1990—12.1%, 2001—14.7%

Poverty in New Zealand

- 1 in 3 children lived below the poverty line in 1995.

- poverty line defined as 60% median equivalent household disposable income

- Poverty in Maori and Pacific Islander families is 2.5x greater (Ritchie, 1996).

- highest levels of income inequality amongst the OECD countries, greater than that seen in Australia, Britain and the United States—1982 to 1996 wealthiest 10% of the country increased income; middle and low income brackets decreased (Braddock, 2000)

- Maori households in bottom income quartile: 1988—23%, 1992—26% (Maori Health Committee, 1998)

- 1997 unemployment benefit—income at 50% of the median household disposable income (after housing costs have been removed). Defining the poverty line at this level identified 4.3% of households (12.3% of the population) living in poverty (Waldegrave, Frater, & Stephens, 1997)

- If the poverty line is 60% of median household disposable income—10.8% of households (13.4% of the population) and 32.6% of all children in New Zealand live in poverty (Waldegrave, Stephens, & Frater, 1996).

- 73% single parent families fall within this definition of poverty, and 64% of families living in state housing

One of the consequences of living on a low income is that families can not afford a healthy diet. A third of low income families in New Zealand reported they often did not have enough food. In these situations, women tended to go without meals in order to ensure their children had sufficient food. Nutritional needs were often not met, even with those families who had enough food. Fruit and vegetables intakes are lower, and fatty foods (which provide more energy per weight) are eaten more often (Else, 1999).

Poverty and nutrition (Ministry of Social Policy, 1999)

- reported running out of food sometimes or often: 31% Maori males, 41% Maori females; 48% Polynesian males, 54% Polynesian females, 14% all males, 21% all females aged between 25 and 44

- use of food banks or food parcels: 4% of population, 9% young people, 19% all Maori people, 14% all Pacific Islander

Poverty not only impacts on peoples' nutritional status, it impacts on their health and well being. Dietry related cancers are found to occur more frequently in families on low incomes. Obesity is also more common in lower income groups (Else, 1999), which increases risks of diabetes and cardiovascular diseases.

The relationship between income inequality and health has been demonstrated across both developed and developing countries (Wilkinson, 1999a). People who live in higher socioeconomic areas, who have higher levels of education and income keep better health and live longer (Howden-Chapman, Wilson, & Blakely, 2000). Males living in disadvantaged areas of New Zealand live, on average, 9 years less than males from more advantaged areas. The difference for women is less; approximately 6 years (Salmond & Crampton, 2000). An increase in income of one standard deviation, was linked with a 4.6% decrease of mortality rates. Socioeconomic grades also impact on developmental outcomes for children, behavioural adjustment, literacy and maths achievement (Keating & JHertzman, 1999).

Peoples' perceptions of inequality within their own society are more important in determining health outcomes, than the actual degree of material deprivation (Institute of Medicine, 2001; Schorr, 1995). When people see others in their society are more affluent than themselves, they feel more stressed and anxious, which increases their risk for poor health outcomes.

The increased stress associated with living on a low income is also associated with parenting style (Pinderhughes, Dodge, Bates, Pettit, & Zelli, 2000). Positive relationships are more likely in families with low levels of stress (Institute of Medicine, 2001). Stress makes it more likely that parents will experience intense cognitive and emotional reactions to their children's behaviour. Stress increases the likelihood of parents' interpreting their children's misbehaviour as intentional. Thus it is more likely they will respond with harsher discipline. Harsh discipline is, itself, further related to poorer outcomes for children (Silburn et al., 1996, Marshall & Watt, 1999). The strong relationship between socioeconomic status and delinquency disappears when child management skills are controlled for (Haapala, Pecora, & Fraser, 1991). This suggests that the parenting style common in families on low income, (particularly the increased use of physical punishment and the non-contingent use of reinforcement) is linked with the development of oppositional behaviour in children which then leads to increased likelihood of delinquency.

Social capital

Definition of social capital focus around strong relationships which provide a foundation to build community relationships (Flora, 2000). Strong community relationships are the building blocks of power, access to resources and information, and a positive identity.

Definitions

- Adler (1999)—a resource used by individuals within their interpersonal networks: the relationships they have with other people in their personal lives, and in their activities within the community.

- networks, norms, values and understandings allowing people to interact and co-operate within their communities (Organisation for Economic Co-operation and Development, 2001)

- Measures—based on the extent to which a society is based on mutuality or power hierarchies, co-operation or antagonism, reciprocity or competition, accepting of diversity rather than a unitary view of 'rightness' (Wilkinson, 1999b)

One form of social capital may be cultural connection. Cultural connection is the degree to which people see their cultural experiences as distinct from those of the hegemonic culture. Ortega (2001) suggests that parents with low cultural connection are more likely to use violent child discipline strategies (such as spanking), are more likely to see the child in control and more likely to feel that their child is beyond their control. Connecting people to their culture was linked to improved feelings of parenting competence.

Individuals' social capital can be 'spent' through supporting others, supporting community projects and may even be converted to economic advantage (community links, for example, may enhance employment opportunities, or create opportunities for informal exchanges of labour) (Winter, 2000). People need to meet and interact in order to maintain their links. Changes in circumstances may result in losses of social capital (for example, when a key person in a network changes employment, the link into the agency previously provided by that person no longer exists). Social capital may also be lost through abuse (for example, damage to a loaned material possession may reduce the likelihood of further loans).

Social capital rich communities form when community members participate in a range of community groups, and through those groups, develop networks of links (Adler & Kwon, 1999).

Opportunities to develop social capital occur through:

- informal neighbourhood networks
- school events
- sporting clubs
- churches
- civic organisations
- interest clubs
- other community groups and activities

Shared norms and beliefs help provide a bond that initially links people together. Participation in community activities helps people build a sense of trust in their community, which then functions to further enhance participation and social capital. Garbarino (1992) refers to socially-rich neighbourhoods as those areas where people have sufficient energy remaining after meeting their own, and their families' needs, to be able to support their neighbours.

Collier (1998) argues that people on low incomes are more reliant on social capital in meeting their needs than are people from higher income brackets. People on higher incomes are able to purchase materials to meet their needs, whereas people on lower incomes are reliant on informal networks, social norms and rules. However, people from higher income levels tend to be more involved in leadership of any community groups to which they belong. As leaders they tend to influence those groups into actions which meet their needs, rather than the needs of group members who may be from lower income groups, thus minimising the benefit of these groups for low income members.

Increases in social capital have been linked to better care for children. Mothers who have greater amounts of social support are less likely to abuse their children, and the children themselves are less likely to demonstrate social problems (Organisation for Economic Co-operation and Development, 2001). Social capital impacts on economic and physical well-being. Increasing crime rates are linked with decreasing levels of social capital (Graycar & Nelson, 1999).

There is a link between trust amongst people and levels of income inequality (Wilkinson, 1999b). Income inequality itself is related to level of individuals' participation in the community. Death rates are two to four times higher amongst individuals who have fewer friends, lower levels of social integration and lower levels of social support (Wilkinson, 1999b). Trust amongst people is related to mortality rates. Animal research suggests the link between low social status (and low social capital) and poor health is mediated by stress. Low social capital creates chronic stress, which increases cortisol levels in the brain, which then impacts on neurobiological functioning. Wilkinson (1999b) suggests that our society represents a culture of inequality, which impacts on social capital formation, and therefore on outcomes for children and their families. Such inequalities are found to be increasing.

Evidence for the decline in social capital in the last fifty years of the twentieth century is strong. Garbarino (1992) argues that people are becoming more isolated as family sizes decrease, people marry later in life, divorce more often, and more often live alone.

Putnam (1996): Evidence for decline in social capital in America

- 25% decrease in informal socialising since 1965
- 50% decrease in time spent in clubs and other organisations
- 25 to 50% decrease in conventional voluntary associations
- 39% decrease in attending meetings related to school or town affairs
- 56% decrease in work for political parties
- 25% drop in overall group membership since 1974
- 33% drop in social trust
- people in full-time employment tended to be more civically involved
- working women tended to be members of more voluntary associations
- women who are not in paid employment may spend more time in voluntary associations
- people born in the 1920s likely to be members of 2x more organisations as those born in the late 1960s.

- this generation are 2x more likely to vote—3x more likely to read newspapers
- people who read more newspapers belong to 76% more civic organisations, are 55% more trusting

The Australian Time Use Surveys (Australian Bureau of Statistics, 1997) show a similar decline in volunteerism as do studies of trust levels.

Australian social capital

- volunteer work: 1992–22.4% of adult Australians—average 89 minutes a week.
- 1997–only 19.8%; average 109 minutes a week (Australian Bureau of Statistics, 1997)
- trust: 1983–46% Australians thought they could trust most people.
- 1995–40% (Hughes, Bellamy, & Black, 2000)
- need to be careful in dealings with others: 1983–51% agreed.
- 1996–59%

The rise of the welfare sate is seen as a cause of the decline in social capital through declines in individual responsibility: people learn to rely on the government to meet their needs, rather than taking individual and community action (Winter, 2000). The welfare state is seen to create a class of welfare dependent people, who are disempowered by monolithic structures centralising power (Lyons, 2000). Bureaucratic structures, emphasising hierarchical authority and accountability, lessen peoples' ability to communicate horizontally and develop networks of associations (Latham, 1998), limiting opportunities to build social capital.

Putnam (1996) proposes that television is a major cause of this observed decline in social capital. Watching television is strongly related to declining social trust and decreases in group membership. Television is a leisure time activity pursued at the expense of other social activities both inside and outside the home. Heavy television viewers are likely to be loners and more likely to over-estimate the risk of crime which makes them more likely to remain inside their homes for fear of their own safety. The resultant isolation is a self-fulfilling cycle.

Low social capital and a perception of high environmental threat leads to high anxiety levels (Twenge, 2000). Most parents today see the world as a more dangerous place than it was when they were children (Scott, Jackson, & Backett-Milburn, 2000). Anxiety is related to higher mortality rates, higher likelihood of asthma, irritable bowel syndrome, ulcers, inflammatory bowel disease and coronary heart disease. In general anxiety levels have increased significantly over the latter half of the last century and typical school children in the 1980s experienced a level of anxiety that would have been diagnosed as pathological in the 1950s (Twenge, 2000).

Existing service delivery approaches

Neo-liberal politicians argue the welfare state is failing. It is the source of social evil through increasing inequality and dependency on the state (Giddens, 1998). Our communities are characterised by increasing levels of social isolation, violence, crime, family break down and poverty. Rather than reducing the incidence of these concerns, existing social services are operating in crisis mode and barely addressing the most urgent needs of our communities (Danziger, 2000). A significant proportion of children and families at risk miss out on receiving services in Australia because of the limitations of the paradigm used to design services for them (Ainsworth, 1999).

Cuts in funding require agencies to do more for less (Ife, 1995). Service managers specify more and more precisely the procedures their workers must undertake to ensure accountability, resulting in fragmented, stigmatising and unresponsive services (Adams & Nelson, 1995). Increasing managerialism results in client disempowerment and a reinforcement of inequities in society (Ife, 1997). Bureaucracy significantly hinders the ability of agencies to make any effective changes in the lives of people (Adams & Nelson, 1995). In order to deliver effective services, the entire nature of our government and our social systems needs to change (Schorr, 1997). Recent Australian social policy initiatives have more noise than performance, with rhetoric taking the place of action (Ife, 1995). These failures, Ife argues, are related to the failure of the current dominant paradigm or worldview.

We need a new paradigm of service delivery in order to meet the needs of children and families in our community who are at risk (Ainsworth, 1999). A similar argument is put forward by Bracken and Thomas (Bracken & Thomas, 2001) who see the need in medicine for a redefinition of roles and responsibilities and a new approach to service delivery. Changing the way current services operate, tinkering with the margins of service delivery, will not provide sufficient change. Existing services are not working, concerns about children and families are growing, and it is time for a re-think about what we are doing and why we are doing it.

A new paradigm

What is a paradigm?

A paradigm is a way of thinking about the world (Guba & Lincoln, 1994). Whilst there are many arguments in the literature about the classification of different beliefs into paradigms, for the purposes of this discussion the three group approach taken by Sarantakos (1998) shall be used.

The three paradigms of Sarantakos (1998)

1: Positivist

- reality exists independently of humans

- reality is governed by universal laws

- reality is perceived in the same way by everyone

- research is aimed at learning the universal laws

- social services manipulate the world using these universal laws to improve things for their clients

- there is a 'right' way to go about things and that 'right' way is the way defined by the laws of nature (eg there is a 'right' way to parent and that way is taught in a parent education programme)

- linked with progress, individualism, technology, capitalism, the industrial revolution, growth, pollution, patriarchy and bureaucracy

2: Interpretivist

- there is no ONE right way in anything

- reality exists only as it is interpreted by humans: as the humans experiencing a situation change, then the interpretation of that situation will change

- social services need to operate from the reality of each of their clients

3: Critical

- reality is created by the powerful in our communities, who then impose their reality on others

- our society consists of people in power, and people who are oppressed

- people who are oppressed may not recognise their oppression, as their perceptions of their life are influenced by the views of the powerful

- social services need to empower clients by supporting them in understanding their oppression, then working to reframe and take control for themselves

Methodologies or models: theory into practice

Methodologies or models translate the principles in paradigms into practice (Sarantakos, 1998). Traditional forms of service delivery to children and families in the community were under-pinned by a positivist paradigm (Kenny, 1999). An emphasis on pathologies, and treatments for those pathologies has led to a service approach focusing on clients' deficits and problems, and the professional strategies implemented to solve these (Leon, 1999). In a positivist approach to working with children and families, behaviour problems, for example, would be diagnosed. Problems are perceived as located in the children themselves, their parents and the interactions between parents and children (Hill, 1999). Programs for parents and children may be imported from other countries (usually America) and replicated, on the assumption that what has worked elsewhere, must work in Australia and other western nations.

In an interactionist approach to service delivery, programs are considered valid only if they are adapted in some way to the needs of the specific communities and target groups with which they are to operate. Politicians, policy officers and others in the hierarchy may be responsible for the choice of specific programs or services, but there is scope for service delivery to be modified at the grass-roots level. Problems are perceived as having wider roots than just individuals.

Despite the ideal of taking a broad approach, it is very easy to slip into an individually-focused approach when situations become stressful or complex (Smale, 1995). Financial pressure on agencies also makes it difficult for programs to maintain an interpretivist focus. This can be a particular problem when successful, small, local programs are replicated on a wider basis. The involvement of bureaucracy, and organisations outside small, local groups, functions to significantly destroy the very factors which caused programs to be successful (Schorr, 1997). Successful service delivery can only occur when there is a radical change in the very structure of our society and its organisations. An interpretivist approach to service delivery does not deliver sufficient change.

Community work underpinned by the critical paradigm has a theme of social justice. Inequalities, once recognised, need to be addressed and overcome. A critical approach to community work incorporates the humanist vision of universal human rights, as well as the interpretivist approach based on interaction and understanding and the relativist understanding of human needs (Ife, 1995). A critical paradigm is explicitly focused on discourses of liberation, change and empowerment within a framework of social justice.

It is inappropriate to expect major changes in society to derive from the very people who are identified as having problems and who are therefore receiving services (Smale, 1995). Not only is this unfair on this segment of the population, it also ensures that people outside the service will continue with existing behaviours, thus perpetuating the oppression which is the cause of the problems. Rather, all members of society should take responsibility for change. The critical paradigm is the underpinning approach to the model of service delivery to children and families discussed in this book.

Conclusion

The western world has become less effective in meeting the needs of children and families. We can see evidence of this in increasing concerns about violence, declining social capital, and increasing rates of poor outcomes. Children and families are living in environments where existing models of service delivery are not succeeding in modifying these trends. We need wide-spread acceptance of new ways to work in communities with families and children, and that these new approaches need to permeate all levels of our social system in order to be effective. Family support programs operate in this new manner and therefore may have the potential to impact on the way our society meets the needs of children and families in the future.

Chapter 2
Aims of family support programs

Introduction

The previous chapter discussed changes happening in our world today. Current service delivery, although clearly shaping the world in which we live, may not be shaping it in the direction many of us would see as desirable. Family support offers a new approach to delivering services. However, the issues faced by our society are complex, and the strategies we need to work with these issues will also need, of necessity, to be complex. Is it realistic of us to expect that family support is the only answer? What is it we want, and can reasonably expect, family support programs to achieve?

The self-serving argument

Children of today will become the workers, taxpayers and parents of tomorrow (Danziger & Waldfogel, 2000). Today's children will develop policy and deliver programs influencing our retirement income, lifestyle, and the support services we will need as we grow more physically (and perhaps mentally) dependant. It is in our best interest to ensure that the decisions they make in the future, are decisions with which we are happy. These decisions arise out of the values we teach our children today.

Values transmitted through early childhood programs and schooling are those associated with the dominant group in our society—a cultural capital consisting of middle class values (Harker, 1990, Bruner, 1996, Viruru, 2001). These values lead them to perpetuate existing power relationships, social and economic structures (Weiler, 1988, Jamrozik, 1994).

Following the same argument, it could be suggested that providing family support to young children and their families, will maximise the chance children will grow up to reflect the values we see as desirable for our own well-being in old age. The more positive their experiences, and the more we provide support to families to ensure positive experiences, the more we are caring for ourselves in the future. The aims of family support programs are therefore, to provide appropriate child rearing environments, in order that children will internalise the cultural capital we need for them to provide for our future.

The social justice argument

Children's rights

Children have a right to develop to their full potential. The United Nations Declaration of the Rights of the Child (United Nations, 1959) and the United Nations Convention on the Rights of the Child (United Nations, 1989)[3] are both key documents which address this issue. The Convention identifies the family as the most important environment for child rearing. It requires the state to provide necessary protection and support to ensure families can fulfil their obligations towards their children. States are required to do all in their power to ensure the economic, social and cultural rights of children. Family support programs are one tool that can be used to fulfil these obligations.

Addressing inequality

Our welfare society reinforces social inequality.

Inequality in access to services (Jamrozik, 1994)

Education

- private school pupils more likely to complete year 12, 2x more likely to enter University
- more middle-class than working-class children have opportunities to develop information technology skills (Valentine & Holloway, 1999)

Labour market

- unemployment—greater impact on lower occupational levels (manual and unskilled labour)

---

[3] Australia ratified the Convention on 17 December 1990 and New Zealand on 6 April 1993 (both with minor amendments).

- growth of jobs in professional and para-professional areas that require higher levels of education

Childcare

- used more frequently by families on higher incomes

Community services have not minimised inequalities in our society and, in many cases, have created new inequalities. Continuing to offer new types of community services without fundamentally changing the underlying paradigm from which they are developed, is not going to change inequalities in our society. Family support programs provide an opportunity to take a completely different approach to the delivery of community services, and therefore have the potential to begin to address some of the inequalities observed.

The economic argument

Research indicates that money spent on early intervention is recouped in the long-term. Graduates of early intervention programs are less likely to be unemployed, engaged in criminal activities and dependant on welfare (see Chapter 8). Long-term savings in education, justice, health and welfare more than offset the cost of early intervention.

For every dollar spent on one programme, the country saved $7.16 in costs related to services required by the comparison population in adulthood (Schweinhart & Weikart, 1993). Forty percent of 8 year olds with conduct disorders have repeated convictions for theft, vandalism and assault by adolescence (Scott, Knapp, Henderson, & Maughan, 2001). Costs associated with crime make up almost 2/3 of the long-term costs of CD, followed by costs of education, foster and residential care and welfare benefits. Long-term costs associated with CD were 10 times higher than costs associated with children who had no identified childhood concerns. children with CD and conduct problems make up approximately 12% of the population but account for 50% of the public expenditure assessed in the research.

California operates a Three Strikes policy, similar to that in operation in Western Australia. This mandates increasingly severe prison sanctions for repeat offending and is estimated to reduce serious crimes committed by adults by 21%. An analysis of the cost of family support compared with Three Strikes (Greenwood, Model,

Rydell, & Chiesa, 1998) suggested the criminal justice system could save $631,000 of every million currently spent on Three Strikes.

Rand Report (Greenwood et al., 1998) cost analysis

- weekly home visits beginning during pregnancy and continuing for 2 years = $2700 per family per year;

- childcare from ages 2 to 5 = $6000 per year;

- parent education programme—classes and one-to-one counselling and coaching = $3000 per family;

- incentives for young people to complete high school = $3130 per child per year;

- supporting young delinquents = $10,000 per youth per year;

- family support programme including all of these components = $54,920 per family per year; $4.325 billion a year; and

- outcome—24% prevention rate accumulated over a 30 year period

Child abuse and neglect rates can be reduced by 50% with appropriate home visits and childcare programs (Carnegie Corporation of New York, 1994). Reduction in child abuse leads to lower offending rates as children develop into teenagers and adults. Early intervention in the lives of children and their families is cost effective. The earlier appropriate intervention is offered, the greater the gains. 'Second chance intervention', programs offered to children beyond the early childhood years (such as school or adolescence interventions) (Danziger & Waldfogel, 2000), are less effective. Heckman (1996, Heckman & Lochner, 2000) argues that for people beyond a certain age, and below a certain skill level, interventions are a poor use of resources. Despite this, most argue that second-chance interventions must still be offered as a supplement to quality family support.

The pragmatic argument

It is tempting to suggest family support programs have the potential to address the concerns addressed to date in this book. However, just as the issues are not simple, nor are the supports needed to address them. Family support programs cannot, and will not, 'fix' children's behaviour problems, nor will they eradicate poverty or violence in our communities. They will not eliminate inequality, nor will they ever remove the need for state provided welfare. However, we CAN expect to increase the ability of children and families to resist being negatively affected by these factors. Family support programs can build resilience.

Risk factors

Risks within the individual

Genetic

A number of genetic conditions have impaired outcomes:

Genetic underpinning (Marshall & Watt, 1999)

- ADHD 60–90%
- ODD 80%
- CD 23–69%

Birth weight and gestation

Infants of low birth weight are slow to achieve developmental milestones, though they tend to 'catch up' by the early preschool years. There remains a link between (Breslau et al., 1996, Breslau, Klein, & Allen, 1988):
- very low birth weight and ADHD at 7 years of age
- low birth weight and teacher rated attention problems, aggression, hyperactivity and delinquency in 9 year old boys.

Arousal levels

Arousal levels define the amount of psychophysiological activity occurring whist an individual is resting and is partly hereditary (Raine, Reynolds, Venables, Mednick, & Farrington, 1998). Low arousal is associated with:
- childhood antisocial and aggressive behaviours (Scarpa & Raine, 1997),
- criminal behaviours in adulthood—when combined with behaviour problems (Raine, Venables, & Williams, 1995).

Aggression

The earlier aggression appears, the greater the risk for long-term problems (Marshall & Watt, 1999) such as Conduct Disorders (Coie & Cillessen, 1993), drug abuse (Farrington & West, 1990), and bullying towards peers and adults (Marshall & Watt, 1999).

Cognition

Other general cognitive limitations linked to developmental risk (Marshall & Watt, 1999) include:
* poor social planning,
* limited ability to channel the expression of strong emotions into socially acceptable behaviours,
* limited ability to concentrate.

Children who fail at school are more likely to demonstrate behaviour problems. In Western Australia, 47% of children between the ages of 4 and 16 who were bullies also had low academic achievement levels (compared with 17% of students who were not identified as bullies) (Zubrick et al., 1997).

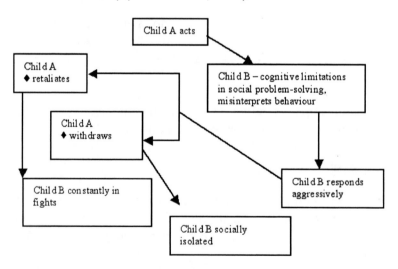

Figure 4 : Aggression as a result of cognitive limitations

Language

Children who experience language delay experience increased risk of antisocial and criminal behaviour. The Dunedin study found language delays in 2 to 8% of children (Silva, McGee, & Williams, 1983) and these may be misinterpreted as inattention and non-compliant behaviour (Cohen, 1996). Language problems are linked to persistence of ADHD type behaviours (Marshall & Watt, 1999) and criminal behaviour up to age 30 (Statten & Klackenberg-Larsson, 1993).

Boys are more likely to have language problems in their early years (Prior, Smart, Sanson, & Oberklaid, 1993) which may lead to problems in social interactions and social skill development. Although boys' language problems ameliorate as they grow older, the social interaction patterns they developed in early childhood as a result of these limitations may continue.

Language ability is significantly influenced by the language children hear around them. Huttenlocher (1998) found that the more often mothers spoke to young children (between 16 and 26 months of age) the better the children's vocabulary acquisition. Turn-taking interactions between caregivers and young children facilitate language development (Berk, 1999), and factors which interfere with these interactions (such as poverty, maternal depression) impact on outcomes.

Physical health

Ten percent of children in Western Australia with diagnosed mental health problems also had physical health problems (compared to 3% of children without mental health concerns) (Zubrick et al., 1995). Similar figures are reported from other studies (Marshall & Watt, 1999) however there has been little longitudinal research investigating the long-term outcomes for children experiencing ill health.

Gender

Gender is linked to developmental risk, but the question remains if the link is through genetic vulnerability, or through socialisation. Boys tend to demonstrate more negative outcomes when exposed to risk factors such as family conflict, divorce and poverty.

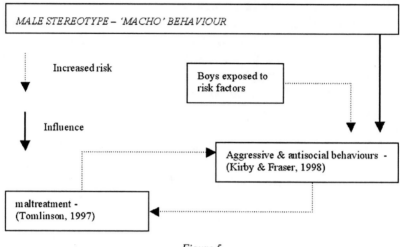

Figure 5

Temperament

Temperament is defined as a stable individual characteristic related to the type and intensity of emotional reactions, activity levels, attention and emotional self-regulation (Berk, 1999). Temperament may be partly genetically determined and does not change much over time (Marshall & Watt, 1999).

Seventy percent of children with difficult temperament are likely to develop behaviour problems by school age, compared with 18% of children with an easy temperament (Prior, 1992). Inflexibility of temperament is a major contributor to behavioural problems (Prior et al., 1993) and boys are more at risk.

Difficult temperament and effective parenting

- effective and supportive family communication
- parents feel in control of antisocial and aggressive behaviours
- parents give and receive affection

Risks in the microsystem

Parenting style

Recent research has challenged beliefs that authoritative parenting is the 'best' parenting. Chinese, Asian and Pacific Island child rearing focuses on higher levels of adult control coupled with high levels of adult (particularly maternal) warmth (Berk, 1999). This is interpreted by families as a high parental commitment to child rearing, without which, children would feel unloved (Sims & Omaji, 1999). In America, black African parents use stricter demands for child compliance and research suggests that when these strategies are used in low socioeconomic environments children experience better outcomes (O'Neil and Parke, 1997, cited in Berk, 1999). Physical punishment, whilst leading to behaviour problems and Conduct Disorder in Caucasian American children, does not do so for African American children (Deater-Deckard, Dodge, Bates, & Petit, 1996). Appropriate parenting style depends greatly on the contexts in which the family are located: there is no 'one right way' to parent.

Parental conflict

High levels of parental conflict are linked with psychological difficulties and antisocial behaviours (Kirby & Fraser, 1998). Parental conflict or psychopathology may influence development through:
- modelling of inappropriate methods of problem solving,
- desensitising children towards violence, which may then impact on children's understanding and use of violence in their own lives,
- less parental ability, energy or time to parent effectively, thus leaving children more vulnerable to other risk factors in their environments.

Divorce

Divorce (Chapter 1) disrupts children's sense of continuity (Butler et al., 2000). Some research identifies increased behaviour problems at the time of the divorce, but this is not repeated consistently in other studies. The impact of divorce depends on a range of factors including consequent daily life[4] and the ability of parents to provide ongoing emotional support for their children (Hetherington, 1992). Children with lower intelligence, difficult temperaments, aggressive and insecure behaviours, and boys have more difficulty in adjusting.

Teenage pregnancy

Pregnant teenagers face greater health risks to both the mother and the infant (Franklin, Corcoran, & Ayers-Lopez, 1997). Many do not obtain adequate pre-natal care and may compete with their foetus for nutrition (Hechtman, 1989). Girls who give birth before they are 16 tend to stop growing themselves, and are five times more likely to die than mothers in their early twenties (Franklin et al., 1997), but this may be related to different socioeconomic levels, rather than age.

Socioeconomic factors in teenage pregnancy

- lower family income levels—4x more likely to become pregnant
- low SES—less likely to receive adequate prenatal care, nutrition, adequate social support, less access to resources
- low achieving girls—37% likely to become pregnant compared with 5% of high achieving girls

Children of teenage mothers face a range of risks (Levine, Pollack, & Comfort, 2000), many of which are linked to low socioeconomic status:

- more behaviour problems throughout their middle childhood years (Fergusson & Lynskey, 1993);
- more likely to be involved in substance abuse and early sexual intercourse;
- antisocial and aggressive school behaviour;
- low school attainment;
- delinquency; and
- boys 2x more offences by age 32.

Adolescent mothers are less likely to have well paying or secure jobs and are more likely to remain on welfare. One study of adolescent mothers found that many were still living in poverty 17 years after becoming a parent (Furstenberg, Brooks-Gunn, & Morgan,

---

[4] Sole parents are more likely to be living in poverty, for example, with all the attendant risks associated with that.

1987). Those who had jobs were working in low paid, low status employment.

Alcohol and substance abuse

Drug use in Australia (Community Drug Summit, 2001a), (Community Drug Summit, 2001e), (Community Drug Summit, 2001i)

- 11% have used illicit drugs excluding cannabis in the past 12 months

- 14% of school children in Western Australia use amphetamines, 10% have used LSD/hallucinogens

- 4 of 10 school children use cannabis at some point, and 1 in 5 are likely to have used cannabis in the last month

- students in rural areas are more likely to use cannabis than metropolitan students

- use of cannabis: Australia—17.9%, UK—9%, US—8.6%, Spain—7.6%

- 8% of all people over 18 years of age are identified with a substance abuse disorder

- Indigenous Australians are more likely to use cannabis than other drugs

- drug use is increasing in many indigenous communities

- Less indigenous people drink alcohol regularly in comparison with non-indigenous people—those who do drink more likely to do so at harmful levels

- 2x more indigenous people smoke tobacco

- the use of volatile substances such as petrol and solvents of concern in indigenous communities

Drug use is related to marginalisation. Young people who are homeless and young offenders are more likely to have higher levels of drug use than others, although there are also higher levels of drug use amongst teenagers whose families are in the highest income brackets (Community Drug Summit, 2001i).

Harm can occur through a single use taken to levels of intoxication (for example overdosing, having unsafe sex). Regular use of drugs can have financial implications and may led to impaired performance at work or school. Regular use of amphetamines can lead to psychosis. Dependant levels of use can result in:

- loss of employment,
- reduction of income,
- break down of relationships,
- health and psychological problems,
- crime (Community Drug Summit, 2001d),
- higher rate of suicide ideation and suicide attempts (Hillman, Silburn, Green, & Zubrick, 2000).

Risk factors commonly associated with drug misuse in young people include (Community Drug Summit, 2001b):

- environmental factors—easy local access to drugs, socioeconomic disadvantage,
- family and social factors—family disharmony and dysfunction, inconsistent or poor parental supervision and monitoring, lack of positive attachment, family history of drug or alcohol abuse, favourable family and/or peer attitudes to drug use and lack of peer attachments,
- individual factors—behaviour problems in early childhood, interpersonal conflict, mental health problems, ongoing social problems, being male,
- life events—past trauma, relationship breakdown, perceptions of academic or career failure.

Research suggests that drug misuse is low until young people experience10 or more of these risk factors. Children of alcoholics from lower socioeconomic class groups and with multiple problems (parental mental illness, criminality, welfare beneficiaries) are three times more likely to have been expelled from school (Miller & Jang, 1997), suggesting an inter-relationship of risk factors.

Parental alcohol abuse increases the risk of children abusing alcohol as they grow. Children from these families are also more likely to have higher cigarette use (Marshall & Watt, 1999).

Parent-child relationship

Infants in the western world tend to establish primary attachments to their main caregivers, normally mothers. Infants from other cultural groups may establish a range of equal attachments to multiple caregivers, which may or may not include biological parents (Jackson,

1993). When these attachments are secure, developmental outcomes for children are likely to be positive. Insecure or disorganised attachments result from unresponsive caregivers which are likely to lead to later behaviour problems: childhood helplessness, unwillingness to try new things, apprehension, weight loss concerns and eating disorders in preadolescent girls (Lein, 2000). Of children with highly externalising behaviours at age 7, 83% had disorganised attachments compared with 13% of children who were not so identified (Lyons-Ruth, Easterbrooks, & Cibelli, 1997).

The adult partners in disorganised attachment relationships are likely to be depressed, have a childhood history of violence and sexual abuse, a psychiatric history, participate in child maltreatment, and are more likely to be negative and intrusive towards the children (Marshall & Watt, 1999). Maternal intrusive and hostile behaviours as early as 6 months of age were related to children's aggression levels at age 5 (Lyons-Ruth, Alpern, & Prepacholi, 1993). Low maternal responsiveness to boys at 10 months is associated with less compliance at 22 months and higher levels of child coercive behaviour at 42 months (Marshall & Watt, 1999).

Alternate measures of attachment, and outcomes

- (Harnish, Dodge, & Valente, 1995)—enjoyment in interaction, sensitivity to child's cues, responsiveness, maternal control and direction, time spent together, clarity of commands, follow through by the mother
- interaction score strongly related to externalising behaviours in kindergarten.
- (Crittenden, 1988)—relationship closeness, reciprocity and responsiveness
- low score strongly neglectful and/or abusive relationships
- used clinically to identify and intervene in 'at risk' relationships.

Paternal factors

Fathers impact on the way their children behave (Ramey & Ramey, 2000):

- fathers' alcohol abuse—child behaviour problems

- smoking fathers—children higher rates of respiratory problems and asthma, birth defects, SIDS, cancer, health risk behaviours, lower birth weights, increases maternal smoking.
- regular contact post-divorce—more positive behaviours, enhanced academic achievement.

Poverty

Longstanding social and economic disadvantage has a significant impact on child outcomes (Joshi, Wiggins, & Clarke, 2000):

- Social impoverishment—children do not experience nurturing care, parents feel ineffectual, unable to respond to their children effectively (Garbarino & Abramowitz, 1992)—may result from maternal depression, drug addiction, or parenting style.
- economic impoverishment—parental stress impacts on ability to provide nurturing and responsive care to their children.

Risks in the mesosystem

Migration

Where children are the only connections between two microsystems their development is at risk. Refugee children need bridges built to connect their experiences at home and at their school/centre (Sims & Hutchins, 2001).

Schooling-home links

In a similar manner, when the home environment values academic learning, children's learning improves (Garbarino & Abramowitz, 1992; Osbourne, 2001). Children exposed to books in their homes, who observe their parents enjoying reading, and who are given many opportunities to interact with books before they begin school are generally more successful in learning to read. In some situations, where families are living in poverty with little hope of employment as an outcome of schooling, girls are encouraged to leave school early. They are required to care for their siblings, or to get pregnant, obtain a sole parent benefit and thus contribute to the family income (Lawrence, 1990).

Risks in the exosystem

Education

Schools operate to perpetuate existing power relations (Hampson, Rahman, Brown, Taylor, & Donaldson, 1998), transmitting hegemonic culture values and beliefs. Where children come from minority groups (such as ethnic minorities) or where families live by values that differ from those of the hegemonic middle class (as is often the case when families are living in poverty), different value systems meet and clash in the school environment. In Australia, for example, some members of Aboriginal communities wondered if they would 'survive' the hegemonic ideas of best practice in schools (Pence, 2001). A common response is to create an oppositional culture involving the rejection of opportunities offered by the school, and the creation of groups such as street gangs. Schools often contribute to the risks faced by these children (Hampson et al., 1998) by failing to create adequate relationships with the children, and failing to create opportunities where children can learn.

Children from disadvantaged family environments are more likely to receive lower standards of schooling (Danziger & Waldfogel, 2000); (Heckman & Lochner, 2000). These children face secondary school with an inadequate foundation upon which to build new learning. This impacts on their ability to succeed at secondary school, and to access further education and training through tertiary education opportunities.

Quality of the education experience impacts on lifetime income and occupational experiences. Changes in class size and spending per pupil represent tinkering around the edges of the problem and do not result in significant changes in student outcomes (Heckman & Lochner, 2000). Dramatic changes in the way classrooms are run, and how schools are structured and organised, are required to make significant impacts on student outcomes (Eccles & Wigfield, 2000).

There are clear links between education and future income levels:
- people with college level qualifications maintained their standards of living over the past two decades,
- lower education levels—more likely to face unemployment (Lynch, 2000),

- one year of post secondary education—increase later family income by between 5 and 10%.
- workers with more education—more likely to receive ongoing job training (Heckman & Lochner, 2000).

Employment

Current economic conditions prompt many mothers to return to employment whilst their children are young. This creates a need for alternative care arrangements for children, which, in itself, does not pose a risk to children's development. However, when low family income limits the quality of alternative care for children, development is at risk.

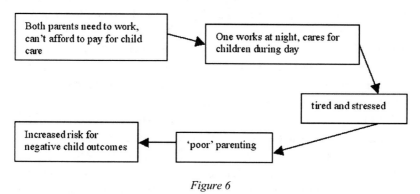

Figure 6

Factors in the exosystem such as employment stress and hours of work increase parental stress and thus impact on children's development.

Communities

When community decisions make parenting more difficult, developmental risk increases (Garbarino & Abramowitz, 1992).

High and low risk communities (Garbarino & Kostelny, 1994)

- two communities selected with the same economic levels
- High compared to low risk community
- higher levels of unemployment
- higher level of transient families

- residents—knew less about available community services, had fewer social networks, less likely to offer informal support to each other
- staff in community agencies—more feelings of depression and hopelessness
- 2x more child deaths due to maltreatment

Risks in the macrosystem

Profit ideology

In simplistic terms, western society is based on an economic model of constant growth with profit guiding economic decisions (Garbarino & Abramowitz, 1992). Ecologists criticise such ideological beliefs as their implementation has led to a depletion of the earth's natural resources, the destruction of many habitats, and an enormous pollution problem. All of these consequences increase developmental risks for children.

Independence

Western cultures assume humans are programmed for individual competition and independence. Dependence is assumed to be immature or pathological: success and failure lie within the individual. However many argue healthy development requires connecting with others.

The importance of inter-dependence

- Maslow (1970)—belonging needs come before esteem and self-actualisation needs
- Erikson Stage 1—importance of infants' establishment of trust in relating to the world around them (Erikson, 1950)
- Vygotsky (1962)—children relate to others to learn

Violence

An individualistic culture accepting competition as a natural consequence of being human, also accepts violence in the home as a natural expression of dominance and stress (Garbarino, Dubrow, Kostelny, & Pardo, 1992).

Acceptance of violence

- 1987—20% of Australians thought it acceptable for a man to use physical violence against his wife in some circumstances
- 50% thought it acceptable for him to shout abuse at his wife (Public Policy Research Centre, 1988)
- follow-up study 1995 - little change in peoples' responses (Laing, 2000)

One form of violence in the home is physical punishment of children.

Acceptance of physical punishment (Boss, 1995)

- US—89% parents had hit their 3 year old children in the previous year
- Korea—97% children had been physically punished, many severely
- Germany—60% fathers and 70% mothers hit their children
- Romania—84% parents thought spanking was normal
- Australian parents (Duke, 1995)
- 79% parents used physical punishment
- 6%—appropriate to smack children at 6 months of age
- 26%—appropriate by 12 months, 20% by 2 years, 18% by 3 years, 3% by 10 years
- Of parents who smacked
- 82% used an open hand
- 12% used a wooden spoon
- 3% a belt
- 46% targeted the buttocks
- New Zealand parents (Maxwell, 1995)
- 87% parents in 1993—smacking appropriate
- 1981—38% appropriate for fathers to hit teenage daughters, 1993—11%
- higher education levels, less use of severe physical punishment

The long-term impact of physical punishment is the cause of much debate in the literature (Boss, 1995), however it is generally agreed that physical punishment models a problem solving approach rooted in violence. It is linked with child abuse, and can also result in delinquency and acting out behaviours.

Sexism

For many years we have understood how sexism forces young males and females into roles which limit self-actualisation. Alloway (1995) suggests that stereotypes are so strong by age 3 children are unconsciously acting them out and reinforcing 'appropriate' gendered behaviour in others.

Patriarchy, the belief that women are secondary in importance to men, also creates developmental risk for children. New welfare policies in America require people to work for their welfare income. Similar ideas are being espoused in Australia and New Zealand (Harris, 2000). However, the majority of jobs obtained by former welfare beneficiaries offer an income below the poverty line (Rice, 2001). This has a particular impact on women: many sole mothers previously on welfare can not lift their families out of poverty through employment in low paying jobs characterised by instability and lack of health benefits. Inadequate access to affordable childcare limits their ability to access employment, which increases the risks they will continue to live in poverty. Patriarchy creates the climate in which social policy requires women to take employment, but fails to offer them choices other than low paid jobs without adequate childcare.

Racism

Racist stereotypes create narrow roles and children's behaviour is expected to 'fit' within these narrow boundaries. Many racist stereotypes categorise groups of children as inferior. Children exposed to low expectations based on these beliefs are more likely to achieve less as they become locked into a vicious cycle of limited expectations (Garbarino & Abramowitz, 1992). In addition to limiting behaviour, racism can profoundly affect children's sense of safety as they experience racial taunts and abuse. Physical abuse in the community is a common experience for some racial groups in Australia (Sims, Omaji, O'Connor, & Omaji, in review).

Accumulating risk

Children's vulnerability to risk increases with exposure to an increasing number of risk factors. Young people who have both family problems and delinquent friends demonstrate very high levels of delinquent behaviour (Howell & Bilchik, 1995). Verbal IQ declines as risk factors accumulate.

Accumulation of risk (Zubrick, Williams, Silburn, & Vimpani, 2000)

- 1 risk = 5 point IQ decline
- 2 risks = 8 point decline
- 3 risks = 18 point decline
- 8 risks > 30 point decline

Risk factors used in the calculation of the risk index in Canada were (Jenkins & Keating, 1999):
- low income,
- alcohol abuse by either parent,
- marital dissatisfaction,
- depression in the primary caregiver,
- large family size,
- teenage pregnancy,
- hostility in the parent-child relationship,
- divorce of parents,
- learning disability in the child.

Approximately 4% of children in the sample were exposed to 4 or more risk factors, and these children were five times more likely to show behaviour problems than children in the 'no risk' category.

Laucht, Esser and Schmidt (1997) suggest that no single risk factor is more important than any other, but that combinations of specific risk factors create risk chains.

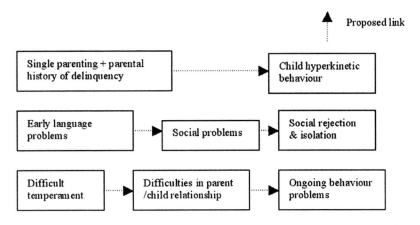

Figure 7: Risk Chains

Resilience

The pragmatic argument suggests that, as a society, we must continue to struggle to eradicate the risks to which children are exposed, but this is a long-term effort. At the same time, family support programs aim to make a difference by improving the resilience of children and parents to these risks. Approximately two thirds of children appear to be resilient and able to achieve positive outcomes despite the risks they experienced (Kirby & Fraser, 1998)

The literature presents the concept of resilience in slightly different forms.

Forms of resilience

Risk

- overcoming the odds (Kirby & Fraser, 1998)

- bouncing back from adversity (Resiliency in Action, 2001)

Stress

- process of coping (Zeitlin & Williamson, 1994)

- possessing learned coping skills

Recovery

- successful adaptation following a traumatic event

- survivors of injury caused by trauma

International definition (Grotberg, 1997)

- Resilient children need at least 2 of: I have, I am and I can

They need to have:

- people they can trust, who set appropriate limits to ensure safety, teach them what they need to know, encourage them towards independence, help them when they need support

They need to be:

- likeable, trustworthy, empathetic, respectful, responsible, positive

They can:

- talk to others to gain support, problem solve, avoid taking unnecessary risks, seek support when they need it.

Protective factors are those factors serving to reduce risk. Many protective factors will operate across several categories of risk. For example, developing a 'socially rich' community functions to decrease parental stress, decrease abuse and neglect, improve schooling, and decrease violence amongst many others. The presence of even a small number of protective factors can have a major impact on outcomes for children. For example the consumption of alcohol, tobacco and other drugs can be reduced by up to 50% when only two or three protective factors are present in the lives of secondary school children (Community Drug Summit, 2001b).

Individual protective factors

Temperament

An easy temperament is one of the most commonly cited protective factors at the individual level (Kirby & Fraser, 1998). The goodness-of-fit model (Thomas & Chess, 1977) suggests that the way parents respond to children with difficult temperaments can either exacerbate the temperament difficulties, or help to overcome them.

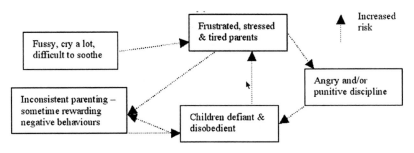

Figure 8 : Goodness of fit model

If parents are able to remain positive, and establish a happy and stable routine despite their children's difficult temperament, outcomes are likely to be much more positive. Difficult and shy children need warm, accepting parenting. Reserved and inactive children need a much more stimulating parenting style: they need encouragement through frequent interactions and ongoing exploration of the environment. Similar parenting styles (frequent interactions) may serve to inhibit very active toddlers and thus not lead to positive outcomes.

Factors other than the relationship between parent and child may also influence the outcomes for children of different temperaments. Difficult infant temperament is an advantage in time of famine (de Vries, 1984). Presumably infants with a difficult temperament make more fuss, are more demanding of their mothers, thus increasing their chances for survival in times of scarce resources. We must ensure that, in our search for protective factors, we consider issues at all levels of the system, and not in isolation.

Feelings of competency and self efficacy

Children who succeed in something feel better about themselves: they develop a sense of self efficacy (Bandura, 1977, Bandura, 1982). Success:

- improves the likelihood of success in other areas,
- increases attempts and persistence at new tasks,
- improves ability to cope with stress (Zeitlin & Williamson, 1994).

Parental self-efficacy is strongly related to positive parenting practices and other factors which influence parenting quality such as child temperament, social support, and reductions in poverty and maternal depression (Coleman & Karraker, 1998).

Programs can:

- improve individual performance
- introduce a range of other tasks in which children/families can succeed.

Self-esteem

Self-esteem is the broader range of feelings about the kind of person one is, and how that kind of person is valued in one's family, community and society. A positive self-esteem is a protective factor and comes from the microsystem. The humanist method of guiding children's behaviour (Marion, 1999) is founded on the belief that children will learn and perform better when they receive guidance that fosters their self-esteem. The role of adults in providing that guidance is crucial. Teaching adults how to interact with children in ways that enhance self-'esteem is one way to improve children's resilience.

Intelligence

Intelligence is linked with achievement in school, and thus to employment status and income in adult life. Children who succeed in school are likely to have higher self-esteem and greater feelings of self efficacy (Kirby & Fraser, 1998). Higher levels of intelligence may increase the mental strategies available to children and improve social competence through ability to attend and interpret social cues more effectively (Marshall & Watt, 1999). Intelligence is subject to manipulation through the environments to which children are exposed. In the same way, academic achievement is also a protective factor.

General wellbeing

Stress and illness are closely related. Managing stress, and maintaining adequate levels of physical health are protective factors. In a similar manner, emotional health impacts on the ability to cope. Maintaining a positive affect facilitates social interaction and the availability of social support, and therefore impacts on coping (Zeitlin & Williamson, 1994).

Children with chronic health problems have 2.2 to 2.4 times greater risk of developing behaviour problems, school problems and emotional disorders (Wamboldt & Wamboldt, 2000). The stress of children's illness impacts on their families. Some families emphasise the development of organisation and structure in order to cope, and this may occur at the expense of spontaneity and warmth.

Protective factors in the microsystem

Positive relationships

Attachment relationships function as protective factors for children. Sensitivity in caregiving helps to establish secure attachments. Sensitive caregivers may only 'correctly' interpret infants' signals 30% of the time, but are skilled at adapting their responses and re-establishing synchronicity (Tronick, 1989). The basis of sensitive care is the ability to 'tune-in' to the infant (Hutchins & Sims, 1999) and to craft an appropriate response, not just to the content of the infants' communicative signal, but also to the emotional tone. Securely attached infants who later demonstrate negative behavioural outcomes have mothers who become less positive and supportive over time (Thompson, 1998).

Emotional availability (Easterbrooks & Biringen, 2000, Emde, 2000) reflects parental responsiveness to a wide range of emotions. Adults who are emotionally available may participate in playful or teasing interactions with their children when this is appropriate.

Adults' ability to facilitate secure attachments with their infants is influenced by their own past history of relationships. Parents' ability to come to terms with negative past experiences, and their ability to understand these experiences in context, appear to function as protective factors in enabling parents to craft secure relationships with their own infants (Steele, Steele, & Fonagy, 1996).

Caregiver-child interaction and measures of the home environment (security, provision of appropriate play materials) have a significant impact on child outcomes at age 4 (Hallam et al., 1998). Relationships outside of the family are also important (National Research Council and Institute of Medicine, 2000). The number of 'good' relationships children have correlates directly with their resilience (Jenkins & Keating, 1999).

Jenkins and Keating (1999)

- 'good' relationships = how well children got along with siblings, peers and teachers

- age 6—1 'good' relationship as effective as 3 in protecting from conduct disorder, hyperactivity, inattention, indirect aggression

- age 10—need more than 1 for same level of protection

- risky environment + good relationship = same protection as non-risky environment

- boys—more difficult to establish 'good' relationships than girls

- boys—protection in high risk environments from 'good' sibling and/or teacher relationships, friendships with peers

In situations of high risk, children need to draw on support from their relationships with other people, and it is then that the presence of these relationships function as protective factors.

Effective parenting

Parenting involves more than relationships. Predictable family routines (such as interactions during mealtimes and bedtimes) act as protective factors against:

- disinterest in preschool and non-compliant behaviour (Keltner, 1990),

- low social competence (Keltner, 1992),

- impaired development of adolescent identity (Flese, 1992).

Family routines can be conceptualised as vehicles for predictable, rewarding and meaningful family interactions (Denham, 1995). Routines are established in families with high parental self-esteem and parenting skills (Baez, 2000, Brody & Flor, 1997). These factors provide the protection rather than routines themselves (Cardamone, 1999). Working with children through family routines produces positive outcomes (Yoos, Kitzman, & Cole, 1999, Sims, 1997).

Parental monitoring is an effective protective factor against unprotected sex, drug use, drug trafficking (Li, Stanton, & Feigelman, 2000) and conduct problems (Kilgore, Synder, & Lentz, 2000). The most effective monitoring occurs when parents obtain knowledge from child disclosure rather than their own active surveillance (Stattin & Kerr, 2000).

Parental expectations of children influence outcomes for children. Parental expectations were linked with adolescents' expectations and motivation (Dai, 1999) and are also related to parenting style. High parental expectations function as a protective factor when coupled with emotional support.

Finally, effective parenting involves the ability of parents to meet children's basic needs: adequate shelter, nutrition, warmth, safety and protection. Parental financial status clearly influences ability to provide these needs. Families require skills to cope with the stress of poverty (Zeitlin & Williamson, 1994). Parental competency in managing finances, cooking on a budget, and negotiating dangers in their communities are all contribute to protection.

Children's experiences in the home environment are complex and can not be measured by commonly used marker variables such as parental income, maternal age, marital status and/or housing conditions (Ramey & Ramey, 2000). The timing of positive experiences, as well as their quantity and quality, have a significant impact on child outcomes. Children themselves impact on the interactions they have with their physical and social environments.

Strong families

Family protective factors help families survive, and even flourish, in contexts of stress and disadvantage. Family recovery factors provide families with resources to bounce back after a crisis (McCubbin, McCubbin, Thompson, Han, & Allen, 1997). Together these combine into general family resilience factors: combining to create strong families.

Strong families

- family members are committed to each other, in both word and deed (DeFrain, 1999)

- commitment balanced with freedom and encouragement to pursue own goals—cohesion: a balance of individuality and togetherness (Silliman, 2001)

- spend time together often through family traditions, celebrations, ceremonies, routines

- enjoy each others' company

- care about each other and appreciate each other (Goddard & adapted by Rodgers, 2001)

- flexible and tend to perceive change positively (McCubbin & Figley, 1983)—sometimes called family hardiness (McCubbin et al., 1997)

- cope more effectively by pulling together, or identifying when they need outside help

- connected to others in their extended families communities, and culture (Silliman, 2001) so have available resources upon which to call for help

- available to help others when called upon (Goddard & adapted by Rodgers, 2001)

- offer support: emotional support (sharing the caring), esteem support (sharing the valuing of each other), network support (sharing the value of membership), appraisal support (sharing information) and altruistic support (sharing the value of sharing) (McCubbin et al., 1997)

- communicate effectively—speak out without judging or blaming

- attempt to resolve differences

- reduce tensions or share joy with humour (DeFrain, 1999)

- share their feelings, dreams and experiences

Strong families are spiritually well (DeFrain, 1999). Some families gain strength through a sharing of religious values.[5] Rituals and traditions associated with belief systems provide vehicles for meaningful family togetherness and provide opportunities for connection with extended family and community. Spiritual wellbeing is the ultimate form of connection; connection to other family and to all humanity which promotes compassion, sharing and love.

Quality early childhood services

Quality early childhood services make a difference to children's long term outcomes. Meisels and Shonkoff (1990), Schorr (1997), Greenwood, Model, Rydel and Chiesa (1998), Marshall and Watt (1999) and Ramey and Ramey (2000) provide some of many reviews of the importance of quality early childhood programs and early intervention programs.

Research focusing on the impact of childcare (in comparison to early intervention programs) on outcomes for children reports conflicting results

---

[5] One study demonstrated that as children's religious commitment increased, so did their academic achievement (Pew Charitable Trusts, 2001).

Impact of childcare

- 40% American childcare of low quality (Ramey & Ramey, 2000)
- 17% of children spending > 30 hours in childcare were aggressive compared to 9% of children who had not spent time in childcare (The NICHD Early Childcare Research Network, 2001)
- BUT these same children increased language skills at 15, 24 and 36 months, improved cognitive skills at 2 years, improved levels of school readiness at 3
- Sydney—children who attended part-time or full-time more likely to be securely attached to their mothers (Harrison & Ungerer, 1997).
- Children—same amounts of social and cognitive stimulation from their parents irrespective of the time they spent in childcare. Fathers of children in childcare increased time spent with their children in physical and emotional care activities (Bittman, Craig, & Folbre, 2000)

Quality early childhood programs (irrespective of their designation as early intervention or childcare) provide protection for children. Quality programs are responsive to the needs of the children and families who use them, thus will vary significantly from community to community, and vary over time within one community. Universal provision of high quality early childhood services can significantly improve outcomes for children.

Schooling

Quality schooling experiences also protect children from disadvantage. Successful schools:
- value academic learning,
- support teachers to constantly strive to improve their performance (Schorr, 1997),
- have flexibility to offer children what they need in order to learn effectively,
- are likely to be small—teachers and students can develop positive relationships, consultation and partnership in decision-making is logistically feasible,
- have high teacher expectations: children from lower socioeconomic groups, girls and minority children experience the

most negative outcomes from lower expectations (Eccles & Wigfield, 2000),
- have orderly and predictable classes,
- give children opportunities to make choices, follow their interests and share in the decision-making,
- focus on quality relationships,
- enhance children's self-esteem, feelings of belonging, and attitudes towards learning.

Successful schools operate in an environment which is supportive of them. This means wholesale changes are needed at the system level to address such issues as increasingly centralised control, inflexibility and bureaucracy. In addition, the intrusion of community issues into the classroom (such as violence) makes learning difficult. More children are attending school without having their lower level needs met (Schorr, 1997); they are therefore unable to make the best of the learning opportunities available to them.

The full-service school model proposes that educational, physical, psychological and social needs of children and families are met through the school (Withers & Russell, 2001). Some provide their facilities for community use after hours whilst others have become partners in community development efforts. For example, the Pacific Foundation in New Zealand runs family support programs, drop-in preschools, and clothing banks out of local schools. Schools are a particularly useful community focal point, as many families have contact with schools through their children. With willingness, and collaboration, schools can play a major role in protecting children from the risks they face.

Protective factors in the exosystem

Social capital

Building social capital in communities (Worthington & Dollery, 2000) involves developing trust between community members through:
- informal community activities—eg. neighbourhood or street parties
- formal interest groups—eg. playgroups, sports clubs, bush fire brigade (Lyons, 2000).

Trust is particularly lacking between people of different cultures and education can play a major role in breaking down this barrier

(Hughes, Bellamy, & Black, 2000). Non-profit organisations play a role in developing social capital (Lyons, 2000) through the provision of services such as health, education, culture and sport in communities. Some are sufficiently large to employ workers; in Australia in 1995-6, almost 600,000 people were employed in non-profit organisations (Lyons, 2000). For every one agency that employs people, a further fifteen use volunteers. Bullen (1998) suggested different types of volunteering produced different degrees of social capital:

- trust, feelings of safety and tolerance for diversity come from direct service delivery,
- participation in the community is associated with management committee work.

Traditionally, business organisations had no role in social capital formation; (Friedman, 1970) but modern business includes concepts of corporate citizenship, social responsibility, community integration and reputation building (Murphy & Thomas, 2000). Social capital can develop through:

- business partnerships with community agencies,
- financial support for community projects,
- corporate volunteering—supporting employees to undertake volunteer work,
- incorporating social responsibility into business planning,
- offering local jobs where possible,
- offering support for staff lay-offs.

There is ongoing debate about the role of the government in social capital formation (Cox & Caldwell, 2000). One position argues that by increasing its involvement in peoples' lives, the government has been responsible for declining social capital and so should restrict its role in direct service delivery, leaving local level service delivery to local level organisations (Stewart-Weeks, 2000). Cox and Caldwell (2000) suggest that this strategy may not work in disadvantaged communities where capacity and resources are distributed unequally. The state's role is to ensure rights, legal protection and fairness. Local communities contribute local knowledge and passion about local issues, and the market offers choice.

Current practice in social welfare appears to be shaped by mistrust and coercive client management. Such policies and programs function to diminish trust in the government, and further decrease social capital

(Cox & Caldwell, 2000). Future policy decisions and government actions need to be shaped by a consideration of the role they play in developing trust in government, and in enhancing people's skills in social capital building, both at organisation and community levels.

Safe communities

Children and families need to feel safe living in their communities. Providing adequate recreational resources, ensuring adequate employment opportunities, and facilitating school success all contribute to community safety. At another level, adequate street lighting, and neighbourhood organisations such as Neighbourhood Watch also contribute significantly.

Economic security

Employment is the accepted route to economic security in most parts of the world. The development of a class of 'working poor' undermines this position. Protective factors addressing economic security need to focus on:
- provision of employment opportunities for people,
- ensuring employment offers adequate financial rewards,
- facilitating educational success.

Availability of physical resources

Communities rich in physical resources are more likely to provide a range of opportunities for children and families. Availability of easily accessible and safe outdoor playgrounds provide opportunities for children to play with others, and for caregivers to meet other parents. Facilities in which to run local playgroups, and to hold local activities (such as craft mornings or budget workshops) make it possible for these activities to occur. An accessible local library provides a source of interesting and fun reading material for children and families. A local skateboard ramp may decrease the damage done by graffiti in the local area. A local youth centre may provide stimulating activities for young people and contribute to a decrease in delinquency. A range of local businesses may provide employment opportunities for parents and for young school graduates.

Protective factors in the mesosystem

Home-school and home-childcare links

Services need to be supported in their attempts to develop relationships with parents. Traditional practices (such as parent-teacher committees and meetings) only function to support some families. Those most at risk, are the very families who are least likely to access these formal meetings.

Effective transitions between home and service increase feelings of belonging (Sims & Hutchins, 1999). Parents need to be involved in these transitions. Parental involvement in daily activities can be encouraged and communication between service and home enhanced.

Centres can involve the wider community in their routines:
- key people—share time with children (eg. local police, local library staff),
- other adults—share expertise (eg. grandparents or other older residents) through storytelling, singing, cooking, taking activities, mentoring programs,
- children—linked with other children in their communities (eg. buddy programme matching a senior school pupil with a junior),
- people from different ethnic groups, religious groups and other minority groups—encouraged to participate. Ideally, the service should reflect the variation present in the local community, so that there is not a discontinuity for children moving from one setting to the other.

School/school links

Children are particularly vulnerable when they transition from primary to secondary school (Eccles & Wigfield, 2000). Most secondary schools are larger than primary schools. Children are taught by several different teachers and have less opportunity to develop positive and supportive relationships with their teachers. Classes are more likely to be characterised by greater levels of teacher control and discipline, and less opportunities for student decision-making and control. Transition programs between schools help children adjust to changes.

School/work links

Students who leave school early to look for employment are at significant disadvantage. Positive relationships between schools and employers can make this transition more effective. Many schools are now offering work experience programs, or linking students into VET programs whilst they are still in secondary schools. Research is divided as to the positive outcomes of adolescent work experience programs (Donahoe & Tienda, 2000). Some argue that students learn essential work place skills whilst others argue that the long-term outcomes do not justify the additional student load incurred. Young women and minority youth benefit more from VET programs but research in America suggests that less than a third actually obtain employment in their fields after graduation.

Employment practices

ILO Convention 156 *Workers with Family Responsibilities* (Work and Family Unit, 1992) captured a growing demand for consideration of family issues in work policies and practices (Seyler, Monroe, & Garand, 1995). Australia ratified the convention, placing an obligation on the Government to encourage the development of family-friendly work policies.

Family-friendly work options

- employer sponsored childcare (on site, or places reserved at a local centre)—preschool and school aged children
- flexi-time and flexible working arrangements
- job sharing
- maternity leave, parental leave
- phone-in lines—children returning to an empty house after school can report to their parents
- working from home some or all of the time

In most cases, employers introduced policies they saw were to their benefit (Seyler et al., 1995). These policies created greater employee commitment to the organisation, and often led to improved productivity (Thompson, Beauvais, & Lyness, 1999). However, Morris (1997) argues that families are often perceived by employers as a major problem. Well-educated men with working wives are paid less, and promoted less, than men with wives who stay at home. The real world of work is often hierarchical and unforgiving of the demands of family. The pace of careers in management and the increasing demands for face-time as a measurement of dedication and commitment to the job are pressures which prohibit many from participating effectively in family life.

Protective factors in the macrosystem

In the past, government services have been characterised by centralised development and control, and the ability to adapt to local needs has been limited. Stewart-Weeks (2000) suggests that we are beginning to see a change. Government can not make local initiatives happen but can create the climate which fosters their development. That financial resources are available to make changes is beyond doubt. The issue is not that there is a lack of resources, but the priorities placed on how such resources are expended. Arias (2000/2001) points out that 5% of the money spent worldwide on military technology and training in 1999 could have provided basic education, health care, nutrition, potable water and sanitation to all of the people in the world.

Conclusion

We know that the world is changing, and that current services are not proving adequate in meeting changing needs. Family support, as a new initiative, is aimed at addressing changing needs in a new manner. Family support programs have the potential to help create a new society but cannot, and will not, change the world by tomorrow. We can realistically expect to ameliorate some of the risks faced by young children and their families by offering opportunities to increase protection from risk. Protective factors can be addressed at all levels of the system, starting from the individual and moving through to the macrosystem level. Improving opportunities for young children and families to develop to their full potential is not just the responsibility of those children and families themselves, it is the responsibility of all of us who live in communities. Our efforts to make positive changes for all will be enhanced when supported by appropriate government policies, but are not prevented in their absence.

Chapter 3

Theoretical underpinning of family support

Introduction

Family support involves a process of supporting and nurturing children, families, and communities. Family support aims to strengthen families by increasing parental confidence and competence in their parenting role, and by creating family and community environments where parents can offer their children their best parenting efforts.

Family support is sometimes seen as a 'treatment'; something that is offered to families to increase resilience and the likelihood of positive outcomes for children, families and communities. However, others argue that family support is not, and can never be, a 'treatment'. Instead, they see family support as a condition of life (Garbarino & Kostelny, 1994): a way of living and being. This diversity of approaches taken makes it difficult to develop an effective and coherent picture of family support. The aim of this chapter is to provide a theoretical framework that, it is argued, underpins all family support programs. The framework is structured around three main theoretical perspectives: empowerment, ecological theory and a strengths focus. All family support programs must be based on these approaches if they are to be effective. Understanding these approaches is the beginning of understanding family support.

Empowerment

Empowerment was originally defined by the Cornell Empowerment Group (1989), and this early definition has guided our understanding of empowerment since that time. Empowerment is an ongoing process, not a specific outcome: process is equally important as outcome (McIntyre, 1995). The process is characterised by mutual respect and caring between participants themselves, and between participants and workers. It involves people who lack an equal share of resources working together at the local community level to develop greater access to resources. The central theme of empowerment is that the very people who lack access to resources, are the people who must be primarily responsible for developing strategies to gain increased control (Cochran, 1992).

Empowerment is not something that workers 'give' to families (Crane & Dean, 1999). It is something that develops through relationships that model principles of respect, equality and trust. The Swahili word 'Harambee' is sometimes used to summarise the concept of empowerment because of its meaning of 'let's pull together (Cochrane, 1991).

The empowerment concept is underpinned by a set of assumptions. These are outlined by the Cornell Empowerment Group (1989):

1. Everyone has strengths

2. Difference (for example ethnicity, age, ability, gender, family type, sexuality) is valued

3. The needs of individuals, families and communities must be considered in a broader ecological context (including environmental sustainability)

4. True democracy ensures all people have choices, and the opportunities to employ those choices

5. The deficit approach can not work with empowerment

6. An understanding of culture and how culture shapes roles and expectations is essential

7. An understanding of patriarchy and how patriarchy shapes roles and expectations is essential

8. Power is the key to accessing resources

9. Power operates directly and indirectly; an understanding of both types of operation is essential

10. Workers have power, and thus control over distribution of resources, because of their status as workers. Empowerment must focus on redistribution of power and resources.

Empowerment occurs at the level of individuals whose recognition of their lack of access to resources prompts them to take action. Individual empowerment is associated with feelings of increased assertiveness and self-confidence (Forrest, 1999). Groups of individuals are empowered when they are encouraged to ask questions about how they are disempowered, and what they can do about it (Jonson-Reid, 2000). Group empowerment leads to collective organisational empowerment where existing social policies and structures are challenged and transformed. The ultimate outcome of collective empowerment is community-based, autonomous services. Collective empowerment may also result in challenging hegemonic ideology as individuals and groups begin to question the ideals and expectations imposed upon them from infancy. It is this final level of empowerment that contains within it the potential to transform society.

Empowerment and power

Empowerment is grounded in the concept of power and involves the transfer of power from the oppressors to the oppressed. Power itself is seen as the capacity of individuals or organisations to have an impact (either planned or unplanned) on others (Cornell Empowerment Group, 1989). Those who do not have access to power often appear to accept inequality without question (Gaventa, 1980). Years of disadvantage shapes thinking through a self-fulfilling prophecy. People stop participating in community affairs because they believe they do not have the skills to participate effectively, they feel uncomfortable and feel they have nothing to contribute. They become increasingly isolated, increasing their feelings of powerlessness.

Different kinds of Power

Different theoretical approaches conceptualise power in different ways, impacting on how empowerment itself is understood. In this book, empowerment is used in the structuralist sense, with some influence from the post-structuralist position. However, any survey of the literature on empowerment demonstrates a wide range of positions taken, and it is useful to understand these positions, in order to appropriately place the perspective used in this book.

Pluralism

- power is spread amongst different interests (Dahl, 1961)
- power should remain distributed to ensure that no one group becomes too powerful

- empowerment—help disadvantaged groups or individuals compete more effectively with other groups for existing resources
- empowerment skills—lobbying, becoming involved in political action, learning how to use the system to ones' advantage, using the media

Elitism

- some groups have more power—are disproportionately involved in decision-making and have greater shares of resources (Leach, 1993)
- empowerment = skills to compete for resources + changing elite groups (from within or from outside)

Structuralism

- associated with Marxism and feminism
- power located in structural inequality
- structures in society such as race, class and gender reinforce inequality through the actions of the dominant groups in society
- change comes through changing structures
- transnational influences make structural changes difficult at the national level—changes at local level are more realistic (Ife, 1995)
- empowerment must address all aspects of inequality (power, gender, race, class, etc) through the development of communities and services where these inequalities are not permitted to operate

Post-structuralism

- Foucault (1980) discourse shapes power: power is seen as coming from the shared understandings people develop through their interactions with each other - understandings are more influenced by the views of some, and thus particular views become accepted as reality.
- empowerment through consciousness raising—an intellectual exercise rather than an activist approach (Ife, 1995)

Empowerment and social justice

The aim of empowerment used in this book is focuses on social justice and the challenging of inequality in our social structures. Inequality comes through unequal access to power. Poverty causes unequal access to resources, restricts individual choice and reduces opportunities. Patriarchy limits the career choices of women, and racism limits the availability of resources and life chances for people from ethnic minorities.

Professionals often have control over decisions relating to the needs of individuals, families or communities. The diagnosis of a behaviour concern by a paediatrician, for example, may open opportunities for family support and counselling, or may exclude the family from certain services. Institutions also demonstrate power over people. The welfare system has created groups of welfare-dependant families, and the health system has created groups of people whose unequal access to services has resulted in poorer health outcomes. Inequalities of power can be seen in access to resources, for example where some communities have large, Olympic-sized swimming pools, whilst others do not have running water to each dwelling.

Ife (1995) argues that those programs and professionals who do not actively challenge oppression, are supporting the dominant structures which create inequality. Therefore, any programme claiming to address social justice issues, must, of necessity, operate in ways that challenge these structural inequalities. Empowerment is the strategy most commonly used to do so.

Relationship between empowerment and community development

Empowerment is fundamental to the family support movement. It is also fundamental to a specific model of community work, that of community development. Ife (1995) argues that community development, as a specific type of community work, is governed by a number of principles, of which empowerment is only one. Some of these principles, such as environmental sustainability, may at times come into conflict with the principle of empowerment. For example, if community members wanted to develop a community-based industry which depleted natural resources and resulted in environmental pollution, whilst, at the same time, considerably improving their short-term economic power, a community developer would be required to counsel against such a move.

Many programs in family support follow not only the principles of empowerment, but also the principles of community development. Numerous researchers consciously use the community development framework for their work in family support, particularly those enacting the ecological approach of locating families in communities (for example, Schorr, 1997). However, the ultimate responsibility in family support work is the family, whereas in community development work, the ultimate responsibility is the community. Therefore, rather than identifying the community development philosophy as one of the underlying principles of family support, the principle of empowerment is preferred in this book.

This does not exclude the use of community development principles in family support work. Indeed, the ecological framework indicates the importance of taking a whole community approach to working with families. If, as argued earlier in this book, real change for families can only come about through radical changes to our political and economic systems, then an empowerment approach alone is not sufficient to create that change. A community development approach, with its focus on building community from the bottom up, is the only approach with potential for success.

Community developers operate under a set of principles outlined by Ife (1995). Community development work focuses on integrated development: social, economic, political, cultural, environmental and personal/spiritual components must all be considered in planning action. Confronting structural disadvantage at the local level requires the community worker to be aware of the subtle operations of power. This involves an understanding of, and commitment to, the principles of human rights. Empowerment ultimately leads to the overturning of existing structures of oppression. This operates in an ecological framework, where the personal is linked to the political; where individual and family needs and strengths are translated into community action.

Community ownership of materials, structures and processes is an important component of community development. Communities learn to become self-reliant, and not dependent on external support. This is particularly relevant to support from the state: true community development work is independent of the state. Community development operates from inside: solutions offered from outside are rarely effective in building communities.

Underpinning community development is a requirement that action is environmentally sustainable. This requires minimal use of non-renewable resources, conservation and recycling are included and pollution is curtailed. Growth must be controlled to ensure sustainability, and occur at a rate determined by the community itself. This requires a balance between short and long-term planning, and a holistic approach to planning. Communities operate as complex systems, and changes in one part of the system will result in changes across the entire system. Community developers need to consider the community as a whole, and encourage it to develop in its own, unique manner.

Neither process nor outcomes alone are sufficient to change oppression: they must be integrated. Just as ethical outcomes (such as environmental sustainability) are important components of community development, so are ethical processes. Processes such as coercion, making decisions for people, and manipulation are not appropriate strategies in community development work. Ensuring non-violence is crucial. Non-violence applies not just in individual interactions, but in community structures and institutions. Violence in communities needs to be addressed, but it must be done so through non-violent means. This requires the involvement and inclusion of all community members. Exclusion is, itself, a form of group violence, and it must be overcome for community development to occur. All community members participate, and contribute their different strengths. True inclusiveness operates when decisions are made through consensus rather than majority. Consensus ensures that everyone has been heard, understands all the issues involved, and agrees on the best form of action in the circumstances. Co-operative community structures are required to ensure that consensus and non-violent processes can operate. The dominance of competition in our communities needs to be challenged.

What is a community?

So far the discussion has focused around communities and the role of empowerment and community development in family support. However, it is necessary to be clear about what is meant by the term 'community'. The term 'neighbourhood' is often used (for example Garbarino & Kostelny, 1994, Schorr, 1997) to specifically identify a geographical community based on location (Ife, 1995). The assumption is that residents in this location have a sense of shared belonging so define themselves as 'insiders' and others as 'outsiders'. Residents share common rituals or symbols, values or norms, have emotional connections and share needs on which they are prepared to work together for solutions (Jonson-Reid, 2000).

Ife (1995) argues that this sense of community often does not exist in our modern social world, particularly in urban areas. Therefore, although the concept of a neighbourhood, or geographical community is the preferred site for community development, sometimes an alternative form of community must be used. This alternative is termed a 'functional community' (Ife, 1995) or a 'community without propinquity" (Wellman, 1979), and consists of people who share common interests or needs. For example, parents of infants may be seen as a functional community, as might families who have children with a particular disability, or families who have a drug dependent teenager. Such functional communities may be a necessary transitional step in developing effective and supportive geographical communities.

Empowerment and professionalism

Some argue that empowerment and professionalism are mutually exclusive (Barr & Cochrane, 1992) and suggest that the role of workers be classified as transforming rather than professional. The purpose for this distinction lies in the connotations of power and authority associated with the term 'professional'. The professional is perceived as (Cornell Empowerment Group, 1989):

- having knowledge drawn from the associated discipline,
- authority,
- community sanction to operate in the professional role,
- a professional culture (which may include a professional code of ethics) which guides practice.

In contrast, the transforming role is one where power is in the hands of the participants, rather than the worker, and where the worker undertakes a facilitation role, rather than one of director or leader. Relationships between participants are the important focus of the facilitating role, rather than relationships between participants and worker. Clients themselves become participants, or consumers whose belief in themselves enables them to take control of their own lives and their own futures. Workers assume that people are basically good and hold high expectations of them. The major difference between workers and participants is not in ability or aspirations, but in access to resources and power. Professionals may hold different views than participants, but these views are not perceived as better. Programs are based on co-operation rather than competition with an emphasis on joint responsibility, inter-dependence and mutual caring. All participants are included, and those who are different are valued as assets.

Strategies to facilitate empowerment

Empowerment can be achieved by developing services reflecting principles of social justice. At the level of policy and planning, services can enact equal opportunities initiatives, and affirmative action. Services can target inequities in society such as unemployment, and access to adequate resources. Services themselves can be accessible and approachable. Locating services in communities, and taking a universal approach to service delivery, ensures that services are seen as a right for all citizens, eliminating the negative impact of labelling. In a community development approach, such services would evolve from the community's own analysis of its strengths and needs, rather than from external agencies' decisions to locate services in certain communities.

Community-based social and political action is another strategy facilitating empowerment. This is an activist approach where community workers support community members to participate in the social and political processes. Finally, empowerment occurs through education and consciousness raising. The aim is to help people understand how they have been oppressed, and offer them the skills necessary to make changes.

Empowerment occurs though commitment over a long period of time to a community. An effective community development programme should be implemented over a period of at least 5 to 7 years (Jonson-Reid, 2000). Within the first 6 months of a project, workers are required to build trust between themselves and community members. They can engage, with community members, on needs assessment and develop groups, encouraging the participation of a wide range of community members. Following trust building activities, workers and community members will engage in capacity building where they will jointly plan actions, reflect on these actions as they are implemented, and continue to engage in further action.

Empowerment-based assessment

The New York State Family Development Credential, developed by the Cornell Empowering Families Project, offers principles of assessment based on an empowering framework (Dean, 2000); (Crane & Dean, 1999) and (Lawrence, Dull, Crane, & Dean, 1999). Assessment is used to help families decide on their own goals and how they want to go about working towards these goals. It is an ongoing process which takes into account families' changing goals and situations. Empowerment based assessment is based on strengths, a theoretical focus discussed later in this chapter. It is family focused, and not controlled by workers or their agencies and undertaken with families, not for them. Only the information needed is collected, and this information is treated with respect and confidentiality.

Assessment which focuses on families' goals and dreams will reflect cultural and other differences in values, beliefs and practices. The Family Development Credential does, however, provide an alternative form of assessment for African American families, the Nguzo Saba which reflects African community values. The Nguzo Saba incorporates the following principles:

1. Umoja: a striving to maintain unity in family, community, country and race

2. Kujichagulia: self definition, speaking for ourselves

3. Ujima: to take joint responsibility with others to work together and help each other

4. Ujamaa: to work together with others to ensure economic wellbeing; co-operative enterprise

5. Nia: to place priority on community building so we can restore our racial respect

6. Kuumba: to strive to ensure that our community is better for our children than it was for us

7. Imani: to believe in ourselves and others so our struggle is worthy and attainable

In contrast to the approach taken by the Family Development Credential, McIntyre (1995) suggests an approach based on change management or participatory action research (Wadsworth, 1991) principles.

Empowerment through:

- engaging in dialogue with the family or community to identify values and views about change opportunities
- common interests and desires explored and strengths shared
- family or community goals set, including mapping future desires and dreams
- plans and strategies drawn up
- resource planning
- implementation
- ongoing monitoring
- reflection

Ecological theory

Ife (1997) argues that the route to changing our society lies in empowering people who are marginalised so that their voices may be heard in policy debates. Empowering individuals to gain the skills to voice their position in a variety of contexts is crucial but serves also to reinforces society's dominant ideology of individualism. Empowerment must also work at the community level if changes are to be made to oppressive societal structures. Thus, empowerment must operate at both the personal and political levels to be an effective process operating in a critical framework.

Bronfenbrenner's theory

Bronfenbrenner's ecological theory provides a framework which helps link the different levels of the system in which empowerment must operate. At the individual level, individuals can be empowered to speak of their own perceptions and issues. Families also can be empowered to speak about protective factors in the family microsystem. Other microsystems in which family members participate (such as childcare services, schools, playgroups) may also need support in order to develop the skills to speak about the issues they face in delivering effective services. All participants in these various microsystems can be supported through empowerment to address risks faced by individuals as they move between the various microsystems. Families operate in wider communities. Community groups have the expertise and understanding of risks faced by local members. They can be encouraged to develop an understanding of the operations of power in their communities, learning to identify the various ways in which different community members are oppressed by the way in which the community operates. Addressing these risks is a community responsibility. Ultimately, ideologies guide the policy making process and influence the willingness of those in power to hear the voices of the people they govern. Unless efforts are made to ensure all voices are heard, little meaningful change can take place. At the macrosystem level, there is a collective responsibility to support the empowerment of all people in our society and to ensure that all voices are heard.

In addition to guiding the operation of empowerment at individual and political levels, the ecological framework allows expression of the complexity of inter-weaving protective factors necessary to address in a holistic family support programme. Children do not grow up in isolation: they grow up in families who access certain types of services, who live in communities with certain types of resources, and in cultures which provide sets of guidelines as to what is appropriate and not appropriate for individuals to aspire to, and the strategies they may use to achieve their goals. Family support programs, if they are to be effective, cannot limit themselves to an individual, or even a family focus. They must take a broader perspective and operate in an ecological manner.

It should be noted that the ecological nature of family support does not require one programme to operate every type of service which might be needed by children and families. Rather, an ecologically based family support programme works through empowerment, mobilising community members to contribute to the development of services and supports which met their own needs. Some risks may best be addressed through the operation of formal human services. Other risks may best be addressed through the development of friendship groups, or informal community links. Some services may need funding to operate, some may not.

Dunst, Trivette and Mott (1994) emphasise the importance of an ecological approach in empowerment and family support. They use the term 'social systems approach' to discuss what, in this book, is simply termed the ecological approach. They indicate the importance of the ecological framework in locating concerns outside of individuals, at the level of other systems: community, social structures and culture. This encourages the view that it is not deficits in individuals which are the cause of their inequitable access to resources, but issues in the wider systems in which individuals are embedded.

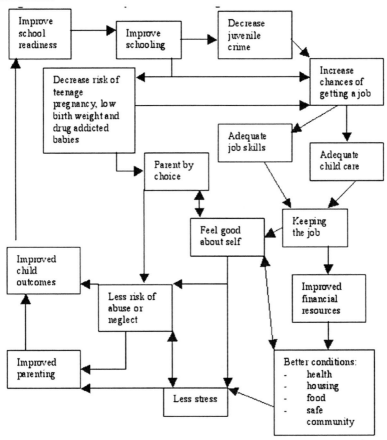

Figure 9: An example of an ecological framework

Interdisciplinary focus

The ecological focus of family support requires interdisciplinary thinking. Services founded in individual disciplines focus on identifying problems and seek solutions for those problems from within their own views of the world (Prilleltensky & Nelson, 2000). For example, Pithouse, Lindsell and Cheung (1998) point out the difficulties their family service workers, grounded in educational pedagogy, had in establishing true and meaningful partnerships with parents. They saw these difficulties as related to the impact of the education ethos which persisted, despite the best, and sincere, endeavours of staff involved. In disciples such as medicine and psychology (Prilleltensky & Nelson, 2000), a strong emphasis on treatment of problems creates a tunnel vision which influences perceptions of, and solutions to, the risks faced by families and children.

A focus on individuals as the source of problems, prompts interventions at the individual level. Once 'correct' diagnosis has been made, individuals loose their identity and are treated as cases (Saleebey, 1992). Information that does not fit the standard model can be ignored, and standard solutions are offered to 'solve' problems. Individuals and families are de-humanised, de-individualised and become simply representations of standard cases and diagnoses. Family violence is 'treated' by anger management programs for aggressors, poverty is 'treated' by budgeting programs, inappropriate parenting is 'treated' by parent education and risk behaviour such as drug taking is 'treated' by prescription of methadone. However, recent analyses of training within different disciplines (Ife, 1997, Abbott & Pugh, 1998, Sims, in review) indicates a growing trend towards recognising the importance of an interdisciplinary understanding of the issues involved in working with children and families in our communities.

Because every community is different, it is not possible to draw up a model of ecologically-based risks which need to be addressed in every community. Risks in communities, and the factors which best protect the members of that specific community against the risks they face, can only be developed through working with members of the community. Working with communities to identify risks and protective factors relevant to them requires professionals skilled in empowerment, but also requires a focus based on building from strengths.

Strengths focus

Taking a strengths perspective is not a new approach in community work (Armstrong & Armstrong, no date), but it is one that many professionals find difficult to enact because of their traditional grounding in its converse, the deficit approach. The strengths perspective has evolved out of the critical paradigm and the concept of empowerment. A strengths approach is used as a tool to overcome oppression; to support and encourage individuals to make changes in their own lives and in the political life of their society.

The deficit approach

One tool of oppression is the deficit approach which has consistently guided service delivery in many areas for many years. Dunst (1995) identifies both the treatment and prevention approaches as being grounded in a deficit approach to service delivery.

Treatment

- fix a problem—for example:
- disease cured through medicine
- stress fixed through stress management
- pathology fixed through drugs or therapy
- child abuse fixed through parent education, intensive family preservation programs

Prevention

- prevent problems from occurring—for example
- pathology prevented through immunisation, or education for a healthy lifestyle
- child abuse prevented through early intervention programs
- school failure prevented by preschool programs

The deficit approach is characterised by a needs analysis (sometimes called a diagnosis) identifying problems owned by individuals, families or communities. In requiring services in the first place, clients are judged as failures (Rapp, 1998). By focusing on problems and deficits during service delivery, expectations are set up which reinforce neediness and failure. The ultimate aim of service delivery is to address problems and return the client to a state of equilibrium aligned to the state they were in before the problems manifested. This, of course, assumes, that a return to a prior state is in the clients' best interests. A 'good' client is judged as one who follows professional requirements, who shows compliance towards professionals. Failures of interventions are often blamed on 'bad' clients: clients who failed to follow appropriate procedures. Following procedures, taking professional advice and support as unquestionably correct are not the skills required to take control of one's life. A deficit approach, aimed a 'helping' clients, functions to further disempower people.

Freire (1973) identifies how the perspectives of the oppressors influence the behaviour and perceptions of the oppressed, who, through time, rationalise their neediness and problems as inevitable, and take on the understandings and perceptions of the oppressors (Foucault, 1980). In developmental literature, at the level of individuals, such a process is called a self-fulfilling prophecy which links outcomes to expectations held about children by others (Berk, 1999).

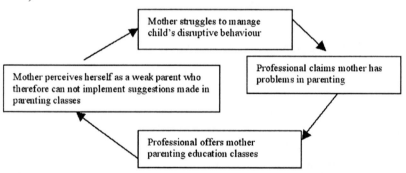

Figure 10: An example of oppression at an individual level

Communities can also be labelled as problematic. Once labelled in this way, services act to increase community dependency on outside sources of support. Kretzmann and McKnight (1993b) point out that many low income communities today have become communities of service where community members believe their well-being is dependant on them taking on the role of client for each service involved.

Communities whose identity is based on their problems experience fragmented service delivery, as each agency identifies need relevant to itself, then delivers services to address that need, and that need only. Families thus may find themselves accessing several different services, each with their own requirements and expectations. Professionals, delivering these services, become the source of solutions, rather than community members themselves. Funding for services is based on demonstration of need. It is in agencies' best interests to continue to demonstrate high need in communities, in order to maintain their services there. Improvements must be overlooked, or hidden amongst problems. Problems have to be defined as worse than in other communities, or worse than in previous years in order to maintain funding. This reinforces the powerlessness of the community itself, the impossibility of change and the negative labels associated with the community.

The risk terminology discussed in Chapter 2 also focuses on problems or deficits. The Commonwealth Department of Health and Aged Care (2000) points out that the extent to which any risk factor impacts on outcomes for children is based on a probability estimate not a direct cause-effect relationship. In addition, the evaluation of which risks are acceptable and which are unacceptable is a value-based judgement and thus influenced by power differentials (such as culture, and gender).

When the focus is on risks, there is a danger that the risk factors themselves will be inappropriately identified, leading to services which are not effective. The compulsory removal of Aboriginal children from their families (National Inquiry into the Separation of Aboriginal and Torres Strait Islander Children from their Families, 1997) is an example of this. At the time this policy was enacted, it was deemed that the risks faced by young Aboriginal children growing up in their families were too great, and that alternative environments had to be provided in order to ameliorate these risks. Hindsight clearly shows the racist and paternalistic attitudes underlying this assessment of risk. Unfortunately risks faced today still result in less desirable outcomes for Aboriginal children and families.

Focusing on strengths

In contrast to the deficit approach, a strengths approach follows a promotion model of service delivery (Dunst, 1995). A promotion model aims to enhance positive growth and functioning through facilitating ongoing development of capabilities which promote resilience. A strengths approach encourages establishing a partnership with clients, so that individual strengths and abilities are used as the foundation for building competence. Individuals and families are supported to identify the strengths they already have which can be used to contribute towards change. Change is more likely to occur when it arises from existing resources within the family, rather than resources brought in from outside (Elliot, 2000). Often people are not aware of the strengths they have, or do not perceive of some of their attributes or experiences as resources upon which they can draw (Saleebey, 1992). A strengths approach encourages this identification and mobilisation.

A strengths approach does not prohibit family members from learning new skills. Instead it requires that new skills are those identified as needed by family members themselves, and the learning is structured so that new content is based on the foundation of existing knowledge and skills (a Vygotskian approach to learning). People with mental illness and people with disabilities can be encouraged to use the strengths they have to create valued social roles (Wolfensberger, 1983) or enabling niches (Rapp, 1998) which provide opportunities for them to succeed. Families can be supported to identify the strengths that allow them to continue to live from day to day, and build on those strengths to develop a way of life they want for themselves.

In a strengths approach, practitioners focus on the abilities already present in the people with whom they work. Their role is to mobilise existing capacities rather than training, treating or educating people to change their behaviour (Chambers, 2000). Everybody has strengths. Often professionals find it difficult to identify strengths, because they are familiar with a deficit approach where their focus is on what is wrong, rather than on what is right (Dunst et al., 1994). Failure to observe strengths is a professional failure to see, rather than a family weakness or absence of strengths.

All families have problems in their lives, and some families face more problems than others. Strong families have resources to deal more effectively with their problems. A strengths focus does not deny the existence of these problems. Instead, it shifts the focus from the problems to the family strengths that are already being used to keep the family alive and struggling on from day to day.

One of the major concerns with the deficit approach is the assumption that 'fixing' problems means that families will function better. It is assumed that families with no problems must be well-functioning families. However, there is evidence in the literature (Dunst et al., 1994) that this is not the case: that the absence of family problems is not associated with positive functioning. A strengths focus avoids the risks inherent in this assumption. By focusing on strengths, families are empowered to improve functioning. Improved functioning may result in a lessening of the problems they face, or it may result in improved resilience to the problems. Either way, families benefit.

Key issues in the strengths approach

Saleebey (1992) identifies the main factors in a strengths approach. Empowerment, as discussed above, is the process by which power is uncovered and nurtured. Empowerment is a crucial component of working using a strengths approach: the two theoretical threads are tightly inter-woven. Practitioners must challenge all forms of oppression (including the power of labels) in their work with children and families and trust that the people with whom they work have the abilities, strength, motivation and energy to uncover and use the power within themselves.

Despite a strong tradition of individualism in western culture, empowerment rarely occurs at the level of the individual; it is a family and community phenomenon. Therefore, membership in families and communities is an important component of both empowerment and a strengths approach. Belonging to family and community groups is considered important in developing a positive inner spirit: at the individual and community levels, those with a belief in their ability to grow and develop will be more likely to show positive progress. Combining families who believe in themselves, with other families who also believe in themselves, creates a synergy which results in outcomes greater than each could have achieved on their own. For this synergy to develop, families need to communicate with each other; they need to interact and develop trust in each other; and they need to be accepted for their strengths and the contribution they can make.

Professionals, in working with these families, take on a collaborative role in order to foster the growth of community synergy. This professional role requires a suspension of belief on the part of the professional. Professionals may, for example, in discussions with family members, attempt to confirm their own hypotheses. Family members may either be inadvertently guided into talking about one part of their story only, or about one way of perceiving their story. This distortion of information may lead to interpretations of the family situation which are not useful for family members. A suspension of belief ensures that all family members are encouraged to tell their full stories and their own interpretations of their stories.

Solution focus

A strengths-based approach focuses on solutions in a different way than in traditional thinking (Petr, 1998). In most forms of practice, traditional problem solving involves identification of the problem, understanding the causes of the problem and finding solutions which address the causes. The strengths approach does not require an understanding of the causes of the problems; the link between cause and effect is not important. Instead of addressing causes, the strengths approach looks for occasions when the problem was not a problem: when children or families demonstrated strengths and overcame or avoided the problem. The strengths approach focuses on what works (Elliot, 2000). The aim is to understand what was done on the occasions when things worked. Once these strengths have been identified, they can be encouraged and developed for use on more regular occasions. Thus the strengths-based problem solving approach involves identifying or defining the problem, understanding exceptions to the problem and finding solutions based on these exceptions.

Assessing family strengths

Assessment of family strengths comes through interview and observation. Families work in partnership with practitioners in compiling their strengths inventory. Rather than asking specific questions, the worker can encourage families to talk about themselves. They can be encouraged to tell their story, describe their daily life and talk about the good things that are in their lives (Dunst et al., 1994). Observations can be made of the family's physical environment. Particular attention can be paid to the things that family members take for granted and therefore do not explain (for example, that the mother returns after school from part-time employment, helps the children with homework, gets dinner on the table and does the family's washing all before 6pm).

Strengths can be seen as the cognitive, attitudinal and behavioural characteristics of families that enhance and promote other protective factors in family functioning. One perspective of strengths suggests they consist of three components: family values, competencies and interactional patterns (Dunst et al., 1994).

Family values

- create family's unique 'culture' or style of functioning
- family expectations of members
- roles members play
- goals and dreams for the future

Competencies

- skills, knowledge and abilities
- how family members perform daily tasks

Interactional patterns

- family relationships
- verbal and non-verbal communication
- the degree to which family members support each other

In contrast to this three component breakdown of family strengths, Cowger (1992) suggests that family strengths are made up of two components: personal factors and environmental factors. In assessing personal strengths, practitioners should consider the cognitive, emotional, coping and interpersonal abilities demonstrated as well as the person's motivation. Sullivan (1992) further explores the role of the environment as a resource. Environmental strengths may be located in the microsystem (for example residence in a house with adequate fencing). Opportunities provided by teachers at school for parental involvement are strength which operates at the mesosystem level. Availability of a safe local park, with adequate play equipment for young children, is a strength located in the exosystem. Willingness of policy makers and town planners to provide infrastructure in neighbourhoods (such as parks, libraries, shopping centres) is a strength operating at the macrosystem level. In any inventory of strengths, it is useful to identify the strengths at all levels of the ecological system.

A framework for strengths assessment

- Individual and family
- cognitive abilities
- emotions
- motivation
- coping skills
- interpersonal skills

Microsystem

- physical environment
- material resources available
- psychosocial resources available

Mesosystem

- relationships with people in other Microsystems
- degree of influence exerted on operation of other Microsystems

Exosystem

- location and accessibility of microsystems accessed
- location and accessibility of other community facilities
- location and accessibility of resources needed outside of immediate neighbourhood

Macrosystem

- values and beliefs
- willingness to facilitate access to power

Another alternative to assessing strengths is to use Maslow's Hierarchy of Needs (Maslow, 1970) as a guide. At each of the different levels, questions can be asked about how the family meet the needs of members. The assumption is that any effort which contributes towards meeting a need is, in fact, a family strength. Ife (1997) reinforces this assumption with his discussion of reframing the concept of needs into that of rights. Using this reconceptualisation, Maslow's Hierarchy becomes a framework of rights. At the most basic level, for example, all humans have a right to adequate nutrition, adequate warmth and adequate shelter. Families, in providing for these rights, are demonstrating strengths.

Discussion with family members will determine if they are content with the way their family meets each need, or if they would like to change the way in which they meet a particular need. Where changes are desired, the existing strengths can be used as the foundation upon which change is built. This process is family-driven, with families making conscious choices about how their human rights are provided for. There are no judgements made about the way families meet members' rights. The framework simply provides an opportunity to discuss family members' perceptions and engage in goal setting.

In contrast to this approach, the Asset-based Community Development Institute provides a framework to use when attempting to map the strengths at a community (rather than a family) level (Chambers, 2000). They argue that strong communities are places where residents' capacities are valued and used to their maximum. In contrast, weak communities fail to use the capacities of their residents.

Mapping community strengths

- interview each resident to identify skills, existing community work, interests etc
- discuss barriers preventing people from participating
- create a community inventory of skills, interests
- the capacity inventory can be down-loaded for free, copied and used (Kretzmann & McKnight, 1993a).

In Australia, the Family Action Centre have developed an inventory of family strengths (Silberberg, 2001) consisting of:

- Communication: frequent, open, positive and honest communication. Humour may be a component of this.
- Togetherness: sharing values, beliefs and morals contributes to a family's feelings of belonging together.
- Sharing activities: this involves family members spending time together through activities such as sports, reading stories, hobbies, socialising, taking family holidays together.

- Affection: showing love, care, concern and interest in each other through physical contact (for example hugs or kisses), words and actions demonstrating thoughtfulness. Greetings, farewells, shared rituals (such as a bedtime story) and celebrations provide opportunities for affection to be shown.
- Support: this involves helping each other, being encouraging, and looking out for each other. Strong families are able to ask for help from each other as well as offer help.
- Acceptance: showing respect and appreciation of each other, understanding each person's individuality. Strong families value each others' differences and allow each member to be who s/he is.
- Commitment: showing dedication and loyalty towards each other, with a recognition of the needs of the family before the needs of the individual are components of commitment.
- Resilience: this involves the ability to adapt and manage change/challenges, having a positive attitude towards change and a belief in the ability of the family to manage.

The importance of valuing difference

The strengths approach requires practitioners to value difference (Goldstein, 1992). In valuing difference they are able to accept that there are multiple ways in which individuals and families can be strong, and that different individuals/families will choose the ways that are most appropriate for them.

Mei Ling and Patti are sole mothers of children (aged 3) who have been identified by the Child Health Nurse as having behaviour problems. Their caseworker, Jondie, summarised their strengths as follows:

Mei Ling

- completed secondary school
- weighs different alternatives in problem solving
- expresses her feelings
- wants to improve her current situation
- attempts to pay her debts despite considerable financial limitations
- has one local friend
- has a sense of humour

- willing to put effort into keeping house tidy despite limited material resources
- creative in finding solutions to need for furniture (eg packing box seats with cushions)
- willing to spend time teaching child
- reads to child and plays table-top activities with him
- willing to attend playgroups or other early childhood services
- lives near a local park

Patti

- cheerful and outgoing
- willing to talk and listen
- chats often with her child—not put off by lack of response
- copes well in chaotic situations
- feeds self and child on regular basis despite considerable financial limitations
- ensures child's safety before she takes drugs
- meets child's medical needs
- manages to provide shelter for child even when homeless
- wants to have a permanent home
- able to establish short-term relationships
- uses network of friends to help meet her and her child's needs
- always organises alternative care for child when she works as a prostitute
- when fencing not available, ensures child can play outside safely by tying him to the clothesline

In the examples above, both women demonstrate a range of strengths in parenting their child. The strengths demonstrated by Patti may not be the strengths that many people would consider appropriate. However, these strengths are significant, and indicate a very skilled degree of control over her life. For example, Patti realises that her child is not safe unless appropriately contained within a fenced yard. There are places in which she has lived where such fencing is not available. Patti also recognises that it is not appropriate for her child to remain inside the house all day with her. When she is tired after a night at work, she knows she is likely to strike her child in frustration. She has decided the best option to ensure her child can play outdoors in safety, is to tie him to the clothesline. In working with Patti, Jondie needs to reinforce the strengths Patti has demonstrated in coming up with such a solution, not denigrate her for tying up her child. Patti has already indicated she would like to work towards a permanent home. Ensuring that this home has adequate fencing will result in the child having appropriate and safe play space outdoors.

Conclusion

Family support programs are underpinned by theories which make these programs very different from many other types of social programs. Family support programs focus on:

- families, not individuals. Families are always considered in community and cultural context.
- offering community-based, universal services rather than crisis-driven, targeted interventions.
- building on strengths already in existence, and not on problems and deficits.
- families controlling their lives. Power and control are owned by families, not by workers.

These principles arise out of the three theoretical approaches discussed in this chapter. The concept of empowerment ensures that the power balance remains with families as participants of programs. They control their experiences and their destiny in the programme. The ecological focus ensures that a wide lens is taken when examining issues: the focus shifts through individuals to families, communities, social systems and culture in the assessment and goal setting processes. The strengths theme ensures that strategies planned to work towards families' goals are based on strengths and capabilities which will, in the long term, result in family and community independence from the service. The ultimate goal of family support work is for the programme to not be needed any more.

Chapter 4

Components of family support: Early intervention

Introduction

Family support operates in different ways in different communities. Some communities offer a range of services from the one agency, in others different agencies offer different programs. Often programs overlap in the services they offer, outcomes they are attempting to achieve, or processes they use to achieve these outcomes.

Different types of services can be categorised in different ways, such as centre-based or outreach, education or support, or on an age continuum. The decision to divide the material about programme components into three chapters is one based on pragmatism (there is simply too much material for one chapter), rather than on any particular typology. Considerable overlap exists between components covered in the chapters.

Targeting of programs

Family support programs vary in the degree to which they offer services to specific population groups.

Universal services

- all children and families entitled to family support
- tend to be locally based
- services are a right
- tend to offer minimal services, at a low cost/head of population

Universal services include health care, education and childcare but power dimensions operate in access and participation. Social class differentials are evident: for example, those from higher income levels are (Jamrozik, 1994):

- more likely to complete secondary and progress onto tertiary education,
- less likely to be unemployed,
- more likely to access childcare.

New Zealand research (Howden-Chapman, Wilson, & Blakely, 2000) demonstrates social class inequalities in health. Gender differentials operate in the employment arena with women continuing to receive, on average, lower pay than men.

Australia November 2000

- average weekly wage: men—$851.50, women—$718.90 (Australian Bureau of Statistics, 2001).

- part-time work 1998: men—12%, women—43.3% (Australian Bureau of Statistics, 1999).

Universal services, although in theory available to all members of a population, tend to be accessed by particular advantaged subgroups. Therefore, some argue it is more effective to offer selective services.

Selective services

- specifically target less powerful subgroups
- these identified on basis of risk factors—age, gender, occupation, income levels or other
- services offered to all members of subgroup
- cost/family > universal services, but overall cost of programme less (targets a smaller population)

Selective services are popular. The Australian National Stocktake of Early Intervention Programs (Davis, Martin, Kosky, & O'Hanlon, 1999) claims approximately 62% of programs for children under 5 years of age were selective. Programs for adolescents were more likely to be targeted at individuals.

Indicative services

- families or individuals at very high risk for negative outcomes
- for example: at risk for child removal because of abuse and/or neglect, parents are diagnosed with mental illness, children diagnosed with severe behaviour problems

- very intensive and expensive but offered to restricted number of people

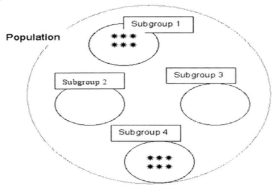

* families/individuals targeted for <u>indicative</u> intervention
  subgroups targeted for <u>selective</u> services
  population targeted for <u>universal</u> services

Figure11: Universal, selective and indicated service delivery

Universal, selective and indicative services focus on preventing ongoing and long-term problems. Other forms of support become available to individuals once treatment becomes necessary (Hillman, Silburn, Green, & Zubrick, 2000), and these are not included in this book.

Alternative, out-of-home care for children

Children's Services (forms of childcare)

Children's Services represent universally available services for children which are often, but not always, centre-based. Formal children's services differ in the way they are conceptualised from state to state (Press & Hayes, 2001), and between countries. Types of care include outside school hours care, childcare (including special types such as Kohunga Reo), family day care etc.

Use of childcare services

- New Zealand (Statistics New Zealand Te Tari Tatau, 1998)
- under 5: 19%—kindergartens, 17%—childcare centres (CCC)
- 5–13 years: 15%—school holiday programs, 20%—formal or informal outside school hours care (OSHC)

- limited access to CCC a barrier to employment: sole parents—30%, 2-parent families—12%, women—22%, men—5%

Australia

- June 1999: 23% children under 12 some form of childcare (Tasman Enterprises, 2001)

- children under 2 in CCC + family day care—15%

- preschool programs: 80.4%—WA, 96.3%—QLD (Press & Hayes, 2001).

- care for work reasons: OSHC—84%, CCC—54%

Alternative care arrangements for children also provide opportunities for parent relief and parent support. The role of childcare workers in providing support to parents is coming under increasing scrutiny (Sims & Hutchins, 1996). The recent OECD Report (Press & Hayes, 2001) identified respite needs of parents, and supporting families at risk as the most important functions of childcare, secondary only to supporting parents to participate in either the workforce or the community.

Good childcare undertakes much of the same functions as parents, including the provision of loving attachments, the foundation of healthy development (McGurk, 1996). However, good childcare is not a substitute for good parental care, but rather a support for parents to enable them to offer the best care possible to their children (Barnardos Staff, 1996). For many families, formal childcare services offer the support obtained in the past through extended family networks. Childcare workers offer advice and support on a range of child rearing issues (such as feeding, toileting, managing behaviour). They may be used as a first step in locating other community resources. In rural areas, and areas where parents have few informal support networks, childcare centres function as a contact point where parents can meet other parents and begin to network into their community. Community-based centres offer parents opportunities to participate in management (through community management committees) and thus enhance social capital.

It is generally agreed that children who attend high quality childcare programs demonstrate long-term developmental advantages but that lower quality centres may put development at risk, particularly in social and behavioural dimensions (Vandell, 2001,

NICHD Early Childcare Research Network, 1998). In North Carolina, policy directives aimed at enhancing access to and quality of childcare (Smart Start) have decreased behaviour problems identified in childcare children by 50% (Fight Crime: Invest in Kids, 2001). Children attending high quality centres demonstrate better levels of achievement in cognitive skills (maths and language) and social skills (interactions with peers, less problem behaviours) through to second grade (Peisner-Feinberg et al., 2000). Children who came from families whose mothers had lower levels of education were more strongly affected by childcare quality, and showed more significant gains in achievements when attending high quality care.

It is clear that benefits from attending quality childcare tend to be more significant in children for whom there is a larger differential in the quality of experiences between home and centre. Childcare plays an important role in reducing the risks associated with living in poverty. In the longer term, reduction of governmental expenditure on health care, remedial education and juvenile justice can accrue from the provision of quality childcare for children who are identified as 'at risk' because of poverty (Childcare Law Center, 1995).

Despite recognition of the benefits associated with childcare, and the intended universal availability of childcare services, access is not equitable for all families (Press & Hayes, 2001). Families on a higher income are likely to have more services available and are more likely to make use of the services available to them (Smith, 1999). Supply of childcare services is limited in rural and remote Australia and there are moves to introduce family day care schemes in areas where centre-based care services are not available. Continuing fee increases from the mid-1990s onwards have resulted in a decline in the number of low income families using childcare and there are claims that there have been more centre closures in low socioeconomic areas than in affluent areas. Indigenous families, families for whom English is a second language, and families who have children with additional needs are all less likely to access childcare, despite extra support available to facilitate access.

Respite Care

Respite care (selective childcare) operates for families who are identified as having a particular need for relief. There is increasing recognition that parents who are under stress (either economic or social) are less likely to be effective parents (O'Brien, 2001). Respite care is commonly offered to families of children with disabilities, children who are chronically ill, families where grandparents are the main carers and families at risk of child abuse or neglect (National Respite Coalition, 1998). It often involves placement of children in out-of-home childcare (centre or family day care during the day; residential, kin or foster homes for more extensive care arrangements) for a specified length of time.

Respite care is needed because family members caring for children with additional needs report increased physical and mental health problems (Stehlik, 1993). Abelson (1999) found that limited respite care for children with developmental disabilities impacted negatively on family functioning.

Costs of caring for children or elders (National Family Caregivers Association, 1997)

- 27% more headaches
- 24% more stomach disorders
- 41% more back pain
- 51% more sleeplessness
- 61% more depression

Communities in America where respite care is offered to selected families report reductions in the more expensive out-of-home crisis services and enhanced feelings of family wellbeing (National Respite Coalition, 1998). Respite care for families identified at risk of imminent break-up resulted in improved parental feelings of control and general well-being, and a reduction in problems: 92% of the families remained intact at the end of the 9 months study (Aldgate, 1998).

Benefits of respite care (Ambler & Kupper, 1996, ARCA National Resource Centre for Respite and Crisis Care Services, 1994c)

- peace of mind
- opportunities to enjoy favourite family pass-times
- improved their ability to cope with day-to-day responsibilities
- support in preserving the family unit

- opportunities to become involved in community activities

- time to go on holiday

- space for each family member to establish their own identities

There are different ways of offering respite care. Some services offer limited services, either in the family home or in the home of another family. This may involve someone occasionally caring for the child for a few hours. The carer may be a person employed by an agency and paid, or may be a friend or family member who is trained through an agency but works on a voluntary basis (ARCA National Resource Centre for Respite and Crisis Care Services, 1994c). Informal respite care arrangements also operate within family and friend networks. Kin-provided childcare, for example, often operates within a network of in-kind transfers between members of extended families (Brandon, 2000) with mothers using childcare based on their estimates of their ability to reciprocate in some way. Many agencies provide specialist camps for targeted groups of children, usually in the school holidays.

Alternative family placements are considered the most appropriate form of out-of-home placement for young children (Shaver, 2001). These can be kinship care or foster care placements (Barth, Courtney, Berrick, & Albert, 1994). Kinship care has benefits for children because of the maintenance of extended family links (Shaver, 2001). It is important that the short-term nature of the placement is emphasised, as research indicates that the longer children remain in foster care the less likely they are to return to their family home (Barth et al., 1994). Foster placements are likely to be more successful when they are located in the communities from which children originate, and are culturally sensitive (Mattingly, 1998). A focus on family-centred practise facilitates the ongoing involvement of parents and their children in order to achieve the quickest possible reunification of the family (Braziel, 1996).

In small communities, it may be impossible for foster and biological families to remain distant from each other, and this can be seen as facilitating relationships, rather than as a problem. For example, Freedman and Stark (1993) report on an Aboriginal foster care programme that addressed the issues of Koori families. Aboriginal families commonly take responsibility for relatives' children. Fear of white authority often results in these families receiving no support from the system at all, which sometimes lead to situations of significant hardship for family members. This programme offered recognition of the already existing cultural practice, and supported its continuance by targeting resources at the families concerned. The programme deliberately challenged existing institutional racism in welfare practices by acknowledging that Aboriginal foster care was different than white foster care, and thus needed different policies and procedures. With adequate resources supporting foster families, children's health and nutrition improved. Stability of placement lead to improved school attendance and social admissions to hospital were reduced. Some families were relocated to adequate housing, which significantly improved conditions of living.

In America, an innovative foster care programme, Family to Family, is run at various sites cross 13 states (Ali & Green, 2001). Family to family consists of networks of neighbourhood-based, culturally sensitive foster care. Children are placed in the communities in which they lived and both foster and biological families are supported in interacting with each other. Biological parents are encouraged to see the foster family as caring for their children whilst they use the time to recover and build their own strengths. Social workers, birth and foster parents are all involved in child placement decisions and in working towards reunification.

An alternative to formal kinship or foster placements is a form of respite care called shared care. Families are matched with second family who agree to share the care of the identified child. The focus is on creating a second family for the child, who spends a regular amount of time with them, and thus develops caring attachments with members of both families. The second family may, or may not, be relatives of the child's birth family. Both families are likely to receive support from the sponsoring agency. In some areas, shared care arrangements are expected to be reciprocal: parents 'trade' respite care with each other (ARCA National Resource Centre for Respite and Crisis Care Services, 1994c).

Foster families themselves, may need respite services (ARCA National Resource Centre for Respite and Crisis Care Services, 1994d). Adequate respite lowers the risk of foster parent stress and burnout and decreases the likelihood of multiple placements for children in their care. Respite carers are more likely to offer quality services if they have received training and ongoing support from sponsoring agencies (ARCA National Resource Centre for Respite and Crisis Care Services, 1996).

The final respite option is that of residential care. In the past, large institutions were common. In more recent times smaller, group homes have become the norm in residential care. There have been many attempts to eliminate residential care for children in favour of family (or foster) care (Barnardos Staff, no date-b, Barnardos Staff, no date-a). The permanency planning approach (Taylor, Knoll, Lehr, & Walker, 1989) requires that every possible effort be made to keep families together. If this is impossible, family placement for children is mandatory. In Maccomb-Oakland family placements are required for all children, including children with severe disabilities. Rosenau (1990) argued that there was no child they had encountered whose disability was so severe that a family could not be found.

However, some children's needs are best met by residential rather than foster placements (Little, 1999, Bath, 2001/2002). Children in residential care tend to have complex and demanding problems (for example, those who have been convicted of crimes and those who have been involved in sexual maltreatment either as victims or perpetrators). These children present with chaotic behaviours, poor impulse control, fearfulness, reluctance to attend school, feelings of being lost, feelings of inadequacy, no hope for the future, offending and inappropriate sexual behaviours. They are likely to have difficulties in their relationships with their parents which makes family reunification challenging. Unfortunately, research suggests that children in residential care are likely to encounter further problems. Sinclair and Gibbs (1998) found that 44% of children in residential homes say they have been bullied, 14% claim they have been sexually abused by other children, 66% say they have been very unhappy in the recent past and 40% say they have thought about committing suicide.

It is generally accepted that good residential homes are small. They are staffed by trained staff clear about their goals and the strategies they use to work towards those goals (Sinclair & Gibbs, 1998). Good homes encourage and support relationships with families (except in those circumstances when this is identified as not in the child's best interests). There is currently support for developing standards for the monitoring of out-of-home care (Scott, 2001/2001).

Rural and remote areas face particular challenges in offering respite care because of issues related to isolation, small populations and large distances between communities (ARCA National Resource Centre for Respite and Crisis Care Services, 1994b). There is limited access to specialists, and limited availability of respite carers. Successful rural services recruit, train and support local para-professionals to network and collaborate with local community resources, and support the work of professionals located outside the community. Local co-operatives and networks may help meet transport needs.

Family Day Care offers opportunities for day respite for targeted families. In Stockport, UK a number of certified caregivers are used by social services to offer day respite (Steele, 2000). The aim of the respite programme is to prevent the breakdown of vulnerable families. Family day carers attend a short training course to prepare them for the additional needs of the children and families with whom they work, and also participate in regular support group meetings. Social workers rated the programme positively, and felt it definitely prevented family breakdown in a number of cases. Family day carers felt the children for whom they cared benefited. They were ambivalent about the impact on families: some felt the programme simply postponed family breakdown rather than preventing it.

O'Brien (2001) suggests that respite care ought to be considered more seriously as an important component of family support programs. Respite care should be one of a range of options offered in an integrated approach to family support and all options should be characterised by a sense of partnership. Respite carers should receive remuneration at a level that recognises the value of the work they are doing and the responsibilities they accept. Low rates of pay tend to result in a transient population of respite carers, with valuable skills being lost as experienced carers move on to other employment opportunities. The fact that Barnardos in Australia pay carers above the award rate explains their ability to place children in respite care within 24 hours of referral (Voigt & Tregeagle, 1996).

Crisis care

Crisis care is an indicative service for families who need immediate alternative care arrangements for their children (ARCA National Resource Centre for Respite and Crisis Care Services, 1994a). Their need may have arisen from homelessness, violence, family breakdown, incarceration, illness or psychological problems. Crisis care provides short-term care for children along with support services for parents to help them resolve the crisis situation. Women's Refuges are examples of crisis care offered specifically to women and their children experiencing violence in the home. Crisis care services offer residential programs (together or separately depending on the types of crisis), childcare and family support services. In many parts of the world, children are placed in foster homes to ensure they continue to receive a family upbringing. Crisis care services place precedence on the safety and wellbeing of individual family members and encourage family reunification where this is appropriate.

Children in crisis care are likely to benefit from routine and structure in order to create a sense of security in their lives. The coping strategies children develop to manage their trauma may be disadvantageous to their development in the longer term (Bloom, 1995, Sims, Hayden, Palmer, & Hutchins, 2000). Calm reassurance of psychological and physical safety is needed for children to feel sufficiently comfortable to abandon previously useful coping strategies.

Parental visits to children in crisis care need to be encouraged. Parents may need support and structure to ensure visits are successful and not unnecessarily stressful. Opportunities to play together with developmentally appropriate activities provide staff with openings to observe and support positive parent-child interactions. Parent training and parent support groups operated from the crisis care service may assist in the development of positive parenting strategies in preparation for reunification. Parents may need access to a range of community-based services such as child welfare, housing support, counselling programs, food banks, alcohol or substance abuse programs, employment services, budgeting support etc. Co-ordination of these services is important in ensuring that parents are able to meet agreed goals and objectives in the reunification plan.

Connecting parents

Research clearly identifies the link between health and wellbeing, and the existence of social support networks (Bloom, 1990). Social support acts as a buffer against stress (Crnic & Booth, 1991) and helps new mothers in adapting to their parenting role (Voight, Hans, & Bernstein, 1996). Mothers' perceived need for social support, combined with environmental risk, tends to increase the risks of maternal depression (Follett, Dayton, Simonds, & Rosenblaum, 1999). Early research identified a link between parental social support networks and children's social and emotional development (Cochran & Brassard, 1979). Support may function to improve developmental outcomes for children by influencing parental sensitivity and expression in unstructured play situations (Contreras, Mangelsdorf, Rhodes, Diener, & Brunson, 1999). Young children, particularly children of preschool age, play a significant role in providing openings for caregivers (usually mothers) to link with other caregivers and develop social support networks (Jackiewicz, 1998).

Many family support programs capitalise on this and provide a range of opportunities for families to connect with other families who have children of similar ages, in the hope that informal support networks will form around common interests and needs. The support provided through groups is different than the support provided to individuals through intimate, dyadic relationships (Felton & Berry, 1992), with most people needing both kinds of support. Opportunities for parents to meet and interact in groups often result in the formation of dyadic relationships.

Scott (2001)

- Long term follow up of a group of first time mothers who met for 6 to 8 weeks within the first few months of their child's birth.

- One to two years later—80% meeting regularly, in informal groups, usually in each other's homes.

- 20% meet with individuals they had met through the initial groups.

Research has failed to demonstrate significant benefits of informal support (Lennon et al., 1997). However, parenting groups, whether formal or informal, offer opportunities to lessen isolation (Carter & Harvey, 1996). Many parents feel inadequate and afraid, loose perspective and do not realise that the issues they face are similar to the issues faced by many other parents. Groups allow parents to express fears and concerns, and to be reassured that such feelings are normal and appropriate. Parent groups encourage diversity as different parents have different strategies for dealing with problems and concerns. Parents are encouraged to demonstrate empathy and acceptance towards others in the group. They can celebrate little successes with others, and share frustrations. Parenting groups need skilful facilitation to ensure issues of power and diversity do not sabotage the group purpose and process.

Indicative parent-to-parent programs match a parent with another parent who has a child with similar needs. This is commonly used in the area of disability, where parents who have children of similar ages with similar disabilities are matched (Klemm & Santelli, 1999). Parent volunteers usually receive training and support from the sponsoring agency. A co-ordinator is responsible for overseeing the programme, following up both the new parent and the volunteer parent to ensure the match is working effectively. The support offered feels personalised, is only a phone call away, and is often available 24 hours a day.

Parent-to-parent programs may also focus on childcare. In Australia, a programme called Matching Mothers matches families on the basis of key criteria (ages of children, care requirements, place or residence) (Jacobsen, 2001). Matched families provide childcare for each other, either permanent part-time or occasional care (such as babysitting). No money changes hands—care is provided on a reciprocal basis.

A slightly different way to conceptualise linking parents is demonstrated in Washington State's family support programme (Nahom, Richardson, Romer, & Porter, 2000). Families who have children with disabilities are matched with a community guide who may be a parent of a child with a disability or volunteers with other links to disability. Case Managers put families in touch with potential community guides, though families have the final choice as to the guide they select. Guides provide families with information, do research and legwork to help families access resources, listen to and support families. Evaluation of the community guide programme suggested that families who had good experiences with community guides were very happy with the service. However, families were better finding their own resources than using a guide who was not effective. Training and supervision of community guides is clearly important in delivering a quality service.

Education programs for parents

Parents learned about parenting from their own parents and extended family networks. However, in more recent times, families have less access to extended family networks and the world itself is changing rapidly. It is not uncommon for today's parents to feel that the experience and wisdom of their own parents is not sufficient to prepare their children for the world they will face as adults (Debord, Heath, McDermott, Wolfe, & Team, 1999, Gonzalez, 1998). Whilst many people recognise that parenting is one of the most important tasks adults will ever face, there continues to be minimal preparation undertaken by prospective parents, and little support available for those struggling with parenting (Pugh, De'Ath, & Smith, 1994). Parent education offers opportunities to fill the gap many parents identify in their own knowledge and skills.

Universal

- any parent who wants to improve knowledge and skills;
- commonly run out of local community centres or schools.

Selective

- run in targeted communities where risks are high; or
- focused at target populations such as parents from minority groups, or sole parents;
- attendance by choice

Indicative

- families with a high risk of breakdown: eg abuse or neglect, children ADHD;
- attendance may be compulsory.

In all of these programs, there is an underlying judgement valuing particular forms of parenting over others (Jones, 1999) and parent educators need to be sensitive to the complexities surrounding this issue. Different desired outcomes for children prompt parents to use different parenting strategies (Julian, McKenry, & McKelvey, 1994). The more conformity is valued relative to self-reliance, the more physical punishment is used as a strategy in child rearing (Boss, 1995). Parenting in violent communities is more effective in the short-term when parents behave in a harsh and punitive manner (Fick, Osofsky, & Lewis, 1997). There is an unmistakable (and incorrect) assumption in many parenting education programs that parents in these situations are parenting 'incorrectly' and therefore need to change (Gorman & Balter, 1997).

Parent education uses a range of strategies to deliver training to parents. Most commonly, parents attend regular meetings or classes, facilitated by a parent educator. Other models may involve parents in on-line groups, or telephone help lines. Education material may be offered to parents to work through on their own. This may consist of videos, newsletters, books, workbooks or television programs. For example, Children's Hands-on Integrated Learning Discoveries—Parents as Co-Partners offers child-sized back-packs for toddlers to take home (Patton & Jones, 1997). Each pack contains a letter explaining the purpose of the activities, instructions to parents on how to play the activities with their child, and all the necessary materials for each activity. All include books parents can read with their children. Tapes are available in languages other than English. Special packs focus on bath-time, bed-time and travelling. Most packs are designed to be used within a week. Parenting education can also be delivered through the mass media using books, magazines, television, radio, newspapers and other channels of communication. However Pugh, De'Ath and Smith (1994) point out that much of the material currently available through the mass media is contradictory, and reinforces common stereotypes.

Another form of parent education is an individualised, in-home approach (Gill, 1998) where a home visitor (sometimes called a therapist or interventionist) works with a family to change the way they interact and handle the target child. This model is the most costly and intensive, and tends to be used for specifically targeted families. Counselling and family therapy are also examples of individualised (or family-based) parent education.

Much of the research on parent education has been undertaken in tightly targeted programs, operating out of ideal environments such as university research laboratories. These programs commonly show significant changes in children's behaviours. Research which investigates the impact of parenting programs on more general audiences, and in less rigidly controlled situations (such as in local centres) has been more likely to show ambivalent results. However,

National Health Service Child and Adolescent clinics operating in real environments with normally referred families, were shown to be effective in making positive changes in parenting behaviours and child outcomes (Scott, Spender, Dolan, Jacobs, & Aspland, 2001). Parents attended group sessions for 2 hours a week over13 to 16 weeks. Sessions addressed issues of play, praise and rewards, limit setting and managing inappropriate behaviour. Children whose parents attended the sessions showed significant improvements in their antisocial behaviours, conduct disorder, hyperactivity and emotional problems. Parents who attended the sessions increased praise in relation to inappropriate commands by a factor of 3.

Parent education programs are commonly based on one of two major theoretical foundations; those of Humanist theories (Rogers or Adler), or behaviourism (with its link to social learning theory). Rogerian programs use techniques such as reflective listening, genuineness, empathy, unconditional positive regard, and an accepting, supportive, non-judgemental attitude (Fine, 1989). Parent effectiveness training (PET) is based on these principles and has proved very popular(Gordon, 2000).

In an Adlerian approach, children's behaviour is seen as purposive, and parents are taught to understand what children aim to achieve by their behaviour (Marion, 1999). The most popular parenting programs based on this approach are the STEP programs (Dinkmeyer, McKay, & Dinkmeyer, 1989, Dinkmeyer & McKay, 1983). It is important to note that both PET and STEP programs have been criticised for cultural insensitivity (Gorman & Balter, 1997) and are inappropriate for families that come from other backgrounds than white middle-class.

Behaviourist-based parenting programs encourage parents to focus on their children's observable behaviour (Smith, 1997). Parents are taught to manipulate the consequences and precursors of behaviour through altering their own behaviour and/or manipulating the environment. Inappropriate behaviour is seen to result from inexperienced parents unwittingly rewarding the wrong outcomes (Pugh et al., 1994). Behavourist approaches are commonly used in parenting programs for children with autism, ADHD and other forms of disability, or in programs focusing on working with children in the juvenile justice system.

The Patterson Model is one such programme (Patterson, Reid, & Dishion, 1992). Parents are taught to observe their children, monitor behaviour, state rules clearly, offer rewards and punishments for behaviours, and negotiate disagreements. Evaluations demonstrate reductions in aggressive and deviant behaviours (Marshall & Watt, 1999). The Patterson Model, in different forms, has been offered to parents with children of all ages. Its effectiveness is more marked with younger children, although changes in the behaviour of delinquent adolescent boys have also been demonstrated. However, the time needed to make noticeable changes appears to increase as the age of the target children increases.

Parenting education can have a short-term impact on new mothers and their infants. Brown, Yando and Rainforth (2000) evaluated a programme which educated mothers through videos and found they demonstrated increased knowledge of child development, were more pro-active in relation to their infants' health care needs and had infants with less illnesses in the first year of life. Other programs focus on older children. In one, families (with children's average ages between 10 and 11) were referred through the mental health or juvenile justice systems (Harrison, Boyle, & Farley, 1999). The programme ran for 12 weeks (2 hours a week) and offered parent education and outdoor recreation activities for children. The programme made changes in family cohesion, family conflict, family time together, time spent in the community, mental health of the parents and parenting styles, but there were no changes in parent-child agreement. Parenting discipline styles changed. There were increases in parents talking to their children, sending the children to their rooms or doing nothing, and decreases in yelling, threatening and physical punishment. The Strengthening Families Programme: For Parents and Youth 10–14 brings parents and children together for 7 weeks in classes (Molgaard, Spoth, & Redmond, 2000) combining parent, child and family skills(Kumpfer & Tait, 2000). The programme reduced youth substance use, conduct problems and gave young participants more ability to resist peer pressure.

Another programme, targeted at families referred through the health system for children who had severe behaviour concerns (Thompson, Ruma, Schuchmann, & Burke, 1996), offered group sessions (12 parents per group) using direct instruction, video modelling, role plays reviews of in-home experiences and assigned reading from a parent manual. Parents who completed the programme reported decreased frequencies of children's externalising behaviours, felt more positive and effective as parents and more satisfied with family relationships. These effects were maintained for 3 months after the programme was administered. However, independent assessment of children's behaviour did not demonstrate significant changes.

Clarke, Harnett, Atkinson and Shochet (1999) report on a parenting programme specifically designed to address the trauma experienced by Aboriginal families through their experiences of colonisation. The Resourceful Adolescent Parent Programme (RAP-P) focused on three areas: parents are people too, families are important, and culture and community. A video offered exercises and discussions for Aboriginal groups to work through with a trained facilitator. The approach uses a strengths focus as parents are encouraged to identify their existing strengths as parents, and the strengths of their communities. Parents are encouraged to reconstruct existing devalued cultural images of themselves and their communities.

Gorman and Balter (1997) claim parent education programs generally fail to demonstrate long lasting, significant changes either in parenting behaviour or in child outcomes. Simply providing parents with information may even be counterproductive (Kumpfer & Alvarado, 1998) but when offered as a component of a wider approach to family support, parenting education can make a difference in the lives of children and families (Lloyd, 1999).

Parent education may be limited in its longer-term impact because parents who are under stress are more likely to continue with familiar patterns of behaviour, rather than attempt new strategies (Brown, 2000). Thus whilst universal and some selective programs may be effective, because parents are choosing to attend out of interest and a desire to learn more, indicative programs may be less likely to succeed because parents attending them are already identified as having problems and experiencing high levels of stress. In these situations, parent education programs may not be the best support strategy to offer families: alternatives such as childcare may be more useful in the short term.

Some programs take a wide focus and attempt to intervene in family issues, such as parental anger management, depression, communication strategies and mood. The Prevention and Relationship

Enhancement Programme (Marshall & Watt, 1999) teaches couples strategies to communicate, resolve conflict, understand gender differences in communication, and addresses other issues in establishing and maintaining intimate relationships. This programme is generally offered to couples prior to their marriage. A 3 and 4-year follow-up of couples showed increased levels of relationship and sexual satisfaction, and lower problem intensity. Similar benefits were found to have been maintained in a 12-year follow-up. Researchers in Australia are currently evaluating the impact of the programme locally.

One alternative to the usual parent education programme is offered through Parents and Teachers (PAT), and its various derivative programs. PAT programs combine home visits (which have an education focus) with support groups (Goldsmith, 1992). PAT originated in Missouri and programme parents were found to be more knowledgeable about child development and child rearing. Programme children were more advanced in language, social development, problem solving and other cognitive abilities. An evaluation of New PAT found that increased parental knowledge was not translated into improved child outcomes; rather it was the quality of the relationship between the home visitor and the parent that influenced children's developmental outcomes (Pfannenstiel & Seltzer, 1989).

Parents as First Teachers is a version of PAT delivered to first-time parents (Winter, 1985). It is this version that initially attracted the interest of the New Zealand government although considerable opposition was expressed about the relevance of importing a programme based on American cultural values and practices (Farquhar, 1990). Parents as First Teachers (PAFT) began in New Zealand in 1991. Parent educators are trained to undertake home visits, offering information and advice on child development and behaviour management (Early Childhood Development Unit, 2001b). Families participating in PAFT also have opportunities to get together. Home visitors link families to community resources and provide referrals to other agencies where necessary. A Maori version of PAFT is available (launched in 1999), called Ahuru Mowai. Maori parent educators are trained to focus on traditional Maori child rearing practices, acknowledging Maori cultural values and preferences.

Family Start, part of the New Zealand Strengthening Families programme, has incorporated PAFT as the education component (in conjunction with health and welfare components) in order to ensure that the needs of at risk, targeted families are met. In Family Start, a home visitor undertakes a needs assessment, teaches parenting skills and links families to community resources. Programs encourage family's links with their *whanau* where appropriate. Family Start offers a more intensive support to families than PAFT.

In comparison, the Positive Parenting Programme (PPP) is offered in Australia. This is a multi-level programme, targeting different services to different audiences. The various levels are (Marshall & Watt, 1999):

- Level 1: brief instructions are given on strategies for handling minor behaviour concerns and developmental issues such as toilet training
- Level 2: minor behaviour problems such as tantrums are addressed through minimal contact (face-to-face or phone)
- Level 3: a brief parent education programme offered for specific problems (eg bed time problems)
- Level 4: intensive programme for parents whose children display a wide range of conduct disorders, oppositional defiant behaviour or aggression. The programme focuses on parent-child interaction and parenting skills.
- Level 5: an intensive programme for families whose children have severe behaviour problems. Issues of family functioning, marital communication, mood management and stress management are addressed as well.

A pilot programme delivered in Perth (Williams, Silburn, & Zubrick, 1998) took a universal focus and was delivered through primary health care. All parents of children aged 3–4 years in the targeted areas were invited to participate. Training consisted of group workshops run for 2 hours a week for 4 weeks, followed by 4 15-minute weekly phone support sessions. Families needing further support were offered home visits, plus modules in mood management and partner support (ranging from 3 to 9 sessions as required). Evaluation of the project demonstrated that 82% of families completed up to 7 of the 8 workshop sessions and 17% were referred to the clinical programme. Follow-up after 12 months indicated that reported child behaviour problems had been halved, as were incidences of seriously dysfunctional parenting. Ongoing evaluations will follow the group for a year.

In Queensland, PPP was offered to a selective group of 300 families whose children were at risk for developing conduct problems (Marshall & Watt, 1999). Four intervention groups were offered.

- Level 1—self-help information and advice
- Level 4—10 week child-focused parent training course
- Level 5—12 week parent training course plus training in marital communication, mood and stress management
- Control group—no services.

All three levels of intervention were effective in reducing children's oppositional and aggressive behaviours. Parents reported using less coercion, were less likely to over react to their children's behaviours and had lower levels of depression. Families in rural Queensland were offered a Level 2 PPP (Marshall & Watt, 1999). They received written materials and a workbook consisting of tasks they needed to complete on a weekly basis. Weekly telephone counselling was offered for 10 weeks, focusing on parental use of the written materials. Families reported fewer child behaviour problems, improved parenting skills, feelings of increased competency and reduced levels of parental stress, anxiety and depression.

Williamson (1997) reports on a parenting programme implemented in Queensland schools (but developed from a programme operating in New Zealand) for school-aged children. Parents attend group sessions where they view videos of their interactions with their children and learn to reflect on what they see. Workshop content evolves out of the issues rising from the videos, taken at the beginning of the programme. At the end of the programme long term support networks are set up and parents are encouraged to undertake further training to function as workshop facilitators. Generally a PATCH programme would take 2–3 sessions to collect assessment and video information, and 12–18 sessions of learning and generalising. Sessions are scheduled at times most convenient for parents.

In an indicative parent education programme, Van den Boom (1994) identified, by means of a questionnaire, infants who were particularly irritable. Mothers were trained to interpret and respond to their infants' signals appropriately. Adult-child interactions improved significantly, and infants became more sociable.

Parent education courses need to offer training in different ways to meet the needs of indigenous families. Tsey and Every (2000) discuss a programme offered to survivors of the Stolen Generation (children who were taken away from their Aboriginal families to be reared in the white world (National Inquiry into the Separation of Aboriginal and Torres Strait Islander Children from their Families, 1997). The Family Wellbeing course ran for 10 weeks and participants attended for 4 hours a week. It focused on basic living and parenting skills and was nationally accredited, giving participants a qualification in counselling. Facilitators were Aboriginal and evaluations indicated participants saw this as very important.

Prenatal supports

One particular type of parental education is that undertaken before children are born. Adequate prenatal care increases the probability of a healthy baby and positive developmental outcomes. Both Australia and New Zealand offer prenatal courses for prospective parents. These mainly cover pregnancy and birth, and offer support and advice on health and personal care during those times. These are often run by midwives or nurses attached to birthing hospitals or centres. Family Start in New Zealand, a selective programme, encourages involvement of mothers early in their pregnancy to ensure ongoing health and positive developmental outcomes for the baby. Pregnant mothers may receive advice, support and be linked into community networks by a home visitor, who will continue to visit after the birth of the baby.

Prenatal programs can also be indicative. For example, in Philadelphia, high-risk pregnant women are visited throughout the pregnancy by both a nurse and a social worker. This programme was found to significantly reduce the number of medically fragile babies left in hospital (Schorr, 1997).

Family planning itself is an important component of family support.

- unwanted pregnancies in America—12% of all births,

- 47%—contraceptive failure.

- 53%—attributed to the 10% of women who use no contraceptive methods, and who are likely to represent an accumulation of risk factors such as poverty, low levels of education and youth (Zuckerman & Brazelton, 1994).

- unwanted pregnancy: less likely to receive prenatal care, less likely to give up smoking.

- Maternal smoking: cause of 20 to 30% of infants with low birth weights.

- Passive smoking: increases children's risks of illnesses such as colds, ear infections, respiratory problems (including asthma), SIDS, behaviour problems.

Research demonstrates that infants whose conception is planned are less likely to experience abuse or neglect (Schorr, 1997) and are more likely to be healthier. Women who are healthy before pregnancy are more likely to have healthy infants (Zuckerman & Brazelton, 1994). Safe sex practices reduce the risk of infants infected with HIV or other sexually transmitted diseases. Preventing unwanted pregnancy, and ensuring the health of women prior to, and during the pregnancy, can therefore be more effective than parent education and support after the birth of an unwanted child.

Information and resources for families

Parents' need for information increases as demands on them increase (Garbarino & Benn, 1992). Information for parents may come through mass media parent education programs. Services such as childcare centres and playgroups may also have a range of information available to parents in the form of pamphlets, booklets or videos. On occasions, larger organisations run a lending library specialising in providing information on child rearing, child development and parenting in general.

Toy libraries are another popular resource for parents Toy libraries provide quality, safe and educational toys. Children and parents can meet and interact at the library, and borrow toys. Some toy libraries also provide opportunities for parents and professionals to participate in training and development courses. Libraries originally served preschool children and their families, but in more recent times have branched out to provide support for older children, people with additional needs, students, teachers, and adults. The Federation of Toy Libraries in New Zealand and the Australian Toy Library Association advise and support new and existing toy libraries, and are referral sources for parents. It is possible to undertake vocational training in toy librarianship through the TAFE system in Australia.

Parent Information Centres (PICs) in Western Australia are run by staff experienced in parenting and child development. They are located in easily accessible venues, usually major shopping centres or community centres. Mobile PICS offer people in rural areas access to the service. PICs provide a range of resources on parenting: videos, books, brochures and audio-tapes. Staff are available to help parents find the information they are looking for. Group sessions are offered regularly on topics of interest in the local area.

Home visits

Home visiting is a common component of family support programs. Because home visiting has been used by a wide variety of models and disciplines, there is often confusion about how it functions within any one specific programme and the following issues need clarification (Wasik, Bryant, & Lyons, 1990):

- Identity of the client: many programs specifically target child outcomes (usually developmental outcomes) and argue that the client is the child. Others identify the primary target as the family. Whilst they may offer developmentally appropriate play opportunities to the child, they may be more interested in focusing on issues which make it difficult for parents to engage in these with their children. An alternative focus is on the family system itself: home visitors may be interested in interactions and dynamics within the family. The ecological approach views the family embedded in wider system of community and culture. In this approach, home visitors may be more interested in the development of community networks and links, and the empowerment of the community as a whole to take responsibility for meeting the needs of its members.
- How the client is served: in the past, home visitors used a directed, 'expert' model of service delivery, offering training and advice to parents in order to shape them towards an idealised version of effective parents. In more recent times, programs based on an empowerment model, require home visitors to develop partnerships with families. Families are expected to learn to take responsibility for negotiating how their needs are met within their own communities.

- The role of the Home Visitor: early home visitors were required to teach, and modify parental practices towards their own understanding of what was 'right'. Family support programs today require home visitors to take on collaboration, facilitation and negotiation roles. Home visitors today are likely to have as much knowledge as their predecessors, however the way they perceive families, and the way they work with families, is very different.

As home visiting has such a long history, there are numerous evaluations of its efficacy across a range of different programs. Home visits during pregnancy and continuing after the birth of the child, resulted in improved outcomes for teenage mothers and their children (Farrington & Welsh, 1999). Babies were born heavier, were more likely to be born full-term, and mothers smoked less during pregnancy. There was a decrease in child abuse and neglect over the first two years of life. Over a period of 15 years, mothers were less likely to have been arrested.

In the United Kingdom, Home Start offers support to mothers of preschool-aged children with the aim of preventing family crisis and breakdown (Frost, Johnson, Stein, & Wallis, 2000). Home visitors are volunteers.

Home Start families

- 61%—economically vulnerable
- 54%—lone parent
- 69.5%—rental accommodation
- 66%—significant health concerns.

Most Home Start families (64%) reported an improvement in their emotional well being during the 6 months of the evaluation. This was attributed to the availability of someone to listen, the availability of neutral support and concern and the level of intimacy that developed in their relationship with the home visitor. All of the families felt they were not receiving sufficient support from friends and family, although over half (55%) thought that this had improved over the duration of the study. Over half (51%) felt their parenting had improved.

The Community Mothers Programme, developed in Ireland, also uses local volunteer mothers as home visitors, in delivering a selective service to new mothers living in disadvantaged neighbourhoods. Home visitors are experienced mothers who have been trained in listening skills, fostering the development of positive self-esteem and in providing information about local resources (O'Connor, 1999). Children whose mothers received home visits were more likely to have been immunised, to be eating an appropriate diet, to have stories read to them and to play 'cognitive' games (Smith, 1999). This programme was extended to offer support to itinerant, traveller families (Fitzpatrick, Molloy, & Johnson, 1997) who lived in caravans, usually without running water and with limited access to toilet facilities and electricity. Many mothers were illiterate. Although traveller children continued to demonstrate low immunisation rates, and high rates of hospitalisation, they showed improved development. Improvements in diet and maternal well being were also demonstrated.

An adaptation of the Community Mothers' programme has been offered in Perth, Western Australia (Marshall & Watt, 1999). Child health nurses and trained volunteer mothers visited new mothers over the first 12 months of their child's life. Although this project was characterised by a high dropout rate (mothers returning to employment, or leaving the area) programme children demonstrated higher rates of immunisation and were breast fed longer. Mothers read more to their children and felt more confident.

The Western Australian Parent Link Home visiting Service is focused on supporting parents who have children under 6 years of age. Volunteer home visitors are trained and supervised by each programme co-ordinator. Volunteers are usually parents themselves who live in the local community. Parent Link aims to:

- assist parents develop understanding, skills and confidence in their parenting role;
- provide information about child development, guiding behaviour and establishing secure relationships;
- lessen parental feelings of isolation;
- provide someone who will visit families in their homes at times convenient to the families;
- link parents into other services as appropriate.

Despite the popularity of volunteers as home visitors, some argue that professionals or other highly trained staff are an essential component of a successful home visiting programme (Brown, 2000).

Nurses are commonly used in programs which focus on pre- and post-natal health and wellbeing. Other programs train para-professionals, and match home visitors and families on dimensions such as ethnicity/ languages spoken.

The relationship established between the family and the home visitor is crucial. In their evaluation of a parent education programme incorporating home visiting, Pfannenstiel and Seltzer (1989) found that the quality of the relationship between the home visitor and the parents was the single most important factor in the programme. This relationship was the major predictor of children's developmental progress, particularly in areas of language development.

Group programs for parents/families and children

The Playgroup Association (in each state of Australia) and the Playcentre Association (in New Zealand) co-ordinate playgroups. Playgroups provide opportunities for parents and carers to:

- socialise;
- share information and ideas;
- support each other in developing parenting skills and confidence;
- play with their own children in a relaxed atmosphere with a variety of developmentally appropriate resources.

Playgroups are often used as meeting places where caregivers (usually mothers) can meet people experiencing similar life events and establish support networks (Jackiewicz, 1998). In a sense, playgroups can see seen as an extension of the family network (Sterpini, 1993).

Children have opportunities to mix with other children, to learn through new play experiences, to learn simple routines and rules, to interact and learn interpersonal skills. Some playgroups offer home visits when a child has a serious illness and can not come to playgroup. Small groups of local parents can get together and run playgroups out of their homes, often borrowing toys from the local Toy Library for each session. Mobile playgroups offer families in new suburbs, or rural and remote areas, opportunities to access playgroup activities. Children in rural areas, who have little opportunity to interact with peers, benefit from the provision of playgroups (Ashby, Boorsboom, & Rosser, 1976).

Playgroups in the past tended to cater mostly for middle class women. In more recent times, specially targeted playgroups (such as for women from culturally and linguistically different backgrounds, women from lower income levels, teen mothers, fathers) are available. Playgroup Officers from the relevant association can provide support and assistance to parents in establishing and running playgroups, as well as providing access to resources, information and inservice training. Playgroup workers contact families, who might otherwise not have the skills to become involved in playgroups, and work along side them in setting up their own services.

There needs to be a range of different playgroup models available to meet a wide range of needs. Some playgroups can be more structured than others. Some may need to have bilingual staff. Others may operate over the weekend where fathers, and other family members such as grandparents and siblings could be involved, thus increasing family involvement and creating opportunities for family social networks to develop (Jackiewicz, 1998).

Playgroups in England run in a different way than in Australia and New Zealand. They evolved as a parent response to minimal preschool provision (Finch, 1984). Children attend several sessions a week (usually 4 of about 2.3 hours each) (Statham & Brophy, 1991). Their main income is derived from parent fees and fundraising. Employed workers run playgroups (an average of 2.8 paid workers per playgroup), but the majority of the staffing is volunteer parent help (Moss, Brophy, & Statham, 1992b). Children attending playgroup are usually aged between 3 and 4 years, though some are younger. Parental involvement in playgroups is variable: most mothers take a turn on roster and a small number are not involved at all (Moss, Brophy, & Statham, 1992a). Mothers from socially and economically advantaged groups were more likely to be involved. Few fathers were involved in any way. Most parents use playgroup to facilitate their children's social skills and to provide learning opportunities through play (Statham & Brophy, 1991).

Drop-in programs for parents and children are another playgroup-type service sometimes offered in family support programs. These are a more casual form of playgroup where facilities are available for parents to drop-in with their children when they choose. Other forms of drop-in services may involve drop-in programs for children or adolescents after school, evenings or weekends. There is little research demonstrating the effectiveness of these services as stand-alone services, as they are mostly used in conjunction with other models of family support.

Family centres

Family centres are community-based family support services that offer a combination of supports to local families (Pithouse, Lindsell, & Cheung, 1998, Andrews & Ellis, 2001/2002). These are often located in disadvantaged areas, thus providing selective services to families. However, other models of family centres may require specific referrals in order to access services (Smith, 1999). Family centres may operate from a range of settings such as schools, community houses or purpose built facilities. They offer a combination of services such as childcare, playgroup, drop-in, child health care, parent education, advice, counselling, resources (such as libraries) group work, and community work. Specialist services may include a residential component where parents are offered intensive training and support in areas related to child rearing and parenting.

Family centres evolved out of family resource centres operating in America in the late 1970s. Family Resource Centres offered opportunities for parents to come with their children, to socialise, learn parenting and other basic skills, have temporary relief from childcare responsibilities and develop co-operative arrangements for sharing goods and services (Chamberlain, 1996). Some family resource centres offered centre-based programs, others included outreach activities (such as home visiting).

Family centres may offer integrated services, or may simply offer co-location of services with little service integration. Co-location offers a 'one-stop-shop' approach to service delivery, where service users do not have to travel long distances to access different services (Donham, 2001). Agencies may benefit through sharing costs (such as sharing a receptionist, computer facilities, conference rooms etc). In setting up a co-located array of services, agencies need to ensure they build on existing community collaboration. Collaboration can be facilitated by the provision of common space (such as a shared staffroom) and through the provision of orientation training.

The Families First strategy in New South Wales explicitly aims to co-ordinate services operated by a range of different government and non-government agencies to support parents caring for new infants and rearing young children. For example, open access, multi-use community-based family centres operate in 2 disadvantaged communities (Pithouse & Holland, 1999) where there are high levels of child abuse and neglect, and up to half of the population are receiving benefits of some kind.

Pithouse and Holland (1999)

- centres offered—play programs, crèche, toy libraries, adult education, parenting programs, social skills classes, parent and toddler groups, after school clubs, advice, counselling, drop-in, antenatal groups, child health clinics, parent support groups.
- Users: women aged between 21 and 30; 48% married, all had children, most under 8.
- Reasons for using the centre: social reasons, to participate in an organised group, access play opportunities for children, somewhere to go for advice and support.
- Non-users: more likely to perceive of them as places for sole parents who were having difficulties, services offered irrelevant

A similar programme operates in Kings Cross in London, one of the most disadvantaged wards in the Borough of Campden with 35% of residents coming from ethnic minority groups, and a 23% unemployment rate (Wigfall & Moss, 2000). However, there are also a significant number of middle class families, and a high student population. Partnership between local agencies resulted in a campus providing:

- Nursery offering care to 108 children aged 6 months to 5 years,
- Parent's Centre;
- 20 place community nursery for children aged 2 to 5 years;
- special needs charity providing services to children with disabilities and their families;
- a family day centre and advice centre for people who are homeless;
- small school for children with autism.

In America the family centre approach is represented by the neighbourhood centres (Leon, 1999), which are required to improve:

- outcomes in reading and math scores;
- truancy rates;
- health education;

- illiteracy rates;
- job training;
- levels of teen pregnancy;
- recreational activities;
- health screenings for seniors;
- job skills for elderly residents;
- case management and levels of community pride among residents;
- using programs most relevant to the community's strengths and needs.

Most centres offered activities and meal programs for elderly residents, health screenings, after school programs for children, drug education, case management, job training programs, meals-on-wheels, tutoring, counselling and home visiting. Evaluation of the centres found improved literacy skills in more than half the students participating in literacy programs. Employment was obtained for 69% of the youth participating in collaborative job training programs. Decreased disciplinary referrals, improved maths, reading and English achievement, decreased absenteeism and increasing involvement in positive youth activities were demonstrated for 85% of the young people who participated in the youth programs. Families involved in the home visiting programme showed improvements in family cohesiveness, and employment outcomes 76% of the time. The evaluators stated that the collaborative approach, resulting in the integration of health, mental health, recreational, social service and other community services, was essential to the success of the neighbourhood centre model.

The Northern Lakes Home Visiting Programme (Bryce, Ellison, Corning, & Curtis, 2000) is an Australian example which uses the family centre concept. The programme operates in an area with a high proportion of young families and children, sole parent families, families on low incomes, families in crisis, high levels of violence in the home and child abuse. The service offers early childhood clinics, parenting groups including a Young Parent's group, and home visiting. A group of volunteers offer transport and respite care. The programme is staffed by social workers, welfare workers and early childhood nurses. The universal approach to home visiting means that families at all levels of risk participate in the programme, with families at high levels of risk tending to remain in the programme for longer. In the evaluation of the service, families reported feeling more confident in their parenting and were able to access a range of other services because of their involvement in the programme.

The Sure Start programme (www.surestart.gov.uk) operating in the United Kingdom uses the family centre approach (Glass, 1999). Partnerships between statutory agencies and voluntary groups aim to develop an integrated approach in the delivery of core services, which are defined as:

- outreach and home visiting;
- family and parent support;
- quality opportunities for play, learning and childcare;
- child health and development advice and care;
- support for those with additional needs.

Local partnerships may operate other family support programs as relevant for their community's needs (for example budgeting, literacy training, English language courses, employment courses). At the Government level, Sure Start is seen as an investment in children (Glass, 1999).

Sure Start, and the Family Centre movement in general, are based on the assumption that integrated services are more effective than uncoordinated service delivery. Integration of services requires communication and cooperation, collaboration and co-ordination, or integration and merging (Hall, 1999). However, research suggests that this is difficult to achieve.

Conflicting goals, perceptions and understandings between staff limit the ability of staff to communicate and cooperate. Staff tend to protect themselves by avoiding situations where conflict might occur (ie inter-agency cooperation for example) (Hvinden, 1994). Co-ordination is often equated with centralisation: a central organising body is responsible for ensuring services 'fit' together. However, centralisation may impede the ability of local programs to meet local needs; to be flexible and adaptive. In a review of outcomes for children placed in state care, Glisson and Hemmelgarn (1998) found that the co-ordinated approach to services delivered worse outcomes for the children than the uncoordinated approach. An attempt to integrate child health and special education services in Ontario (Kauppi, 1997, cited in (Hall, 1999) found that, despite an attempt to decentralise and create multi-disciplinary teams, central control was maintained and local flexibility declined. Different professional groups continued to maintain boundaries within the teams. Collaboration between agencies is difficult when agencies have different cultures, policies and procedures, different professional roles and different conditions of employment (Hall, 1999). Effective collaboration needs to occur at the local level, where it is dependent on relationships between individual staff, and their willingness to work together.

Conclusion

Programs such as those discussed in this chapter have provided the foundation upon which both Australia and New Zealand have crafted their recent programs aimed at strengthening families. In Australia, the Good Beginnings National Parenting Programme offers home visiting (using both trained volunteers and professionals), parenting groups, networking opportunities for parents, and opportunities for parents to link to other local services. Parents and agencies are encouraged to develop partnerships increasing community participation. Family Start, part of the New Zealand Strengthening Families programme, also offers a combination of home visiting and parent education.

There is increasing recognition that support provided to families in the early years has a major impact on long-term outcomes. Family support programs are moving from early pilot versions, into national programs aimed at operating in as many local communities as possible. Ongoing debate continues about the respective roles of families and the state in providing appropriate child rearing environments for young children.

Children's rights before parental rights

- It is the state's ultimate responsibility to ensure that all children receive appropriate opportunities to develop to their potential.

Parents' rights before children's rights

- parents have rights to rear their children in ways they believe are appropriate;
- it is not the state's role to impose a set of standards (underpinned by a particular set of values) on parents.

Community responses to New Zealand's Code of Social and Family Responsibility (The Response Analysis Team, 1998) suggests community opinion is strongly in favour of family responsibility, with the State playing a strongly educative rather than punitive role. In offering family support programs, the State can ensure a safety net exists for children. Families are empowered to rear their children in ways appropriate for their own values, and achieve positive and desirable outcomes for both children and, in the long-term, the state itself.

Chapter 5

Components of family support: Community-focused

Introduction

This chapter continues the discussion, begun in Chapter 4, of different models of service delivery commonly found in family support programs. This chapter discusses programs operating in different microsystems accessed by various family members (such as the school, workplace and community).

School linked programs for children

Children spend up to 6–7 hours a day over 10 to 13 years in school. Research continues to demonstrate that smaller schools (with enrolments less than 600 in years 9 to 12) provide better learning environments for children (Garbarino & Garbarino, 1992). Smaller schools encourage participation and discourage elitism and staff inflexibility. In smaller schools, children who are academically marginalised have more chance to feel involved and this can improve academic performance, A sense of belonging to the school may improve resiliency, motivation and emotional wellbeing (Gilligan, 2000). Positive school experiences assist women live with episodes of sexual abuse in childhood (Gilligan, 1998). Socioeconomic status is the major predictor of children's academic performance when they begin school, however once in school, academic success breeds further academic success and is linked to other behavioural and social outcomes (Sylva & Evans, 1999).

Children who come into schools with behaviour problems are more likely to experience alienation and lack of success. They take up a disproportionate amount of teacher time, disrupt and intimidate other children (Lupton & Sheppard, 1999). When schools respond by excluding these children, they may exacerbate the problems, laying the foundation for longer-term social and economic disadvantage. The FAST (Families and Schools Together) programme is a selective programme, developed and implemented across a number of countries in the western world, which attempts to address these issues (Bierman, 1997, Hernandez, 2000). Some FAST programs target children who are identified as at risk by their teachers, others are more universally available (McDonald & Frey, 1999).

FAST

- run by accredited FAST personnel only;
- weekly (8 x 22 weeks) group sessions of parent management training based on social learning and behaviourist principles;
- 2-weekly home visiting or telephone support;
- parent graduates meet for further 2 years;
- children—weekly social skill training in groups, academic tutoring in reading;
- teachers—trained in behaviour management;
- peers—social skills training 3x weekly in class for first 5 years of schooling.

Graduate FAST children were less likely to be perceived by their classmates as aggressive. They were more likely to be liked by their peers and have better understanding of emotions. Reading and social acceptance improvements have been demonstrated for a year after the completion of the programme. Improvements in maths were initially identified but did not prove durable. Negative peer initiations were decreased and positive peer relations were increased after a year (Marshall & Watt, 1999). Parental involvement in the school is increased, and parents are likely to maintain friendships with other FAST parents (McDonald & Frey, 1999).

Lupton and Sheppard (1999) report on their attempt to implement a FAST programme in the UK. They were unable to duplicate the programme in its entirety because of funding limitations and staffing issues. Their programme offered parent home visits, group-based social skills training for children, academic and behavioural support in the class through the use of individualised education plans and teacher-based classroom intervention. Evaluation of the programme indicated that parents perceived the home visitor as a befriender, but the teachers saw the home visitor as a parent educator. Communication problems between parents, teachers and home visitors limited the effectiveness of the programme. Despite this, parents and teachers agreed that up to 50% of the children demonstrated positive behavioural changes, more evident in the home than in the school. These changes were less likely to be observed in those children with the most difficult behaviours, and there was concern expressed that intervention, by age 7, might already be too late for these children.

A FAST programme is being offered in socially disadvantaged primary schools in Australia (Scott, 2001). Parents attend an 8 week intensive parent education programme. Each family takes a turn at offering a meal to other programme families (with financial and volunteer assistance). Parents are encouraged to maintain contact when the sessions are completed. Graduates of the programme are encouraged to become involved in new programs. Evaluation of the programme is not yet available.

The Resourceful Adolescent Parent Programme, RAP-P (Ham & Schocet, 2001) aims to prevent adolescent depression by reducing family-based risk factors (such as parent-adolescent conflict, affectionless control) and increasing parental ability to support adolescent independence and foster secure attachments. The programme operates on the assumption that parents who are poorly differentiated from their children feel rejected as adolescents seek independence and react by struggling to hold on and maintain control. Parents are taught, using cognitive behavioural techniques, to manage stress, restructure their perceptions, challenge negative self-talk and self-manage behaviour changes and emotions. They are given information on adolescent development and the developmental needs of their children, building on existing strengths and competencies, and increasing differentiation by increasing self-esteem. The programme operates through three parental workshops of 2–3 hours each offered through schools. Evaluations indicate the programme results in improved adolescent attachment to parents and decreased parent-child conflict.

Children from minority cultures are particularly at risk of school failure because of the different values and beliefs they hold in comparison with those of the school and the hegemonic culture. Hampson, Rahman, Brown, Taylor and Donaldson (1998) report on a programme they offered to Grade 4 African American students in an urban school. The aim of the programme was to connect the young people to their own culture; to affirm the value of African American ways and beliefs. Students were given opportunities to learn about their ancestors, and biological and cultural inheritances they have from their ancestors. An empowerment approach was used to encourage students to take control of their own futures and to develop their own community-focused problem-solving skills. Children participating in the programme were found to have significant increases in self-esteem, self efficacy and social problem solving skills.

Bullying programs commonly offered in schools focus on skills training for children. Olweus (1994) reports on a national campaign in Norway to address bullying in schools. Workshops were provided for teachers and parents and children and resulted in a 50% reduction in bullying, reductions in antisocial behaviour, vandalism, fighting, pilfering, drunkenness, and truancy. Students reported greater satisfaction with school life and schools reported improved discipline, more positive relationships and attitudes and a general improvement in school 'culture'.

Bullying programs need to take an ecological approach (Arnette & Walsleben, 1998). Linke (1998) summarises the work of a number of researchers and suggests that programs must include:
- policies and procedures for dealing with bullying;
- commitment from all staff to understand and implement the policies and procedures;
- procedures for prevention;
- clear messages that bullying is unacceptable;
- social skill and anti-bias behaviour training programs for children in the early childhood years;
- no-blame, no-labelling approach for bullies or victims of bullies;
- strategies to recognise and support positive behaviours;
- strategies to build positive relationships between staff and children;
- strategies to ensure collaboration between staff and parents
- an understanding by staff that their behaviour provides a model for children to follow.

In Melbourne, the Creating New Choices violence prevention programme operates in schools with the aim of using a community development approach to develop partnerships between communities and schools to address violence (Sidey, 2001). Intervention uses a whole-school approach including developing curriculum and policies, training staff, offering public forums and creating initiatives. Parents, students and community members are involved in education activities then in developing appropriate initiatives for local needs.

Roots of Empathy is another programme which aims to teach children empathy, and, at the same time, prepare them for their future role as parents (Gordon, 1999). It operates in schools from kindergarten to Grade 8 and is run by certified instructors. Local parents visit the class monthly with their child and visits are used to focus discussions on emotional literacy, caring, violence and aggression.

These programs address concerns by teaching children and parents within the existing school environment. Zigler suggests that improving outcomes for children involves a radical re-think about schools and how they operate. In his School for the Twenty-first Century (Finn-Stevenson & Stern, 1997) he suggests a family centre approach to schooling.

Schools should include

- full time care for children aged 3–5;
- outside school hours care for children up to age 12;
- parent education and support for families with children under 3;
- information, referral, health, and nutrition services;
- linkages to other services such as family day care.

This model is being applied in more than 400 schools across 13 states of America. An evaluation of one of the earlier sites found that parents reported an increase in the amount of time they spent with their preschool aged children, and a decrease in the different types of care the used. In the early years of school, children showed improved performance on standardised achievement tests.

Zigler's model requires schools to become involved in family services. However, Schorr (1997, p. 240) argues that most schools do not understand children under 5, so locating services for children under 5 in schools is not necessarily a positive move. An alternative approach is the School Development program introduced by Comer (1993). Comer's aim was to change the climate of the early school years to take more account of child development, to make school management more participatory and to strengthen the relationships between parents and schools. Schools, according to Comer, are an ideal locus for change, and have the potential to bond a community together to work for the benefit of children.

The programme aims to change schools through developing a School Planning and Management Team, a Student and Staff Support Team and a Parent Team. The teams use a no-fault, consensus decision-making procedure to develop policy and goals, and to evaluate school performance. Over 600 schools are using the Comer approach and children in these schools demonstrate improvements in maths and reading achievement, school attendance, school adjustment, teachers' ratings of classroom behaviour, attitudes towards authority, group participation ad self-esteem (Finn-Stevenson & Stern, 1997). Seven years after implementing the model, one of the schools has now been ranked in to top 5 in the city for performance, and has eliminated serious behaviour problems (Marshall & Watt, 1999).

In 1992 Zigler and Comer created a new programme which combined elements of their individual models. By 1997 there were 14 'CoZi' schools across America.

Bowling Park Elementary School in Norfolk, Virginia, 1st CoZi school

(Finn-Stevenson & Stern, 1997)

- 92% of families—at risk due to poverty, single, teen parenting, unemployment, substance abuse, crime and hunger;
- majority of families are of African-American origin;
- children began school with no preschool experience and with low school readiness scores;
- community planned & developed childcare, outside school hours care, PAT home visiting programme, vacation care, adult education programme leading to a high school diploma, family literacy programme, school health clinic;
- Year 1 of programme: 81% of staff at the school felt more positive about their jobs, 80% of parents now felt welcome in the school, children higher test scores, 97% attendance rate;

Schorr (1997) suggests that schools can become the focus of community development initiatives because most community members are involved with schools in some way or another. Schools can become the hub of networks of community services (Corter, 2001). However, the responsibility for the development of such a hub can not rest on schools alone; community members, agencies and community groups need to work together to revitalise disadvantaged communities.

One example of this occurs in Papakura, Auckland where the Pacific Foundation has set up a family support programme based at a local primary school. The programme operates out of a building on the school campus and offers home visiting support to families who have children at the school, or whose preschool children live in the area and will attend the school in the future. Home visitors are locals: people respected in the community, who have received training from the programme co-ordinators and who work for the programme part-time. Some of the home visitors have children attending the school. Home visitors are expected to work with families on goals selected by the families themselves. Facilities on the school site are used to offer regular health clinics and specialist clinics from the local hospital (three bus trips away). A drop-in playgroup runs for infants and children up to 5. A food bank and clothing bank are also on site, run by parent volunteers.

Another example is the Thornberry Centre for Youth and Families in Kansas (Fisher, 2001). The centre combined an existing Boys' and Girls' Club and an alternative middle school. Community action raised the necessary funds to create a new centre which has two gymnasiums, a swimming pool, teen centre, library, classrooms, media centre, 4 computer labs, performing arts area, kitchen and dining area serving more than 750 children a day. A range of services also now operate out of the new service including a family court, public library, literacy programme and a university outreach. The school serves children who need educational support, or who have dropped out of the public school system. It focuses on literacy and critical thinking using a communications/arts focus emphasising self sufficiency. The centre emphasises community partnership and participation, combining schooling, outside school hours (including weekend) youth and family activities and additional tutoring. Parents, local businesses and community members are involved.

Schools as Community Centres is an Australian example which locates a community centre within a school (Starr, 2001) targeting severely disadvantaged areas and providing integrated services for families in those areas. The programme uses a community development approach to work with families who have children under 8. The aim is to ensure families have access to services through interagency collaboration at the community centre and to support families in their parenting roles. Families are encouraged to contribute to community decision-making. The services operating out of the community centres vary depending on the needs of the local population. Evaluation of the programme indicated the following were important in programme success:

- collaborative approach which involves joint funding and management;
- community participation prior to the establishment of the programme and ongoing collaboration;
- targeting disadvantaged areas and working with all families in the targeted area;
- support from the school encourages families to access the ranges of services available on the school site;
- community development approach focusing on specific local needs;
- a facilitator who is not aligned with any of the sponsoring government departments, and who is not involved in casework. Facilitators are selected by local community management groups;
- state-wide co-ordination providing appropriate support and training for personnel involved in service delivery;
- focusing on early childhood (birth to 8);
- ongoing evaluation and monitoring.

Evolving from this is the concept of full-service schools (Withers & Russell, 2001), which have a primary emphasis on education but, through changes in power and structure, include a wide range of support services (health, basic services, mental health, family support etc). Collaboration of professional and community members is required. Withers and Russell report on a number of initiatives in Australia beginning to take a full-service approach.

Vocational training and employment programs

Adolescents and young school leavers

Within the past few decades, requirements for qualified workers have grown, and employment opportunities for unqualified workers have declined. This means that adolescents who do not undertake some form of tertiary training face significant disadvantages in the labour market. In America, the unemployment rate for black male high school drop-outs is 70%. Up to 60% of high school drop-outs are likely to be either unemployed, underemployed, or a member of the working poor (Pouncy, 2000). Employers tend not to hire recent school graduates, preferring employees in their mid-20s, so that even those who graduate find it difficult to get employment. Schorr (1997) argues that young people need not face such significant disadvantages if schools better prepared them for employment, and if there were closer links between schools and the labour market.

Some schools offer work experience opportunities to students with the aim of facilitating their transition into the workplace. However, Donahoe and Tienda (2000) point out that if work experience programs result in students undertaking less formal school learning, then they may, in fact, be detrimental in the long term. Where young people are employed, the longer the hours they work, the more they are likely to withdraw from school and the less likely they are to continue into tertiary training. However, those who do not work at all face the highest risk of dropping out of high school.

There is disagreement as to the value of skills students learn in work experience placements to their long-term employment career. In some work experience placements youth are segregated from other workers, serving to increase the influence of peer culture, and increase deviance. In addition, youth employment tends to decrease parental monitoring. However, as employment is highly valued in western society, participation in the workforce has the potential to increase youth self-esteem and psychological well-being.

There is a growing trend to offer specific vocational training opportunities in schools for those students who elect not to pursue further academic studies. In Australia, links between secondary schools and the TAFE (vocational education) sector are increasing, with a number of high schools now offering students opportunities to complete some TAFE modules whilst still at school.

Workers who are disadvantaged

Training for employment occurs in various educational institutions and on the job. On the job training occurs formally (through competency-based learning, inservice training courses, apprenticeships, traineeships etc) or informally. People who are disadvantaged qualify for assistance in accessing certain training programs. Occasionally, community agencies can obtain funding to run targeted employment programs for specific groups of people. For example, a group of long-term unemployed youth can join together to form a co-operative and build inexpensive housing for their community, or playgrounds for the local municipal park. Supported work programs provide a job coach to work alongside a worker (or a group of workers) to ease their transition into the workplace. Such support may be short-term(with the expectation that, once adapted to the workplace employment can be maintained) or longer term for those workers whose disabilities limit their workplace performance.

Skills for daily living

Parents who feel capable performing daily tasks experience lower levels of stress and thus are more likely to have energy to parent more effectively. Parental proficiency in basic daily living tasks contributes to meeting children's basic needs. Some family support programs offer parents opportunities to learn a range of relevant daily living skills with the aim of improving parental efficacy and self-esteem, improving children's likelihood of having their basic needs met, and ultimately, improving parenting itself. Daily living skills might include tasks such as cooking nutritious meals, laundry, managing the shopping, planting a vegetable garden, and learning how to clean (vacuum, sweep, wash dishes hygienically).

Craft-type activities are a popular focus in parent support groups as they serve to bring together a number of isolated women. Through working together in craft classes they establish friendships and networks which have the potential to extend beyond the classes and link them with other members of their community. Craft classes vary, depending on the interests and needs of the group. Sewing and/or knitting classes provide opportunities to learn fundamental skills enabling participants to provide clothing for themselves and their families. Other craft classes provide opportunities for participants to learn skills they can use to improve their homes (for example upholstery, lace making, weaving, patchwork etc). Generally craft classes are attended by women as gender roles assign these tasks to women. Offering other types of classes, such as car maintenance, brick laying, or making wooden furniture, offer opportunities for women to move into less traditional (but equally useful) activities, as well as opportunities for men to participate in community networking activities.

Effective management of family finances is essential for family stability, and many families require budgeting support. Whilst it may be appropriate for family support workers to give basic budget advice, it is generally considered that budgeting support is best offered by someone with specific training in that area. Effective family support programs will have links to local budgeting services, or may include their own budgeting service.

Accessing the community

Participation in community activities functions to improve support networks, develop skills and feelings of self efficacy, and increase resilience.

Community participation (Gilligan, 2000)

- caring for animals;
- sport;
- helping and volunteering;
- part-time work;
- attending local dances;
- joining a local or church choir;
- taking part in a local art class;
- joining in a group to prepare a float for the local street parade;
- joining a local band, music group;
- joining a local reading group;
- other community options.

Pets are recognised as having a beneficial impact on stress levels, and pet ownership encourages independence, autonomy and may also encourage community participation. Walking a dog often creates opportunities to meet and talk with others engaged in a similar pursuit and joining shared interest groups is possible (such as puppy preschool, dog obedience, tropical fish club etc).

Involvement in sport can also increase resilience and foster community links. Sporting clubs provide opportunities for people with similar interests to join together and share in activities. Those who do not play sport may still be involved through coaching or managing teams, or helping in with such activities as manning the snack counter at games. In one study, a group of young Africans formed their own soccer team, creating strong support networks amongst themselves, in defiance of the racism they experienced in community teams (Sims, Omaji, O'Connor, & Omaji, in review).

Through helping out and volunteering, networks and community links can be fostered, and feelings of self-esteem and self-efficacy enhanced. For example, research consistently demonstrates the advantages of peer tutoring, not just for the learner, but for the tutor (Gilligan, 2000). Many youth programs now encourage youth to be involved in community activities such as helping out at the local Anzac Day service, or running errands for those in the community who have mobility problems. These activities promote a sense of belonging in the community, which facilitates feelings of security and attachment. Little (1999) suggests the creation of a Children's Advice Bureau (along the lines of a Citizen's Advice Bureau) would provide young people with access to information which could help them become more effectively linked into their community through leisure time activities. Programs such as Big Brother Big sister also facilitate the development of community connections (Bownes & Ingersoll, 1997).

Many family support programs act as brokers, linking families to existing community support agencies. Referrals between agencies need to happen smoothly, so that families do not find themselves being shuffled from one agency to another, with no-one taking the responsibility to support them. Communication between existing agencies works most effectively at local levels, where it is dependant on relationships between staff members themselves. Family support workers must ensure that they keep their local networks up-to-date; that they know the relevant workers in other agencies.

It is also appropriate for family support workers to have links with the media. Relevant publicity can be most useful in raising the profile of the service, developing publicity for community events and increasing business and corporate interest leading to fundraising opportunities both for the service itself, and for resources for families and the community. Many communities have a local newspaper, and it may be appropriate for the service to have a regular column in this. Alternatively, the service may find it useful to have its own, regular newsletter which is circulated widely (not just to members) to increase public awareness and community involvement.

Community building

Some family support programs operate with an explicit mandate to contribute to the development of the communities in which families live. In the Northern Territory of Australia the Strong Women Strong Babies Strong Culture Program had the specific aim of increasing infant birth weights by improving prenatal and antenatal care (Mackerras, 2001). In this program Aboriginal women were trained to work with the women emphasising the value of both traditional practices and Western medicine. The use of local, Aboriginal women, and the valuing of traditional practices, created a foundation upon which women built trust in the programme. The programme was successful in increasing infant birth weight and increasing maternal weight (though this was still below the average weight for non-pregnant women).

Myers (1993) discusses the important contribution a family support/early childhood focus has in developing communities in majority world countries (developing countries). He argues that investment in early childhood care and education facilitates the success of other programs such as education, and health care. For example, parent education programs not only improve parental literacy and employment opportunities, they improve child rearing, and parents' ability to access other services such as health. Children provide an acceptable common rallying point often crossing boundaries of beliefs and practice. He cites cease-fires between warring groups obtained in order to carry out national immunisation campaigns as powerful examples of peoples' willingness to place children's needs first. Children's welfare is often perceived as apolitical, and this provides an opportunity for people to agree and work together, even when they may violently disagree about everything else. Communities, for example, may co-operate in order to develop sources of clean drinking water for children, but would not do so if they thought of the water as being for themselves. Many programs now operating through Aid agencies, the United Nations, and other agencies working in the less privileged parts of the world, take a focus on children and families. This is seen as the most effective and appropriate way to make longer-term changes and improvements in the quality of life for all people (Young, 1995).

Shorr (1997) outlines a number of programs where family support is integrated into a community development initiative. The South Bronx was one of the most infamous American cities with burned out building, high levels of crime and unemployment and a general aura of hopelessness. In 1986 the attempt to revitalise the South Bronx began with a number of not-for-profit organisations beginning to build low cost housing for families. The Comprehensive Community Revitalisation Programme (CCRP) offered expertise and advice to community members to access the necessary funding, technical advice and expertise. CCRP identified strong community groups and worked with them to make them stronger. The programme worked at involving members of the community in planning new services (such as playgrounds, health services, stores, banks). CCRP provided funds for the development of a new shopping centre, bringing new jobs into the area. They created links between police and community members who were concerned about crime. Social workers, involved with each family as they move into new housing in the area, help connect families to local resources and make home visits where necessary. The HIPPY (Home Instructional Program for Pre-School Youngsters) programme is used to support parents in becoming more effective teachers of their young children. Local parents are trained to become HIPPY workers. Local residents' groups continue to identify issues of concern in their community, then act to address these issues. One local group conducted training in domestic violence for local police, and developed a support group for families experiencing domestic violence. Other local groups addressed issues relating to care of elderly relatives and another sponsored the opening of a Head Start programme in their area. Job training and job placement was part of the early CCRP initiative and now a range of employment supports are available (new models for the transition from welfare to work, English as a second language courses, a database of available training programs throughout New York). A range of community-based employment opportunities have been made available. Schorr points out that the important factor, in all this activity, is the role of the community members themselves; services were not simply developed for them. Community members were an integral part in identifying what needed to be done, how it ought to be done, and in actually undertaking the necessary work to make things happen. CCRP's main role was in connecting people so they could work together to jointly problem solve and develop strategies for improving their own community.

In New Zealand, the Awhina Maatua programme uses a community development approach to reach and work with young families who are not already involved in early childhood services (Early Childhood Development Unit, 2001). Low income communities with high density housing or isolated rural areas, characterised by a lack of services and transport, are targeted. An early childhood development officer (ECDO) works with community groups and local families to determine what is wanted in the community. A core group of parents and community agency staff is formed who plan the development of the programme and network in the community to extend the group. The ECDO may initially be involved in home visits, contacting the media, door knocking and community meetings. However, this involvement is gradually scaled back as the parent group develop confidence to take control for themselves. One common outcome of the programme to date has been the establishment of playgroups such as Pacific Islands Language Groups.

Counselling

Sometimes families will need specific counselling in order to address the issues they face. Whilst some programs may have trained counsellors, others need to refer families to relevant counsellors. Family support workers need links with local counselling services to ensure that families they refer do obtain the services they need.

There are a range of counselling services that may be relevant to families. Couples may benefit from couple or relationship counselling. Family counselling helps family members understand the way they relate to each other, and to establish more positive patterns of interactions within the family. Brief Strategic Family Therapy is claimed to be of particular benefit in families experiencing delinquency and violence (Robbins & Szaporcznik, 2000).

Auxiliary support

Various other auxiliary services may be useful, either included as part of a family support programme, or as separate identities to which the programme links as necessary. Many charitable organisations operate food banks, redistributing food to those families who need it. Large organisations collect food from manufacturers, growers and retailers, parcel it up and distribute it to relevant families. Often members of the public are requested to donate items to be included in food parcels. Many agencies keep records of families who receive food parcels, and require that families do not use their service too regularly. The expectation is that food parcels are for crisis situations, not regular supplements. Other agencies offer discount price schemes, where food is collected and sold to qualified families at very low prices. These agencies often give a form of identification to qualifying families who can then purchase food from the store when-ever they choose. Many of these services offer food in bulk parcels, so there is restricted choice.

Food kitchens are another source of food for those in crisis situations. Food kitchens offer a free meal, often for those living on the street. Food is donated, or paid for by agencies raising the necessary funds through public donations or other activities. Food kitchens are usually staffed by volunteer workers.

Clothing banks operate in a similar manner to food banks. Some services offer free clothing to qualifying families. Other agencies use recycled clothing as a tool to raise money to fund other social service activities. St Vincent de Paul, and Salvation Army second hand clothing shops, for example, are scattered around many cities and towns in Australia. Anyone can buy from these shops, and the money raised contributes towards their other charitable activities.

In some communities, community development activities result in the establishment of co-operatives. Co-operatives may form in order to share transport, or to buy food in bulk (which is cheaper) and distribute it amongst members. For example, purchasing vegetables at a market or direct from a grower is often much less expensive than buying them from shops. A group can organise one person with transport to purchase in bulk, then redistribute the vegetables amongst contributing co-operative members.

One co-operative activity that often proves popular, is that of members sharing transport (perhaps through hiring a mini-bus or using the vehicle of a member) to visit factory seconds outlet shops to purchase clothing. Factory seconds shops often have very inexpensive clothing, but are usually in places quite difficult to access for those without transport. Many communities find a seasonal outing around several shops in one day provides an opportunity to purchase inexpensive clothing for the family in preparation for the season ahead. The shared experience of shopping often creates friendships between shoppers that endure beyond the one-day shopping outing.

Programs which combine a range of features

This section discusses programs that combine elements of family support. In reality, there is little clear distinction between the categories, and significant overlap. Comer and Fraser (1998) provide an evaluation of six programs, all combining home visiting, child developmental screening (medical, social and health) parent education and parent support (social, emotional and educational). Some of the programs offered childcare, referral and advocacy information, organised activities or sporting events, prenatal or neonatal care and adult education. All evaluations showed reductions, after 12 months, in pregnancy complications, and gains in quality of prenatal care, parent-child interaction, parental knowledge, child health and development. Parents reported improved levels of self-esteem and feelings of efficacy. Four of these programs provided 2 year follow up data which suggested that these gains continued. A further two provided follow up data after three years which indicated improvements remained stable. A five-year follow up of one programme found that programme children performed better in school and had better school attendance. Educational achievement gains continued in a ten year follow up of the same programme. Families, at the 10-year point, had better educational, financial and housing outcomes.

In the UK recent attempts to reduce crime have resulted in the development of a crime prevention programme focused on children at risk called On Track (Johnston, 2001). Pilot On Track programs have been established in high crime, deprived, small, local communities.

On Track programs are administered by local partnerships and are expected to develop a range of core services such as structured preschool education, home visiting, home-school partnerships, parent training and family therapy. Programs focus on children aged 4 to 12 years and aim to significantly reduce antisocial behaviour and offending.

In Missouri, a programme called Parent Link (not to be confused with the Parent Link Home Visiting Programme operating in Western Australia) uses an ecological approach to integrate levels of the ecosystem so parents can obtain support when and where they need it (Mertensmeyer & Fine, 2000). Parent Link offers information, resources and emotional support addressing social, health, safety, mental health, education, economic and community development issues. A range of agencies and organisations share in the Parent Link Coalition which acts as a broker in guiding families to existing programs and resources, and as a collection point for multi-disciplinary sharing of ideas.

High/Scope Perry Preschool Project

A group of 3 to 4 year old African American children living in poverty in Ypsilanti, Michigan were identified at risk for school failure through intellectual delay at the time of the project (Schweinhart, Weikart, & Larner, 1986). The children were offered one of three different centre-based education models (Schweinhart et al., 1986):

- Distar direct-instruction—based on behaviourist principles, required teachers to initiate activities to which children respond.
- High/Scope Cognitively Oriented Preschool Curriculum—a Piagetian approach to development, offered opportunities for children to practice key developmental skills. Children and staff are expected to work together.
- Traditional nursery—focused on children initiating and teachers responding to those initiations. Children were encouraged to participate in free play.

In all the classes there were usually 15 to 16 3–4 year olds with a teacher and a teacher assistant. In addition, a female special education student was employed to undertake custodial care tasks. The programme ran for three years, involving three cohorts of children.

Parents received a two-weekly home visit (of about an hour and a half) and attended regularly scheduled group meetings (Schweinhart, Barnes, & Weikart, 1993). Home visits included discussion and modelling of activities (using the curriculum approach of the group to which the child was assigned) in which parents could participate with their child. The home visitors' role was solely to focus on the parent-child relationship, not to address other issues within the family.

Detailed discussion of the outcomes of this project are presented in Chapter 8. All children showed significant gains in development in the short-term which disappeared in the longer term. However, over a period of 27 years, the intervention children continued to show advantages over their peers in increased earning capacity, and decreased welfare dependency and participation in criminal activities. The High/Scope Perry Preschool Project is one of the few projects able to report financial data. Schweinhart and Weikart (1993) report a savings of $7.16 for every dollar spent 27 years earlier. This analysis is commonly used across a wide range of literature as a justification for offering early intervention programs.

Abecedarian Project

This project operated in Chapel Hill, North Carolina (Campbell & Ramey, 1995, Ramey & Landesman Ramey, 1998). All children in the project were full term, 98% were of African-American background, all had normal birth weight and were healthy at birth. The home environments of these children were all significantly lacking in positive developmental opportunities for the children (Ramey & Ramey, 2000). All were identified as 'at risk' on a risk index which included items such as family income and mothers education (which averaged at 10th grade level). The average maternal age at the beginning of the study was 20 years.

Some children were offered nutritional supplements, social services and follow-up paediatric services. Others were offered a 5-day-a-week centre-based programme from the ages of 4 months to 5 years as well. Throughout this time, children in the centre-based programme demonstrated significantly higher IQ than children receiving nutritional supplements only. This difference, though decreasing in magnitude, continued through to age 21 (Campbell, Pungello, Miller-Johnson, Burchinel, & Ramey, 2001). The children achieved more at school and were more likely to go on to tertiary education. Interactions between mothers and children were more positive and mothers rated their children as having an easier temperament. Mothers themselves were more likely to continue their education and be employed.

The long-term advantages in intellectual development and school achievement demonstrated in this study were not reflected in the Perry High/Scope research samples. The Abecedarian researchers (Campbell et al., 2001) suggest the explanation for these differences might be the young age at which children were recruited in their study. The Abecedarian project began intervention at 4 months of age whereas the Perry High/Score children received intervention at ages 3 and 4 only. However, the authors caution that the explanation for the difference may also be associated with the duration of the intervention (5 years compared to 2). Other differences between the programs included programme intensity and the service delivery models used. The Abecedarian project used a child-centred curriculum, whereas the Perry High/Scope Project used a range of curriculum, only some of which were child-centred. The Perry High/Scope children were specifically selected because they had low IQ scores at the age of 3. The Abecedarian children were selected because of their at risk status, and not on the basis of their development. The Abecedarian families all lived in a community which was committed to providing adequate housing, low-cost medical care and public transportation. Schools in the area were generally of good quality, with extra supports available for teachers in reading and maths when required. Bronfenbrenner's theory of ecology (Bronfenbrenner, 1979) indicates that all of these factors will have contributed to the differences in outcome.

Head Start

President Johnson announced the war on poverty in America in 1964. A range of programs were initiated and funded aimed at addressing poverty. Towards the end of 1964 it became evident that many of these programs were not as effective as expected. By December that year a planning committee was formed to develop the programme which became known as Head Start (Zigler & Muenchow, 1992). The planning committee were given 6 weeks to come up with a proposal for a major programme to address poverty and disadvantage in up to 100,000 American children across the country. The first 8 week Head Start summer programme was expected to cost $US18 million and was planned for implementation that summer. By May 1965, the budget was increased to $50 million, and the number of children expected to be served rose to over half a million. Before the first programme began, plans were made to include over $150 million in the following year's budget in order to offer the programme year round.

Head Start provided basic health care, medical check-ups, immunisation, dental care and two nutritious meals a day. Parents were encouraged to be involved. Centre-based education programs were considered of little importance in comparison to the heath components. However, for many, (including politicians) it was the lure of potential IQ gains which made the programme sound attractive and this created unrealistic expectations which were to reflect negatively in evaluations for some years.

Different communities were required to apply for funding to run a Head Start programme to ensure that programs were designed in ways that met the needs of individual communities. Some programs delivered centre-based services to children, others were home-based. The curriculum offered to children varied, as did the way health and nutritional needs were addressed. The degree of diversity in programs made it very difficult to ensure quality, and this continues to be a problem today. In addition, lack of trained staff made a huge impact on programme quality.

Early evaluations showed a significant gain in IQ for Head Start children, but this gain soon 'washed out' when children began school. This 'washing out' of IQ gain had a tremendous impact on support available for early intervention initiatives, and for a number of years programs such as Head Start were extremely vulnerable. However, when longitudinal research began to demonstrate that early intervention did result in long-term gains (but not in direct measures such as IQ), programs became popular again. Head Start graduates, though not demonstrating the degree of improvements shown in more intensive programs such as High/Scope and Abecedarian, still tend to show improvements in school functioning compared to children from similar backgrounds who have not attended Head Start.

Chicago child-parent centres

These began in 1967 (making them the second oldest federally funded early intervention programme in the United States) and were based in

11 Chicago schools located in areas of social and economic disadvantage (Reynolds, 1994). They began offering a structured half-day preschool programme to children aged between 3 and 5 years, aiming to prepare the children for school. In addition to pre-academic preparation, children and families were offered comprehensive health and social services, and parents were encouraged to be involved. Over the past 20 years, the programme has expanded and now offers outside school hours support to children through to Grade 3 (some children therefore receive intervention for 6 years).

By age 9 the children were achieving better results in maths and reading, and were less likely to have repeated a grade in school. Differences in maths achievement remained significant at age 14. Children who had attended the programme were less likely to be involved in delinquent activities at age 14, but the difference was no longer significant at ages 15 and 16. Children who had participated in the programme for four or more years were likely to demonstrate the greatest benefits (Karoly et al., 1998). Children who participated in the programme for longer were less likely to drop out from high school (Temple, Reynolds, & Miedel, 2000). Recent reviews of the Chicago Child-Parent Centres (Strauss, 2001) indicate the important contribution family support makes to the prevention of juvenile delinquency, particularly in arrest rates for violent offences.

Parents are expected to be present in the centres for at least 2.5 hours a week, helping in the school, learning about health and nutrition and developing life skills. The programme aims to help parents (who generally have negative personal experiences of the education system) feel positive about their children's school. In more recent times, maintaining parent involvement has become more difficult as American welfare reform has required parents to work. The centres have responded by attempting to run parent workshops at the weekends and having more flexible schedules overall. In addition to changing amounts of parental participation, welfare reform in recent years has also resulted in cuts to the funding of the preschool components of the programme, those very components that have been identified in research as crucial contributors to positive outcomes.

Elmira Prenatal/Early Infancy Project (PEIP)

First time mothers prior to their 30th week of pregnancy and mothers with new babies who were judged to be at risk were enrolled in this programme (Olds, Henderson, & Kitzman, 1994). Nearly 25% of participants were young, unmarried and of low socioeconomic status. One group received home visits during pregnancy, whilst another continued to receive visits until the children were 2. Both were offered free transport to prenatal and well-child health services. Home visitors were registered curses with additional training in parent education and developing social support networks.

Outcomes (Olds, Eckenrode, & Henderson, 1997)

- For mothers during pregnancy
- less likely to smoke;
- better nutrition;
- more likely to attend child birth classes;
- better social support networks
- For children heavier at birth
- decreased risk of child abuse and neglect
- more developmentally appropriate resources available in the homes
- in adolescence, less likely to—run away (60%), arrested (55%), convicted of a crime (80%), smoke, consume alcohol (Olds, Hill, & Rumsey, 1998)
- For mothers by age 15 of child
- less likely to be involved in criminal activities
- less likely to be using drugs and alcohol in amounts which impaired their functioning
- few subsequent pregnancies
- longer intervals between children
- less likely to be on welfare

Healthy Start

The Hawaii Healthy Start programme began in 1985 (Kapi'olani Health, 1998, Duggan, McFarlane, Windham, Rohde, & al, 1999). Strength and need assessments are carried out on all newborn infants, and all families receive information about available community services. Home visits by trained para-professionals are offered to families who are identified as at risk for child abuse or neglect.

Criteria to identify risk

- unmarried parents
- unemployment
- low income
- insecure housing
- no phone
- low education levels
- lack of emergency contacts
- marital or family problems
- attempts to procure abortions (either successful or not)
- substance abuse
- psychiatric problems
- depression
- inadequate prenatal care of newborn infant.

Home visits focus on strengthening families, promoting positive attachment and relationships, facilitating child development and empowering families. Home visitors link families to community resources where relevant. In the pilot, home visits began weekly then gradually decreased in frequency as families became more confident and capable.

Healthy Start families demonstrated a decrease in the frequency of reports of child abuse and neglect and a decrease in the levels of family stress. Interest in the Healthy Start prompted the development of a range of Healthy Start-type programs in other states of America and by 1997 there were nearly 270 programs in 38 states (Evanston et al., 2000).

Conclusion

In this section a range of models of family support are presented and discussed. The ecological approach to family support suggests that no one model on its own will have as significant an impact on family functioning and resilience, as a combination of models. Family support is more successful when different components are combined in a multipurpose approach. The impact of intervention in the home is lessened when children go outside the home to attend schools where they are exposed to a range of risk factors. Intervention in schools is compromised when children participate in community activities where they are exposed to risk factors. Interventions need to target individual, family, and community risk factors to ensure that all children have opportunities to develop to their potential.

Chapter 6

Targeted family support

Introduction

This chapter discusses programs targeted at selected groups, individuals or families. These are commonly run by agencies identifing with the particular targeted group (for example, agencies for people with disabilities often run family support programs for families who have children with disabilities).

Teenage parents

Teenage girls who are mothers experience conflict between their own developmental needs, and their responsibilities towards their child.

Risks of teen parenting

- adolescents self-centred (Erikson—identity formation)
- forming identity—may see baby as means to fulfil own un-met needs for love and trusting relations
- immaturity—difficulties in providing adequate nurturance—difficulties mother-child relationships
- less prenatal care than desirable—increased risk difficult births
- premature infants—2x more likely
- infants smaller birth weight—higher probability for developmental concerns, 40x more likely die in the first months of life
- prematurity plus low birth weight 39%—increase in infant health problems, birth defects
- little understanding of child development—unrealistic expectations of child—child abuse
- more impatient and punitive (Lowenthal & Lowenthal, 1997)
- less likely complete school—greater likelihood of long-term unemployment, poverty—inefficient financial management—increases impact of poverty

- feel socially isolated as peer group not share experiences—loneliness and depression—ineffective parenting—more likely to become pregnant again (33%—another child within two years)

Little research focuses on teen fathers and their needs are often overlooked (Lowenthal & Lowenthal, 1997). Teen fathers have lower incomes and lower levels of education than their peers. Many refuse to be involved in their children's lives as they may have experienced blame and criticism for their role in conception. Some fear the long-term financial commitment involved in supporting mother and child.

Teenage sexual activity and lack of contraceptive use are complex issues that are not simply solved by offering sex education programs in schools (Berk, 1999). Teenagers need support to link what they learn in sex education classes, with what they do in practice. Some argue that easy access to contraception will result in undesirable increases teenage sexual activity. However in Western Europe where school-based clinics offer contraceptive services, teenage sexual activity is not increased and there are lower teenage pregnancy rates. Ultimately, teenagers who have a future to look forward to are less likely to become pregnant, so prevention programs which focus on providing teenagers with options for their future contribute towards lowering the teenage pregnancy rate.

Once teenagers become pregnant the aim of support programs is to increase their resilience.

Supports needed

To remain in school

- school-based prenatal classes—nutrition, health care, child development
- ongoing parenting classes—school-based classes may be compulsory (Butterfield, 1996)
- school-based childcare

To develop/maintain friendships

- enhance self-esteem
- develop social skills
- emotional support
- respite care (babysitting)

- encouragement

Adolescent parents who have adequate support systems are more likely to complete their education, obtain employment and feel more comfortable in their parenting roles (Lowenthal & Lowenthal, 1997). More effective parenting increases positive outcomes for the children of teen parents.

Incarcerated parents

Imprisonment of a parent breaks up families, and children experience stress and trauma when they loose a parent in this way. The long-term consequences of such stress and trauma can be social, emotional and physical problems such as school failure and delinquency (Adalist-Estrin, 1995).

Women inmates face a double burden. Women who are imprisoned are seen as not only breaking the law, but also as failing in their natural role as children's main caregivers (Teather, Evans, & Sims, 1997). Single mothers are likely to loose custody of their children. In contrast, when men are imprisoned, care arrangements for their children are rarely considered.

Imprisonment interferes with maintenance of parent-child relationships. Children of women prisoners are particularly at risk for future mental health problems (Aldridge, 1993) because of the difficulties faced in maintaining secure relationships between mother and child. There is evidence that where these relationships can be maintained through the time of imprisonment, families are more likely to remain together after the women are released. Family stability is linked to lower rates of re-offending (Benjamin, 1991).

There are a range of ways in which parent-child relationships can be maintained.

Mother-baby units in prison

- for mothers with infants or young preschool aged children
- depends on the length of the sentence and what the authorities believe is in the best interests of the child (Farrell, 1994)
- some concern that mothers in these units are doing 'easy time' (Teather et al., 1997)

- infant development not impaired by time in prison compared to fostered infants (Catan, 1989)

Supported prison-visiting Relais Enfants-Parents (Ayre, 1996)

- volunteers accompany children on visits to prison
- special visiting areas for parents and children
- additional time allowed
- volunteers facilitate interaction
- complex cases (eg one parent murdered the other) volunteers will be professionals (eg counsellor)

Often, parents are offered parenting education classes in prison with the aim of facilitating future family reunification. Other sentencing options may also be explored for parents. Sentences such as supervised group housing (Hartz-Karp, 1983), day prisons, bail hostels and community-based correction (Benjamin, 1991) all offer alternative forms of punishment with less severe impact on parent-child relationships.

Disability

Families who have children with a disability must cope with negative social constructions of disability so may feel embarrassed, ashamed or that the disability is their 'fault' (Sims, 1997).

Risks

- High levels of stress—family breakdown, and divorce (Sims, 1997)
- social isolation through lack of alternative care options, societal attitudes towards disability
- additional financial stress
- increased risk abuse and neglect

Family support programs focus on coping with high levels of stress. Individual counselling, developing alternative childcare arrangements and encouraging parents to spend time with each other alone, and with siblings, are all important for these families. However, the establishment and maintenance of support networks is crucial (Thompson et al., 1997) in helping families develop resilience.

Support networks not only assist in providing emotional support, they can be viable substitutes for limited services such as respite care or transportation. Emotional support is often best provided by other families who have experienced similar feelings, and thus empathise with the confusion of emotions. Shared Care helps parents cope with additional stress. Services match families with another family whose role is to provide alternative care for the child on a regular basis (for example every second weekend, or once a month).

Siblings are affected by having a child with a disability in their family (Seligman & Darling, 1989). Siblings may feel:

- over-burdened with additional responsibilities,
- resentment that their opportunities are limited by their sibling's needs,
- resentment of parental attention directed away from them.

Open communication within the family, and the ability to share feelings (both positive and negative) can help achieve positive outcomes for all family members (Lobato, 1990). In the long-term, siblings may be required to take on the responsibility of care when their parents become too old to manage. Positive resolution of conflict and stress in their early years will help siblings take on this responsibility when the need arises. At this time, siblings need access to the ranges of services offered to parents to ensure they receive the necessary support to be effective caregivers (Moore, 1998).

Traditional early intervention focused on parents taking a teaching role. Professionals 'trained' parents to implement professionally-predetermined programs in the home. Children's lack of progress was often blamed on parental inability to teach effectively, or to put aside sufficient time to implement the programme properly. Some parents felt the conflict between their parental and teaching roles resulted in a huge burden of stress. For example, only a small number of mothers who have young children with disability return to the workforce.

Supports for families caring for children with disabilities can include (Sims, 1997):

- Architectural modifications to the home
- Childcare
- Counselling and therapeutic resources
- Dental and medical care beyond what is normally available in the community
- Specialised diagnosis and evaluation

- Specialised nutrition and clothing
- Specialised equipment and supplies
- Home-maker services
- In-home nursing and attendant care
- Home training and parenting courses
- Recreation and alternative leisure activities
- Respite care
- Transport
- Specialised utility costs
- Vehicle modification

In America, increasing numbers of states have adopted legislation requiring family support services for families who have children with disabilities (Agosta & Melda, 1995) with the aim of preventing out-of-home placements. Where children have been in out-of-home placements, services are required to focus on reuniting families where possible.

One area where family support services have yet to develop effectively is in supporting families who have an adult member with disabilities. In America, at least 80% of adults with intellectual disabilities live in their family homes, being cared for by elderly parents (Heller, 1998). Generally, as children grow into adults, they are eligible for less support and less services, and many families exist with little or no support from outside agencies. The Home-based Support Services Program (HBSSP) in Illinois is an example of a family support programme aimed at supporting adults with intellectual disabilities either living with their parents or living semi-independently. The components of the programme used most often were respite care, transport, vocational services, leisure services and dental care. Families in the programme were less likely to need out-of-home placements (13% compared to 27%) and reported greater caregiving satisfaction and feelings of competence. Significant cost savings were demonstrated.

Comparison of costs (Heller, 1998)

- HBSSP—$US10,668pa
- supported community residence—$US17,091 p.a
- state developmental centre—$US75,091 p.a

One final area is family support for families where parents themselves have a disability. In the past, parents with a disability were strongly encouraged not to have children. In more recent years, women with disabilities are having, and keeping, their children and some agencies offer support to enable them to do so (Meadow-Orlans, 1995). There is some suggestion parents with disabilities and their children are at risk for a range of psychosocial problems, but little evidence is available to support this claim (Kelley, Sikka, & Venkatesan, 1997). Parents with intellectual disability are at risk for neglecting their children because of their limited parenting skills, and this may result in their children being taken from them (Greene, Renee, Searle, Daniels, & Lubeck, 1995).

Self-learning, pictorial manuals have been successfully offered to mothers with low IQ (less than 80) showing basic childcare skills such as changing nappies, treating nappy rash, bathing and safety (Feldman, Ducharme, & Case, 1999). Skills increased further when the manuals were combined with face-to-face training. Direct instruction has been offered to mothers whose resumption of child custody was contingent on their demonstrating they had gained specific parenting skills (Greene et al., 1995). Mothers demonstrated gains in parenting skills initially, but once in their home environment, with other factors impacting on them, these changes were not maintained. Parents with disabilities are better serviced by an ecological approach to family support, with services including advocacy, home visits, behaviourally-based education, client control of decision making and collaboration between all involved (Pomerantz, Pomerantz, & Colca, 1990).

Chronic illness

Children who have chronic illnesses require additional support from their families in managing the illness and the associated emotional, physical and economic burdens.

Risks associated with chronic illness

- families may need to learn specific medical techniques—eg using a nebuliser, resuscitation, tube feeding
- additional costs—eg running an electric oxygen supply, finding accommodation near to the hospital

- side effects of medication—lethargy, pain, nausea, weakness
- increased vulnerability to infection—limit families' ability to participate in family and community activities
- treatments, eg radiation therapy—lower ability to learn, particularly in the areas of reading comprehension and mathematics—lower self-esteem
- frequent hospitalisations—socially isolated from their peer group, difficulty forming friendships
- children's misconceptions about illness—siblings socially shunned
- siblings—conflict between supporting their ill sibling, and being accepted by their own peer group—stress, unexpressed feelings of anger and resentment
- parents focus a significant proportion of their time on the ill child—sibling jealousy
- siblings left in others' care for long periods of time whilst parents at hospital.

Hospitalisation is a stressful experience for children and parents. Unexpected hospitalisation can negatively impact on children in ways that last into adolescent years (Gibbs, 1991). Children may think their hospitalisation is a punishment for wrong-doing. They need support to make sense of their hospital experience. Parents need support to enable them to stay over with their child in hospital. This may involve alternative care arrangements for other children, accommodation (Ronald McDonald Houses for example) and emotional support.

Family relationships can be significantly impaired. Separation anxiety may develop, negatively impacting on both children and parents. Parents feel anxious about sending children to school, because of concerns about the impact of the wider school environment on the children's vulnerable health. Children respond to this unease, and feel uncomfortable about separating from their parents, particularly if their peer group is not accepting and welcoming of them (Sexon & Madan-Swain, 1988).

Families who have children with life-threatening illnesses have to come to terms with the prospect of their children's death. Children's understanding of death varies depending on their developmental stage and depends on context (Kellehear, 1992). Children who are facing death tend to have more realistic ideas of death.

Many children with life-threatening illnesses feel uncomfortable talking about death with their parents as they observe the distress their parents feel and do not wish to increase this distress (Thomas, 1988). These children need support to talk about their death, and support to include their families in these conversations.

The support needs of families who have children with chronic illnesses vary.

Support needs—Queensland families children with life-limiting illness (McGrath, 2001)

Support received from

- close family members—46.7%

- support groups—29%

- friends—29%

- church groups—6.5%

- no support—21.5%

Problems with support received

- inability of supporters to deal with the condition or medication

- living a distance away

- reluctance to ask for help from family members who were carrying their own load of responsibilities

Support needs—trained volunteers to

- babysit—38.3%

- help with household chores—42.1%

- help with physical care—36.4%

- offer emotional support and/or company

- help with siblings

- assist in running errands

Times of particular vulnerability

- after the birth of a sibling

- when the child is sick and/or the condition degenerates

- when they needed to attend medical appointments

- when parents needed a break away.

Autism

Children with autism have difficulties in establishing and maintaining relationships, and in adjusting their behaviour to different contexts (Sims, 1997). Generally, programs offered to families who have children with autism result in some improvements in behaviour: the Lovass programme claims significant success (McEachin, Smith, & Lovaas, 1993). This approach requires intensive work by therapists in the home using a strict behaviourist-based approach and physical punishment. A form of this programme (without the physical punishment, and involving volunteers working collaboratively with parents) was offered in the Murdoch Early Intervention Programme (Birnbrauer & Leach, 1993). Children received between 8–25 hours of intensive training depending on other family commitments. Approximately half of the children demonstrated significant improvements in functioning over the 2 years of the programme. Clear gains were made in compliance and co-operation and less in independence and social play. Families felt, despite the involvement of volunteers in their home, and the intensity of the programme, their stress levels were decreased through participation.

Anderson and Romanczyk (1999) suggest that applied behaviour analysis (ABA—the technique upon which the Lovass approach is based) offers the most effective intervention for children with autism. The focus of ABA remains on changing children's behaviour, with parents involved as teachers. However, it is unlikely that one approach will be effective for all children (Dunlap, 1999, Brown & Bambara, 1999). An alternative discussed by McGee, Morrier and Daly (1999) takes a family focus.

Walden Toddler Programme

- 30 hours a week of centre and home based intervention
- incidental teaching
- half-day centre programme alongside children without autism
- home visitor—4 hours/week—embedding teaching in normal routines
- parents—10 hours/week teaching child

- parental support network
- parent education classes
- parental social events

Toddlers involved in the programme demonstrated increases in functional language, peer proximity (time spent playing near peers), social responsiveness with teachers and parents, levels of engagement in toy play and independent self help skills.

Domestic violence

These programs need to take a multi-system focus (Laing, 2000). Firstly, services need to be available to ensure the safety of women and children who wish to leave a violent living environment. Women's refuges offer practical and emotional support, assist women to find somewhere to live, access necessary finances, and link with other women who provide support, reassurance and comfort. Programs for children offer opportunities for children to express their concerns in a safe and supportive environment. Many services offer childcare so women can have time to deal with the many issues that must be addressed.

Community education aims to develop understanding of the roots of violence in our society, and how violence is reinforced by our societal structures. In New South Wales, curriculum materials on child protection education for students from kindergarten to year10 are available (Alford, 2000). These cover learning about all forms of abuse (harassment, bullying, dating violence, physical, sexual and emotional abuse, neglect, domestic violence and organised paedophilia). The aim is to teach students how to:

- recognise and respond in unsafe situations,
- seek assistance,
- establish and maintain healthy relationships focusing on quality, respect and responsibility.

A similar programme is being developed in Queensland (the 'Savvy Schools' project) (Parker & Ireland, 2000). The Building Safer Communities project in NSW (Venkatraman, 2000) offers lessons to students built around stories which address issues of violence and the rights of children to feel safe.

Some programs are targeted at specific groups rather than offered universally. The Responsive Adolescent Guys Education project

(RAGE) is offered to young men (aged 12–18 years) who have witnessed or experienced domestic violence (McVeigh, 2000). The project offers specific skill training (conflict resolution, safety planning, choice and consequence training, assertion versus aggression and identification of immediate and long-term goals). Traditional attitudes to the male role are challenged as are issues of homophobia and racism. Group work focuses on the socialisation experiences of men, men and emotions, violence and responsibility, men who are different and relationships.

A number of programs in both Australia and New Zealand are based on the Duluth Model (Pence & Paymor, 1993). Violence is seen as consisting of coercion and threats; intimidation; emotional abuse; isolating others; minimising, denying and blaming; using children; male privilege and economy abuse. Perpetrators are required to be accountable for the behavioural choices they make by both the woman and children involved and a community which enforces consequences for abuse.

Another option is to offer support groups and Szikla (1995) discusses the evaluation of one such where separate support groups for women and children were offered. The groups met weekly for 1.5 hours over 10 weeks. Women attending the groups did so to seek support, gain information and develop a network of friendships. All felt these needs had been met and, in addition, children's behaviour had improved.

In South Australia, a collaborative effort between the justice system, human service agencies, voluntary agencies and the police offers a programme operating on the principles that (Duigan & Felus, 2000) :
- safety of women and children is paramount,
- men who abuse are responsible for, and should be held accountable for, their actions.

Team members working with women offer support to aid women in identifying their own safety needs. Support is provided in obtaining Domestic Violence Restraining orders. Workers with children aim to promote child protection strategies. Workers with perpetrators focus on responsibility for violence, facilitate violence groups and collaborate to ensure that victim experience informs their work. All workers take opportunities to educate and inform the wider community about the non-acceptability of violence.

Family violence is a significant issue in many Aboriginal communities (National Crime Prevention, 2001). Programs addressing family violence need to involve community members themselves in taking ownership of the problem. One example of such a project is the project auspiced by the Northern Rivers Community Legal Centre in Lismore (Bardon & Walk, 2000). Community consultation is being used to develop a programme to make it easier for Aboriginal women to apply for an apprehended Violence Order and to follow the application through to completion. Local radio and local schools are used to involve and educate community members.

A final component is visitation or contact centres (Laing, 2000). These provide a safe place where non-resident parents can either spend time with their children in a supervised visit, or children can changeover from resident to non-resident parents. Evaluation of these services indicates that staff require more training to be able to recognise when children are distressed by the visit. Contact centres could play a more active role in supporting both resident and non-resident parents to make changes that would benefit children.

Alcohol or drug dependency

Drug policies in Australia are based on an attempt to reduce the harm caused by illicit drug use (Community Drug Summit, 2001g). Within this framework operate a range of programs which also contribute to supporting families. Universal approaches aim at developing community attitudes that do not support drug use. Schools offer drug education programs with varying levels of success. One assumption often made by these education programs is that drug use in students arises out of peer pressure. The Life Skills Training Programme (Community Drug Summit, 2001h) aims at enhancing individual competence, which is thought to be linked to ability to withstand peer pressure. Evaluation of this programme across a range of studies indicates some success in reducing alcohol, cannabis and tobacco use. Peer leaders are often used in drug education as they are more likely to be perceived as credible by other young people.

Education needs to be offered before drug-taking behaviour is established; it is more difficult to change existing patterns of behaviour than to prevent their acquisition (Community Drug Summit, 2001b). Late primary and early secondary years are the ideal time to target preventative drug education programs. The way the programme is delivered also impacts significantly on outcomes, with interaction style and processes being extremely important in engaging young people's interest. It is most effective to target 'gateway drugs' such as alcohol and tobacco, as early use of these is linked to use of illicit drugs (Community Drug Summit, 2001c).

Members of the local community can be involved in school-based drug education programs, and families can be supported to model appropriate attitudes and behaviours towards drug use. Schools need to move away from a disciplinary approach to students involved in drug use, and become involved, in conjunction with community workers, in the development of care plans for those students (Community Drug Summit, 2001c).

The Community Trials Programme in California and South Carolina (Community Drug Summit, 2001c) is a prevention programme which mobilises community members, trains bar staff in responsible beverage service, targets drinking and driving, and underage drinking, and restricts the availability of alcohol. Evaluation of the project showed a 10% decrease in alcohol related traffic accidents per year. In Western Australia Community Mobilisation for the Prevention of Alcohol Related Injury operated in Geraldton and involved community development activities, local networking, provision of alternative activities, health education and public education. Outcomes indicated that some measures of alcohol related behaviour showed changes, but that community-wide changes are slow to occur.

Community Drug Service Teams work through offering counselling and support to other local services and communities. Some offer direct services to young people, whilst others focus on working with other agencies in the community to make them more accessible to young users. Local Drug Action groups are responsible for local public education campaigns, and provide opportunities for parents to develop networks and support (Community Drug Summit, 2001b).

A range of treatment options are available for family members who have a drug problem (Community Drug Summit, 2001f) and no one treatment meets all needs. Generally treatments work, when compared to the no-treatment alternative. Detoxification is the first step of treatment, and the longer people remain in a treatment programme, the more likely they are to be successful. Many of the young people who develop drug problems were marginalised before their addiction further socially isolated them. Treatment programs therefore need to address their integration into society through addressing their(Community Drug Summit, 2001h):

- physical capital: these are the material assets available such as a place to live, a car to drive, employment etc
- social capital: these are the relationships still maintained, and which can be used to develop further attachments and relationships
- human capital: the skills individuals have including self-esteem, efficacy, etc

Harm-reduction programs (Community Drug Summit, 2001d)

Needle and syringe programs

- reduce sharing of needles
- provide injecting equipment, treatment referral, other assistance (health, legal, social)
- significantly reduce the transmission of HIV, Hepatitis B and C
- do not result in increased injecting drug use
- do not increase needle and syringe litter in public places

Supervised injecting facilities

- operate in Switzerland, Netherlands and Germany,
- Australia's 1st—Kings Cross, Sydney, 2001
- provide sterile injecting equipment, supervision for safe injecting, immediate overdose treatment, primary health care, treatment referral.
- reduce overdose death rate
- improve health and functioning

Families of drug users report feeling isolated because of negative community attitudes towards drug dependency (Community Drug Summit, 2001f). Individuals who become involved in treatment programs are entitled to confidentiality which also isolates their family. Little attention is paid to the needs to the family, and the family context. Where family are considered, they are often perceived to be part of the problem, rather than part of the treatment.

Needs of family members (Community Drug Summit, 2001f)

Information

- issues related to the drugs taken
- different harm minimising strategies available
- ranges of treatments available
- rights and responsibilities regarding concentual/non-concentual treatment

Support groups

- meet families with similar issues
- siblings – conflict between loyalty to sibling and parents—may resent parental attention on target child
- Kids Helpline

Family members may also be victims of the crimes of their drug-taking family member. This may result in considerable financial hardship and is the cause of much emotional stress as families grapple with the alternative actions available to them:

- unwillingly supporting the drug-taking behaviour;
- requiring the child to leave home and live independently (with all the attendant risks associated with probable poverty and homelessness);
- enrolling the child involuntarily in a treatment programme;
- reporting the illegal behaviour to the police in the hope that the justice system may provide effective treatment and rehabilitation.

There are increasing numbers of grandparents caring for grandchildren and increasing numbers of children in alternative care because of parental drug problems (Community Drug Summit, 2001f). When parents have drug problems their children are likely to be neglected. In Western Australia, one study indicated that of the families who had substantiated cases of abuse, 22% combined drug abuse with serious injury to children. Between 65 to 70% of care and protection orders taken out for children in 1999/2000 state that alcohol and/or substance abuse are a serious concern.

In Western Australia a programme offered through the Women's Health Centre (Community Drug Summit, 2001f) attempts to reach parents who use drugs. Support and outreach services are provided during the pregnancy and the early years of the children's lives and attempts are made to include fathers. Early evaluations suggest the programme significantly reduces harm to children.

Post-natal depression

Biological (Dalton & Holton, 1996)

- hormonal imbalance
- treatment—diet, natural progesterone

Psychological (Thurtle, 1995)

- role change
- loose figure, freedom, employment

Social (Nicholson, 1998)

- gender role expectation—fulfilment in child rearing
- if not—failed as a woman

Although the incidence of PND may be relatively high, there are few services available (Aiken, 2000). Addressing PND is important as research consistently identified less positive outcomes for children of depressed mothers (Stein, Gath, Bucher, & Bond, 1991, Marshall & Watt, 1999).

Preparation for parenting course are sometimes offered. One such course consisted of 6 2-hours classes held prior to the birth, and an after-birth reunion (Brugha et al., 2000). Classes were specifically focused on strategies for tackling depression using cognitive and problem-solving approaches, and strategies for developing support networks. However, although the parents indicated they enjoyed the classes, and felt they benefited from them, evaluation failed to demonstrate reductions in PND. Similar programs in Australia also failed to demonstrate significant impacts. For example, two antenatal and one postnatal support groups were offered to women who were identified as at risk for PND (Stamp, Williams, & Crowther, 1995). Attendance at the sessions was low (31%) and at 7 weeks after the birth 15% of women in the control group and 11% of women in the intervention group scored high on the PND scale. In Western Australia, Pope and colleagues offered 6 support groups for women identified at 2 weeks with PND (Marshall & Watt, 1999). Women reported they enjoyed the groups, and felt they benefited from them, but evaluation failed to demonstrate a significant impact.

In contrast, an ecologically-based approach is claimed to be more beneficial (Honikman, 2001). Hanley (2998) described a selective programme aimed at encouraging mothers to socialise and develop support networks. Support groups were offered and mothers received home visits from a health visitor who listened to their concerns, offering advice and support. Some mothers received training and became involved in home visits. The health visitor referred mothers where additional support was required. Mothers were also able to access practical help in the home, including childcare.

Another programme (Meager & Milgrom, 1996) offered of educational, social support and cognitive-behavioural components in 10 90-minute weekly group sessions. Depressed mothers tended to have poor parental relationships, poor social supports, higher levels of stress associated with childcare and a previous family history of depression. However, after participating in the programme, depression levels were significantly reduced, suggesting that a cognitive-behavioural approach to PND is efficacious.

Mental illness

Extent of the problem

- 35% of mental health clients are women with children under the age of 18—majority have children under the age of 6

- 33% of these have a history of drug or alcohol abuse (Australian Infant Child Adolescent and Family Mental Health Association, 2001)

- 10–20% of the general population likely to experience some psychological disorder; 1–2% a psychotic disorder during childhood, adolescence or adulthood

- children whose parents have a mental illness experience a higher risk of developing mental illnesses themselves (Dean & Macmillan, 2001): 25–50% for a psychological disorder and 10–14% for psychosis (Australian Infant Child Adolescent and Family Mental Health Association, 2001)

- 33% of children in out-of-home care have a parent with a mental illness (Cuff & Pietsch, 1997).

Mental illness impacts on parental interactions with their children (Australian Infant Child Adolescent and Family Mental Health

Association, 2001). Family relationships are at risk and parenting skills are generally poorer. Infants whose mothers experience mental illness are likely to have lower birth-weights and to be born prematurely. They have delays in cognitive, language, physical and psychosocial development. Impact is influenced by timing: the earlier in children's lives the illness manifests, the worse the outcomes (Australian Infant Child Adolescent and Family Mental Health Association, 2001). Intensity also matters, with less positive outcomes associated with increased degrees of parental disturbance. Children may be protected from some of the impact if the family is stable and harmonious, and if an alternative, healthy caregiver is available.

Family support aims to:

- enhance parenting skills
- support parents to meet the needs of children
- minimise parental discord
- increase parental social support networks
- children need positive attachments (inside or outside the immediate family group)
- opportunities for children to understand their parent's actions and to assess them against a realistic framework (reality-testing)

The Sutherland project in South Eastern Sydney (Dean & Macmillan, 2001) uses a child risk checklist to identify the impact of the mental illness on children. Workers develop plans for children as well as the adult, linking families to other services in the community. Telephone support groups involve small groups of children linking up in a conference call with 2 facilitators, aiming to build networking and coping skills. The service also offers support to schools so they are better able to support specific children.

Divorce

Pedro-Carroll and Cowen (1985) offered a support programme to children aged between 10 to 12 years whose parents were divorcing. Children participated in 14 one-hour weekly classes covering issues such as conflict resolution, anger management, and understanding feelings. Two weeks after the intervention, children in the programme were rated by their teachers as having improved behaviour and social competence. Parents reported improvement in the children's school performance and peer relationships. The children were less anxious about the divorce.

A similar programme was offered to children aged 8 and 9 years whose parents had been separated, on average, 3–4 years prior to the intervention (Alpert-Gillis, Pedro-Carroll, & DCowen, 1989). This programme included children from different ethnic groups, and offered a more culturally-appropriate curriculum. Children were taught strategies to deal with infrequent contact with their non-custodial parents and how to identify caring adults and seek support from them. Four weeks after the intervention, the children were rated as having improved coping skills, attitudes towards their families, parents and themselves. Parents rated them as having improved behaviour and problem-solving skills, and teachers thought they were more assertive, had increased tolerance for frustration and improved peer social skills. Long-term follow-up of children undergoing these programs has not been attempted. The authors suggest that these relatively brief social competence interventions have an impact on the stress children experience as a consequence of divorce.

Extended family

The grandparent role has changed significantly in the latter half of the twentieth century as populations become more mobile, retirement ages change and women enter the workforce in increasing numbers (Thomas, Sperry, & Yarbrough, 2000). Often grandparents are unable to be closely involved in the lives of their grandchildren and must maintain contact through telephone, letters and cards, email and, in some cases, occasional visits. Other grandparents are able to have more frequent contact with their grandchildren through regular visits, childcare (Gattai & Musatti, 1999) and sleepovers. Where a positive relationship is established between grandparent and grandchild in the child's early years, it is likely that that relationship will last a lifetime (Ramirez Barranti, 1985). Grandparents can offer practical and emotional support (Tinsley & Parke, 1987).

Programs aimed at supporting grandparents maintain positive relationships with their grandchildren (Koser, 2001) include inter-generational gatherings such as picnics, parties and other recreational activities. Older people can participate in reading and academic support programs with children. Children can visit seniors' homes, and grandparents can visit early childhood centres and schools. Children whose parents work can be matched with a local older person who can call to check they arrived home safely. Children can call to remind the older person about appointments, and to chat. Resources can be shared. For example one community uses the same van to transport children to their early childhood programme, seniors to the senior centre, deliver meals on wheels and collect children for an after school hours programme (Butts, 2001). Other inter-generational programs include foster grandparents, and programs linking children from different cultural backgrounds with elders from their culture.

When families separate, and divorce, the needs of extended family members such as grandparents are often overlooked. Matthews and Sprey (1984) found that the relationship between grandparent and grandchildren varied depending if the custodial parent was the child or former in-law child. Some grandparents found it difficult, or impossible, to maintain contact with their grandchildren when the custodial parent was the former in-law child.

In America, nearly 1 in every 10 grandparent will have the responsibility of rearing grandchildren for at least 6 months (Thomas et al., 2000). This is often the result of family crisis, stress and/or breakdown (Koser, 2001), all risk factors for negative developmental outcomes. It is therefore likely that grandparents find themselves raising children who demonstrate behaviour problems, emotional and mental health concerns.

Whilst grandparents may access a range of family support services, they also have special needs (Cox, 2000).

Special needs of custodial grandparents

- more likely to experience depression, particularly if they are in poor health themselves (Musil, 1998)
- increased stress if grandchildren have behaviour problems
- Grandmothers may experience physical and emotional health concerns (Roe, Minkler, Saunders, & Thomson, 1996)
- financial hardship—limited retirement income (Kelley, 1993)

Programs to support grandparents focus on providing information and education in handling the behaviour concerns (behaviours they may not have had experience with in rearing their own children). Programs also provide emotional support for grandparents who may be torn between the needs of their children, the needs of their grandchildren and their own needs. Links to community services are important, as communities and services are likely to have changed significantly since grandparents last accessed them as parents.

The Skip programme in New York supports grandmothers (and one great-grandmother) rearing grandchildren (Turner, 2001). Grandmothers are connected to each other via a hotline, and volunteers call regularly to remind them of support group meetings. A car pool operates to share transport to meetings. Grandmothers are offered information specific to their needs at the meetings and given general information on child development and child rearing. Childcare is offered during the meetings.

Abuse and neglect

Parent education is often offered to families who are identified as at risk for child abuse or neglect. Parent education implies the existence of 'good enough' parenting, but attempts to define this fail because of lack of agreement about what is good and bad parenting (Tomison, 1998). This is particularly problematic when parents are required to improve their parenting in order to keep their child, or to be reunified with their children

Parents who are at risk of abusing or neglecting their children seldom do so simply because they lack parenting skills. There are usually other factors contributing towards the risk of abusive and/or neglectful behaviours.

Combinations of risks in abuse and neglect

- substance abuse problems
- unemployment
- minimal social support
- poverty
- unrealistic expectations of children
- limited social and cognitive problem solving skills
- mental illnesses

- rely on punishment to control their children (with its concomitant underlying values relating to violence, power and oppression)

- impaired relationships between themselves and children.

Given all these risk factors, parents may engage in abusive behaviours if they find themselves in situations of high stress. These situational stressors may occur regularly in their lives, or they may be infrequent.

Universal programs are aimed at preventing child abuse and neglect through educating all parents. Resource kits offer awareness raising activities, videos and booklets. Parenting education programs offer families opportunities to access information and develop skills. Home visiting services offer individualised, home-based support. Education programs for children in schools teach personal safety (for example the Protective Behaviour Programme - (Tomison, 1998).

Selective programs usually combine parent education and home visiting. The Family Support Team from Anglican Community Services in North Adelaide offer a home-based skills intervention programme. Home visitors offer opportunities to gain an understanding of child development, parenting, behaviour management, budgeting and household management. Group activities are offered to facilitate the development of social support, communication and social skills and to link families to community resources.

In the past, children were removed from their families when abuse was identified and placed in institutions or foster homes. In more recent times the focus has become one of family preservation. Intensive family preservation services (IFPS) (Maluccio, 1998) are offered to families where there is immanent risk of out-of-home placement: children will be placed within the week unless alternative action is taken (Pecora, 1991). Evaluations of IFPS indicate some degree of success in maintaining children in the home and improving parenting (Kirk, 2000).

IFPS services can include a range of components.

Components of IFSP in Wales (Pithouse & Tasiran, 2000)

Most used services in home

- practical advice
- financial support

- counselling
- child accommodation
- given/loaned goods

Less popular

- other residential
- other day care
- family centre drop-in
- help in the house
- family therapy
- medical appointment
- child and adult out-patients appointment
- education services

Least popular

- mediation
- connection to voluntary organisation
- holiday
- voluntary befriender
- alcohol/drug treatment
- remedial teaching
- special adolescent services

Services never chosen

- marriage guidance
- special adult services

IFPS are thought to be more effective when home based. Where 50% of caseworkers' time was spent in the home, families were able to keep the child at home. In contrast, only 22% of families kept their child when case workers spent 25% of their time in the home (Berry, 1994). However, other research (Showell & White, 1990) shows the opposite effect, thus it is not clear how important it is for family support workers to spend time in the family home.

One early IFPS is the Homebuilders which is offered in slightly different forms in different areas. In Washington, workers spend about 36 hours over about a month in the homes of families (about 72 minutes a day) (Berry, Cash, & Brook, 2000). In Utah, the average daily contact time is less (between 30 and 40 minutes a day).

The aim of IFPS workers is to do 'what-ever-it-takes' to increase the child's safety and reduce the risk of abuse or neglect. The components making up the 'what-ever-it-takes' approach vary from family to family.

What-ever-it-takes (Berry et al., 2000)

- 30 minutes a day including in-home work, agency paperwork, supervision of:

- client-centred skills—problem-solving, cognitive-behavioural strategies, psychosocial, behavioural, Adlerian and experiential skills.

- concrete services—parenting, transport, childcare, food, financial and medical services, home, bills, moving, recreation, cleaning, job services

A large number of the families receiving these services remained intact (89%) and 4% had their children placed in foster homes. At the one-year follow-up, 36% of families had had another reported of maltreatment but only 11% were sustained. Some of these families were referred for IFPS again and, of these families, 11% eventually had their children placed in foster homes.

A broad-based evaluation of IFPS in Utah and Washington based on Homebuilders showed that 92.9% of the families served were able to remain together (Haapala, Pecora, & Fraser, 1991). Just over two thirds of the families were still together 12 months after the programme compared with 14.7% of a small control group. Families referred to IFSP were characterised by high levels of coercive relationships, poor parenting and children who were oppositional and non-compliant. IFPS offers parenting education in the home, in the context in which parenting occurs, and the study found that parenting generally improved as a result of this. Parenting education and support served to break the cycle of coercion and allow families to begin to establish more positive relationships. In addition to parenting education, family support workers also provided counselling, clinical services (such as anger management, conflict resolution), family therapy, crisis interventions and concrete services. When family support workers empowered families to seek concrete services themselves, positive outcomes were more likely. Families who did not succeed in the IFPS, were those whose child/children were already in an out-of-home placement, where the target child was suspected or confirmed to have drug or alcohol abuse issues, or there was a history of out-of-home placement.

IFSP have been used to facilitate the reunification of children with their biological families (Kirk, 2000).

Reunification IFSP (Lewis, Walton, & Fraser, 1995)

- IFSP 15 days prior to the reunification and 75 days after, compared with routine foster care support

- 92% IFSP children still in the home compared to 28.3% foster care children

- factors contributing to success: relationship building, crisis and conflict management, self-esteem and mood management, parenting skill building, time and money management, ability to access outside resources

6 year follow-up: (Kirk, 2000)

- IFSP children—less case supervision time in the intervening years, lived at home longer

The consensus from a number of research projects reported in Kirk is that successful reunification is facilitated if IFSP services are delivered for between 60 to 90 days, and that more intensive support is more beneficial than less intensive.

Indicative programs depend on accurate identification of families at risk. Houston and Griffiths (2000) suggest that this focus has created an emphasis on investigation and gathering forensic evidence. The use of a risk framework assumes risk can be predicted, and accurate assessment of risk will prevent abuse occurring. It also categorises families at different levels of risk, often with only those at the high end of the scale eligible to receive services. There may well be many other families who are not identified in this category, who are just as in need of their services.

Forms of counselling can be effective in supporting families where there has been sexual abuse. The Giarretto Child Sexual Abuse Treatment Programme (Bagley & LaChance, 2000), evaluated in Britain, was found to be 100% successful in preventing re-abuse (although researchers were unable to follow-up families who dropped out without completing the programme). A replication in Canada was slightly less successful. However, the programme is very expensive (approximately $US10,000 per family in 1995 costs). It offers individual counselling for the victim, her mother and the offending father, dyadic counselling for victim and mother, and separate group counselling for mothers, female victims, father-offenders and, where the father was to be re-united with the family, whole family groups. With calls for increased sentences for sexual abuse, there is very little community and political support for expensive programs such as this, despite apparent success rates.

Another programme with some success in working with families is the Signs of Safety approach, developed in Western Australia (Turnell & Edwards, 1999). Child protection workers follow six principles in working with families:

1. Seek to understand the position of each family member—the values, beliefs and understandings they have of their situation

2. Look for occasions when maltreatment has NOT happened—these indicate alternatives that have been tried in the past

3. Identify family strengths and resources

4. Focus on developing goals using the family's ideas. Goals ensure safety of the children and use a treatment rather than therapy approach. Child protection workers build a picture with the family of what safety will look like, then work with the family towards achieving this.

5. Keep focus on the family's sense of safety and progress

6. Determine the family's willingness, confidence and capacity to work towards goals

Conclusion

Selective and/or indicative family support is offered to a range of targeted groups who are identified as having particular needs. This chapter has reviewed a range of these targeted groups and discussed the components of family support identified as necessary for their special needs. In some areas, family support has been offered, in various forms and under various guises, for a number of years. In other areas, the concept of family support is new and programs have yet to become readily available. All of these programs offer different combinations of the various components discussed in the previous two chapters. Components are assembled based on needs of the targeted groups and the likelihood of families being able to access comparable universally available services. Family support programs can not be characterised by simple models and standard services.

Chapter 7

Staffing

Introduction

The early motto of family support, *whatever it takes* (Bergman & Singer, 1996), reflects the ranges of challenges staff may be required to face in their daily work lives. In performing *whatever it takes,* family support staff demonstrate a diverse range of skills and knowledge which could represent the beginnings of a new profession. Roles and responsibilities, training and professionalisation of staff are examined in this chapter.

A new profession?

Those who work in family support in the United States are called Family Support Workers (for example see Family Support America at www.familysupportamerica.org), or simply family workers (Dean, 2000). Many see family support work evolving into a profession with its own specific sets of knowledge and skills. Norton (1994), for example, developed sets of basic knowledge, specialised knowledge and practice skills which represent the necessary professional grounding for effective family support work.

Family support is community work. Ife (1995) argues that effective community work cannot be undertaken by professionals. Professionalism, he states, is characterised by specialised skills and knowledge which set professionals apart, as 'experts', from the people with whom they work. Indeed, many professional groups actively work to exclude others from their professional knowledge and skills through requirements such as registration to practice, and through the use of professional. Such a separation between professional and 'other' is antithetical to the theoretical foundation of family support work (Kagan & Weissbourd, 1994). Sharing skills, empowerment and acknowledgment of the expertise of family and community members can not occur in a professional framework.

There remains a need for workers to behave 'professionally', or in other words, ethically. Standards of conduct and expectations of workers need to be clear. Ife (1995) argues that a passion and commitment to the moral principles related to social justice are essential as this provides a far more effective guide for ethical behaviour than a surface commitment to a code of conduct. This passion is considered detrimental to 'professional' behaviour in the usual definitions of 'professionalism'.

One criteria for defining professionalism requires a coherent knowledge base derived from theory and research which is transferred to 'professionals' through appropriate training (Kagan & Weissbourd, 1994). In Australia, the National Training Packages (Australian National Training Authority, 1999) define the skills required of community workers in aged care; alcohol and other drug work; children's services; child protection, statutory supervision and juvenile justice work; community housing work; community work; disability; mental health (non clinical) and youth work. No specific training is available for family support workers, whose skills bridge between those associated with several of the areas. However, Ife (1995) argues that workers will develop their own style of work which can not be constrained by professional definitions of appropriate roles and standardised procedures. Individual style arises from individual knowledge and practice experiences, as well as life experiences, values and personality factors in a constructivist view of learning (Sims, in review-b, Sims, in review-a). Attempting to define these too closely, he argues, removes the core elements of flexibility, commitment and empathy from family work.

The final criteria for professionalism is that of professionally developed and recognised standards of knowledge, training and performance to which all practitioners adhere. However, Kagan and Weissbourd (1994) argue that one of the strengths of the family support movement lies in the blending of a range of differently skilled workers with different backgrounds and different experiences. Some of these people are professionals, professionally trained and recognised as such by the relevant professional registration bodies (such as social workers). Others, who have equally important contributions to make, may have local skills and knowledge, or specific life experiences which make their contributions essential to the specific programme in which they are employed.

In an attempt to facilitate the development of family support as a new profession, Family Support America have begun to develop a system to accredit family support programs (Mason, 2001). All types of family support programs can apply for certification. They are required to undertake a self-assessment and peer review process focusing on the way they implement the principles of family support practice. Programs who are successful in obtaining certification are identified on the website of Family Support America and will be able to use the Family Support flag as their symbol.

Family support workers

Most family support programs will consist of teams of workers, each with different skills and expertise to contribute to the team (Norton, 1994). Practitioners in family support undertake a range of roles depending on the programme, their own skills and expertise, and the needs of the children, families and communities with which they work. Despite this variation, there are likely to be some roles and functions many programs hold in common (Stott & Musick, 1994). Teams are likely to consist of the following types of workers undertaking some of the following roles.

Family support co-ordinator

Generally this person is responsible for the running of the programme. This means that the person is accountable to the funding and/or sponsoring body for financial management, supervision and conduct of staff and outcomes for children, families and communities. The role must operationalise the underpinning principles of family support with staff as well as with children, families and communities. A collegial, supportive approach to management (rather than an hierarchical and bureaucratic) is essential. This can often be difficult if the programme is sponsored by an agency, which itself runs along bureaucratic lines. Co-ordinators often find themselves in the unenviable position of trying to empower staff, and work using consensus decision-making strategies, in an environment where they are simply told what to do and when to do it. Negotiating the tricky boundaries between hierarchical and non-hierarchical management requires skill and a deep commitment to the importance of the principles underlying family support.

Skills

- financial management and budgeting

- fund-raising may be required

- allocating and prioritising funds in relation to the policies of the organisation and the programme

- staff recruitment

- supervision

- performance appraisal

- relevant unions

Co-ordinators must ensure they receive adequate support, and this may be difficult to receive from management in their own organisation when sponsoring organisations are bureaucratic. Supervision may be sought outside of the programme, and co-ordinators need to plan the necessary financial support for this.

Workers with families

These workers have skills in working with parents. They may have training in relationship counselling, social work, psychology, or in family studies. They are responsible for issues relating to family dynamics and family functioning, communication within families, roles within families and family culture. They are involved in the assessment of family strengths. They may also be involved in issues of domestic violence and child abuse and neglect so need relevant skills and understanding.

Workers with children

These workers have skills and expertise in working specifically with children. They have a sound knowledge and practical experience in working with children of all ages, particular skills in working with infants and toddlers, expertise in child development, and in strategies for guiding children's behaviour. They may have training in children's studies, or early childhood education. Some workers may also have training in working with older children or in youth work. In addition, there may be workers on the team who have experience in atypical development (such as working with children who have disabilities, or children who have been traumatised). Specific professionals such as physiotherapists, speech and language therapists and others who have particular skills to contribute may also be involved in teams of workers focusing on children.

Other workers

Family support programs in America often include para-professionals. In other countries these workers may not be perceived as para-professionals (with its implication of hierarchy of status) but simply as differently skilled workers. These are workers who have little or no pre-service training, but whose contribution to the team is specifically related to their life experience. Many family support programs explicitly state as their goal the employment of local people rather than outside professionals. The aim is for local people to work with other local people, thus empowering communities. The expertise these workers bring is their local knowledge, and their personal standing and reputation in their communities. Workers may also bring specific language skills to the team.

They require in-service training to ensure they develop necessary skills and knowledge. Training often needs to be personalised to ensure that individual issues (such as the worker's own experiences of child abuse or domestic violence) do not hamper them. Sometimes these workers experience conflict in their own families as they grow and develop skills: they feel they are 'growing away from their family' (Stott & Musick, 1994). Appropriate supervision is necessary to ensure that workers are adequately supported to work through these issues.

Some programs may choose to use volunteers as well as, or in place of, paid staff. Volunteers are not cost neutral. Volunteers face similar issues to those discussed above. Appropriate training and supervision of volunteers is essential to ensure that the service they offer is of high quality, and to ensure they, themselves, do not suffer because of their involvement in the programme. The cost of training programs, and regular support for volunteers, as well as reimbursement of expenses incurred in delivering services, must be included in the programme budget.

Administrative workers

Some programs may have the luxury of administrative support. Programs where workers are out in the field most of the time, for example, may require a person at the end of the phone all the time to take calls and inquiries from families. Where those calls are likely to involve serious issues, existing family or children's workers may need to be rostered on to phone duty. However, in other programs, a receptionist may be appropriate. As this person provides the public front to the programme, the role is crucial. A sound understanding of the principles underlying the programme, and the ability to operationalise these in interpersonal situations is necessary. Training in the programme policy and philosophy, and specific skills necessary for the position is required, along with appropriate supervision and support.

Other administrative workers may include clerical, fund-raising, or financial management support workers. In a large organisation, of which the family support programme is one component, these may offer a centralised support system. An understanding of the programme, and its methods of operation, are essential if these personnel are to be able to undertake their roles effectively as they too, may straddle the divide between a larger bureaucratic organisation, and the power-sharing approach used in the family support programme. Smaller programs may operate using community members to fulfil these roles, perhaps as volunteers. Again, volunteers require appropriate training and support to work effectively, and these costs must be included in the budget.

A new approach to training

Knowledge presented to practitioners becomes incorporated into their thinking. Information presented, through training and practice, will be 'learned' differently because each practitioner has a unique model of the world or framework into which the knowledge is integrated (Sims, in review-b).

The role of values

Practitioners work more effectively when their beliefs and values match those of the context in which they work (Hasazl, Johnston, Liggett, & Schattman, 1994; O'Loughlin, 1989, O'Loughlin, 1989). When family support workers work in a system that expects behaviours which do not fit with their own personal value systems, they will not be able to deliver quality service. This will not only impair the quality of the service they deliver to families, it will also impact on their personal functioning: they are more likely to experience stress and burnout.

Thus training for family support work is not values free. There is an explicit aim to shape values towards forms congruent with quality practice. It is important for both educators and practitioners to be clear about the values they are imposing on others. Ife (1995) argues it is appropriate to impose on others the values associated with high quality practice, but it is not appropriate to impose other values on others.

Values congruent with high quality family support practice

- empowerment—partnership and shared power
- need for support is not through failure
- all families have strengths
- valuing of difference and diversity
- families alone are not totally responsible for their circumstances
- role of family support worker is wider than simple responsibility to families alone
- value their own abilities

The role of praxis

Family support programs operate out of a critical paradigm. Practitioners need to integrate theory and knowledge in order to operate effectively in an environment where they are constantly required to problem-solve in unique circumstances.

Conventional learning theory suggests that action comes from understanding; training presents of theory which practitioners later convert into practice. The reverse of this position is associated with the competency-based learning approach (Smith, Lowrie, Hill, Bush, & Lobegeier, 1997): understanding is expected to come from practice. In family support, effective practice requires an integration of both learning and doing; understanding and practice must occur together. The term 'praxis' distinguishes this new form of learning from others (Ife, 1995). Praxis implies a constant cycle of doing, learning and critical reflection.

Praxis skills

Different workers will develop different skills as they experience different situations in their practice. Ife (1995) argues that gut feelings, arising out of experience and reflection, may often be more relevant to a community worker than clearly defined and learned skills. Despite this, underpinning all the different roles that may be required of different family support workers are core requirements related to the theoretical foundations of family support.

Critical reflection

Critical reflection, or reflective practice, is the basis of sound family support work. Practitioners are required to constantly reflect on their practice (Allen, 2000). Reflective practice enables the practitioner to link theory to practice, and elucidates theory through practice.

Making time available in busy work schedules is a crucial requirement for effective family support practice. Effective practitioners realise the importance of time to reflect through:

* setting aside a regular time for reflection—such attempts often go awry and this is generally not an effective strategy for most people.
* keeping a reflective journal using one of several different structures.
* formal supervision—collegiate, supportive- supervisor listens, asks challenging questions, supports the practitioner in self reflection.
* supervision outside agency—supervisor not have same taken-for-granted assumptions
* Informal interactions—networking meetings
* Increasing general knowledge through reading—gain different perspectives on the world

Critical incident approach to reflection (Frankrijker, 1998, Newman, 1987, Newman, 2000)

* identify a specific incident
* ask questions: what happened? how did I contribute to this incident? what did I do? what did others do? how do I feel about this? how would I change my behaviour next time? what have I

learned from this incident? now this has happened, what am I going to do now?

- journal confidential—never leave unattended

Reflective practice is not only essential for the practitioner, it is a skill that can be taught family and community members. The ability to reflect on one's own experiences of power and powerlessness, as well as on one's strengths and successes is an essential pre-requisite in creating opportunities for change. Effective practitioners model reflective practice, and offer opportunities for families to develop the skill in order to take control over their own lives.

Vision

Effective family support workers are committed to their work because they believe that they can make a difference: that their work with families is contributing to making the world a better place in which to live. Effective workers see their employment as more than just a job: it is a vocation requiring a personal commitment to social justice. Family support workers may finish work at the end of the day, but their commitment to social justice runs through all aspects of their lives, both the public and the private.

Technical skills

Not all workers will need all of these skills, and there will be many other skills that workers in different positions will need to acquire to become effective in their specific positions.

Writing

Family support workers need to write clearly and precisely to produce:
- reports (including assessments).
- funding submissions
- media release and publicity material (such as brochures)
- newsletters or other less formal written networking and communication devices.

Writing needs to be grammatical and spelling correct. The ability to express ideas clearly and concisely in simple English is essential. Coupled with writing skills is the ability to engage in critical reflection about written work, so that the worker can modify the writing style to different purposes, and check if the purpose is achieved.

Computing skills

There is a general expectation that most workers will be computer literate as workers may need to:
- use word processing
- use mailing lists
- keep up to date with recent information - internet
- use email and chat lines for networking
- use database and financial management programs

Public presentation

Some family support workers may spend all their time working directly with families and not need the skills of public presentation. However, many will find there are occasions when they are required to speak in public. This may occur through a need to speak at community meetings, or meetings of several families. It may occur through networking meetings where groups of workers share their experiences and talk about their programme. Some workers may be involved in conferences and be expected to present papers or workshops about their work. Workers in family support programs are ideally placed to talk about the work they do, and share the value of that work. The ability to speak well in public helps to convey this important message to others.

Working with media

The most effective media release is one which can be used directly, without having to be rewritten by the journalist involved. Media writing is a specific form of writing that most practitioners will not have experienced. Read the papers carefully before attempting to write. Practice writing in the style used in the paper being targeted. Use critical reflection skills to evaluate what has been written and rewrite as often as necessary.

Some workers may find themselves involved in an interviews which may be taped for later presentation or live. Always check which applies in each situation. Watch interviews on TV and listen to interviews on the radio. Reflect on how interviewees handle difficult questions. How does the message get across when the interviewer does not ask the necessary questions? Take time to think and answer questions. A pause before speaking is preferable to a string of 'ums' and 'ahs'. Practice identifying the really important issues to convey, and ensure that they can be communicated in 20 seconds.

Management and organisation

Family support programs should reflect, in their structure, a strength-based empowerment approach. Traditional management skills are not relevant but strong interpersonal and group skills are. Staff management skills (such as supporting staff performance, ability to identify and work through change management for staff who are not performing effectively) are essential. Despite a collegial environment, the manager or co-ordinator of a programme is ultimately responsible (in this bureaucratic world) for the performance of staff in the programme.

Financial management requires an understanding of budgetary processes, financial accountability and simple bookkeeping skills. The non-hierarchical nature of family support programs makes it very difficult to manage financial data using standard financial management systems. However, legal liability for money mismanagement may make it difficult to have alternative systems of financial control. Record keeping skills are related not just to financial management, but to managing information in general (such as family information, information about staff, information about the programme).

An organiser is someone who makes things happen; who does what is necessary so that others can get on with doing what they need to do. Organisers attend to details. With an empowerment focus, the worker does not undertake the organising tasks; rather the role involves supporting others to take on these responsibilities. This involves interpersonal skills needed to encourage, tactfully remind and support others through their organising tasks. Effective family support workers are, themselves, organised. They ensure that they have the resources they need. They ensure they have time available to undertake the tasks they have promised to complete. They are effective time-keepers, and become skilled at estimating how much time particular tasks will take.

Research

Basic research skills are required to undertake research about specific communities, perhaps through accessing census records, community profiles, community records, and needs surveys. Some workers will be involved in evaluation research. Research skills include:

- the ability to determine appropriate research methodologies,
- knowledge of different research methods and techniques,
- knowledge in data collection and data analysis (both quantitative and qualitative).

Process skills

Personal communication

Roberts, Wasik, Casto and Ramey (1991) suggest that interpersonal skills are so fundamental and important to the role of family support, that workers should be required to have them before obtaining employment in the field.

Communication

- model empowerment & strengths
- communicate trust and respect
- communicate location of power
- gentle reminders without nagging
- ask questions, listen to answers, interpret
- make people feel comfortable
- keep conversations on track
- sensitive to cultural differences
- provide information clearly

Family support workers need to be comfortable dealing with conflict using negotiation and mediation skills. Workers need to be particularly sensitive to power issues when working through conflicts, to ensure that all participants are accorded dignity and equality during the collaborative conflict resolving process. Generally workers do not initiate confrontation as this acts against the empowerment focus of their work. However, there may be occasions when confrontation is necessary.

Family support workers may also work with children, and must develop skills in interpersonal communication with children. An in-depth understanding of guiding children's behaviour is an essential component of effective communication with children.

Groups and meetings

Family support workers also work at the level of communities. They need to be able to use all the above interpersonal skills with groups of people as well as with individuals. Workers need to be able to read and interpret group dynamics, and have strategies they can use to ensure everyone in the group has a fair opportunity to contribute. They need to have strategies they can use to ensure those who often do not participate equally (women, people from minority cultures, people with disabilities for example) are given, and supported to take, appropriate opportunities.

In formal group meetings, family support workers will need facilitation skills. These include the ability to reflect back decisions to the group for ratification, to keep the group working together and on track, and the ability to support a group so they move towards consensus. Organising skills both before and after meetings ensure that the physical environment is appropriate and comfortable, and that where appropriate, an agenda is circulated, people are adequately prepared, minutes are taken and, after the meeting, circulated (Sims, 1997).

When working with groups of children, family support workers need to skills associated with appropriate oversight and supervision. Understanding of children's development and learning are necessary for workers to provide appropriate physical and human environments for groups of children. Understanding of, and adherence to, legislative requirements may be necessary if workers are providing childcare.

Community education

Education, as a process, implies a transfer of knowledge or skill from those who have them, to those who do not. Linked to this is an assumption that power accrues to those who have the knowledge and skill. Aligning education with the principles underlying family support is therefore a difficult, but important task for family support workers. Workers are required to support families who make their own decisions about what they want to learn and how they want to learn it. Workers need to have sensitivity in order to craft the education they offer to the specific needs of the family concerned. Training is based on principles of equality and respect, where the worker learns as much from the parents as the parents learn from the worker.

Obtaining Resources

Family support workers require knowledge of the communities within which they work, and must have established networks within those communities. Family support workers are not required to know everything that a family might need. Some family support workers, for example, may become familiar with budgeting processes and be able to work with families on simple budgeting issues. Other workers would know to whom families should be referred, and may be involved in supporting families through the referral process. Family support workers understand the resources available to families, and how to access these resources when necessary. Knowing when to refer families is an important skill. Having referred families, workers may need to work with families so they develop skills in managing a number of different professionals in their lives.

When working on resources with families, it is important for workers to remember that the purpose of their work is to develop family self sufficiency. The best answer to family support needs is not always to locate resources outside of the family itself. Often families can resource themselves and the role of the family support worker is to encourage families to seek their own strengths and build on these.

Motivating

Family support workers who are enthusiastic and committed are likely to find that they engage with families easily, and that families are motivated to work with them to set and achieve family goals. These characteristics are personality traits, intrinsic to individuals. However, communication-based skills, the ability to be self aware, to critically reflect on one's own performance, learning from experiences and sensitivity to the communications (both verbal and non-verbal) of others all help facilitate motivation.

Advocacy

Worker involvement in advocacy implies the inability of families to advocate for themselves. Advocates have power: those on whose behalf they advocate are seen as powerless and needing others to speak for them. Family support workers need to think very carefully before they take on the role of advocate. Advocacy skills involve the ability to speak at hearings, presenting concise arguments, writing skills and using the media.

Sharing skills

Family support workers share their skills as widely as possible. They need to develop and understanding of the skills they have in order to demystify them and make them capable of being understood and learned by all family members. In this process workers identify the skills and strengths of family members, and make these available to share with others.

Family support workers have opportunities to continually learn new skills from the families with whom they are working. The relationship between worker and families is one of power sharing, where both emerge from the relationship having changed and learned. Family support workers are constantly learning and developing new skills. Critical reflection throughout this process ensures that workers combine learning and practice in an effective praxis.

Understanding

Family support knowledge can be grouped and presented in various ways. The New York State Family Development Credential offers one way of categorising this knowledge (Dean, 2000). This training programme has been developed for workers across a range of services who are involved in supporting families. Some of these workers will have other training, for others, participation in this programme is their first experience of training. Workers will already be employed in a family support role, and will be required to integrate their training with their practice as they work through the course materials. Currently this curriculum has been adopted, in various ways, in a range of states including Alabama, Alaska, California, Connecticut, Missouri, North Carolina, Rhode Island, Colorado, Iowa and Massachusetts.

The New York State Family Development Credential

- Families and family development—empowerment, ecological model, self reliance, family development, family forms, family systems.
- The worker—setting their own vision, prioritising, support systems, managing stress, balance between their own work and family lives.
- Relationships—demonstrating respect, setting appropriate boundaries, strengths perspective, confidentiality, how to terminate their relationship in a positive manner.
- Communication—basic communication skills, alternative strategies for families with language barriers or low literacy skills.
- Different cultures—cultural competence, migration, trauma, language barriers, racism, powerlessness and oppression, and family role changes.
- family assessment—empowerment-based assessment, Family Development Plan, Family Circles Assessment.
- Specialised services—referral.
- Group work—different group roles, facilitation skills, leadership.
- Collaboration—how to collaborate.

An alternative framework

Norton (1994) uses a framework for knowledge and understanding that is linked more strongly to the ecological underpinning of family support. She sees that the common threads across all family support programs are the focus on improving parental child rearing by creating settings in which parents become empowered and by creating communities which provide the appropriate resources for parents.

- Biological/physical—development, health care needs, environmental impacts, risk and resilience, atypical development, attitudes towards disability, resources available for different types of disability.
- Cultural, socioeconomic and racial—families and family systems, race and gender, attitudes, social policy, economics and politics, and how these impact on children and families.
- Psychological and emotional—development and facilitating development, attachment, relationships, play, risk factors, abuse and neglect, child protection system, mental health expertise, resources and referral options.
- Cognition and language—development, facilitation of development, impact of different cultures on development, literacy programs, parent-child interaction.
- Prevention—primary, secondary and tertiary prevention, ethical and policy issues, funding sources, different types of intervention methods.
- the early years—development, parent-child relationships, cultural differences, relationship development, the importance of the early years.
- Parenting—family life-cycle, family processes, adult stress and coping, self-esteem, fatherhood, impact of socioeconomic status, ethnicity or disability on parenting.
- Social support—group and informal supports and networks.

Qualifications

Interdisciplinary foundation

Family support workers require interdisciplinary training enabling them to work at the level of children, families and communities, to provide support in the tasks of child rearing, parenting, adult and community development. Internationally, the move to prepare community-based workers with a broad grounding in a range of disciplines is well established. In Norway, as early as 1992, the role of social pedagogue was defined as one who operated in a community setting using universalist approaches and undertaking a generalist role which included advocacy, community work, and community change (Bradley & Blaney, 1996). Social pedagogues are trained to use community-based, generic approaches to build family and community capacities, rather than focusing on deficits and rehabilitation.

Other countries in Europe were quick to join the growing focus on interdisciplinary training (Oberhuemer, 1998). Some opted for age-related training; developing courses which focused on the early years, school age years, adolescence and adulthood. In countries such as Belgium, France, Italy, Luxemborg and the Netherlands education services (such as schools) are administered, at the state level, differently than other services for children and families. Often this administrative division is reflected in training courses (Oberhuemer, 1998).

Many training courses are now being offered at University level. For example, at Manchester Metropolitan University (Fawcett & Calder, 1998), (Abbott & Pugh, 1998), a broad, interdisciplinary degree in early childhood is the foundation upon which students move into a range of employment options. Graduates add relevant postgraduate qualifications (for teaching or social work for example) onto their undergraduate qualifications where required (Powell, 1998). Such training is ideally suited to prepare workers for the new Early Years Development and Childcare Partnerships currently mandated by the Department for Education and Employment (Department for Education and Employment, 1999), focusing on combining services with children with support services for their families.

In Australia, the interdisciplinary approach to training is being offered in a small number of Universities, for example, Edith Cowan University in Perth (Sims, in press). The inter-disciplinary nature of this specific degree enables graduates to move into a wide range of community based services for children and families. With the ongoing growth in areas such as family support and parent education, graduates are able to make significant contributions. Meerilinga Young Children's Foundation in Perth also offers an interdisciplinary Certificate in Family Support based on competencies selected from both the Community Services and Children's Services training packages. This Certificate training is developed especially for volunteer home visitors working in the Parent Link programs sponsored by Meerilinga.

Other universities are developing postgraduate and masters taking an interdisciplinary focus. One course is the new masters programme being developed at City University in London for those who are working with survivors of violence: rape, abuse, family violence, road traffic violence and violence associated with war and refugee experiences. This course was developed through collaboration with institutions in Australia, Canada, Portugal and the United States, so has a strong international focus.

Specialisations

Most family support teams include a range of workers with different specialisations, as well as workers who have appropriate interdisciplinary qualifications. The types of specialisations represented in a family support team will vary depending on the particular communities involved. Programme may choose to employ workers with qualifications in special education, occupational therapy, physiotherapy, speech and language therapy, nursing, paediatrics, audiology, psychiatry and/or psychology, teaching, and youth work. Many services will choose to employ workers who have special expertise in child development and families. Other relevant, community-based areas of expertise may include health or addiction studies, family counselling, and budgeting expertise. Where families are identified as 'at risk' for child abuse and neglect, social workers will be involved in the family support team.

Workers with no formal qualifications

Effective family support involves the coming together of a range of workers with a range of necessary knowledge and skills. Some of these workers will not have formal qualifications. Instead, these workers will bring a range of different skills and experiences to family support work. In some programs, workers may be specifically recruited because of their expertise in a specific culture or language. In other programs, workers may be recruited because they have a common bond with the children and families who are receiving support. Some of these workers will be in paid positions, others will operate as volunteers.

Volunteers may be involved in direct service provision in roles such as crisis or respite care provider, home visitor, educator, or group facilitator. They may support qualified service providers through offering transport to families, running errands, offering encouragement and support, offering back-up services, or sorting, cataloguing and/or allocating resources such as food for a food bank. Volunteers may also offer administrative support in areas such as organising mailing lists and mail-outs, writing newsletters, working as a receptionist, providing clerical support, organising special events or recruiting other volunteers.

Conclusion

Is family support a new profession? Perhaps so, but only if the understanding of what constitutes a profession is suitably modified. Family support work involves a common body of knowledge, but that knowledge is actively shared with the families and communities with whom the worker engages.

Some family support workers will gain background knowledge and skills from pre-service training, but continue to learn new knowledge and skills for as long as they work with children, families and communities. The most effective knowledge and skills are context based, so that knowledge and skills gained out of context can only be transferred and modified, they can never be applied unchanged in toto. Other family support workers will gain knowledge and skills from the job. They are experts in their specific context and may have limited ability to transfer those skills to other contexts. Training for family support work can only be context independent to a limited extent. The potential for professional accreditation or registration is therefore limited, unless a sufficiently flexible system can be developed which recognises the relative value of both context independent and context dependant skills and knowledge.

Despite the current uncertainty about the evolution of family support into a profession, there is no question about the need for workers to behave professionally. However, again, professional behaviour in family support needs to be defined differently than professional behaviour in more traditional, and higher status, professions. In family support a professional worker is one who is passionately committed to social justice, and all the ramifications that are associated with social justice: valuing of diversity and difference, power sharing, strengths-based approach, and a bone deep understanding that services can not be limited arbitrarily but must address the entire family experience at all levels of the system. Family support workers become deeply involved in the communities in which they work: some will live in, and participate in, these communities as part of their personal lives. Family support workers represent a new breed of professionals in whom the public and the private are no longer entirely separate. Family support workers undertake their work because they believe it is the right thing for them to do.

Chapter 8
Evaluation

Introduction

For many community-based programs, evaluation is required to demonstrate to funding bodies that projects are worth ongoing funding. To researchers, evaluation is necessary to determine cause and effect: to decide if certain interventions make a significant impact on defined outcomes. To practitioners, on a day to day basis, evaluation is linked to reflective practice, and helps determine one's daily actions. This chapter addresses evaluation at the programme level. Formal evaluations of well-known programs are reviewed and the chapter concludes with a discussion of more practical evaluation strategies for those delivering community-based services to families on a limited budget.

The research basis
of programme evaluations

In order to determine if interventions work, the research world requires a specific type of programme evaluation. Much of the formal evaluation literature comes out of demonstration or pilot programs, associated with Universities or organisations undertaking the evaluation component separately from service delivery. Such evaluation opportunities are not usually available to practitioners. Much of this evaluation work comes from the 20 years between 1960 and 1980, a period referred to by Newburn (2001) as the golden age of American evaluation research.

Formal research evaluations are based on the positivist paradigm and use an empirical method of data collection (Zimiles, 1993).

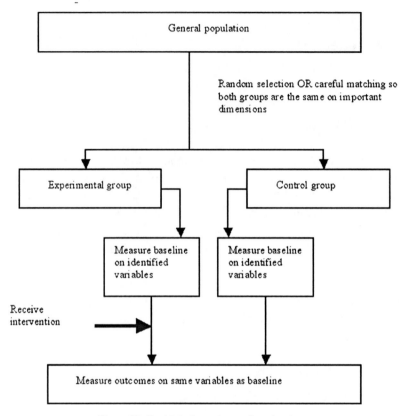

Figure12: Positivist/experimental evaluation

Group selection requires:
- Experimental (intervention) and control groups as similar as possible on variables identified as important (such as gender, socio-economic status, family size etc)
- Similarity created through random or matched sampling from the target population

Expected outcomes of the intervention are clearly stated. In many early intervention programs outcomes were expected to be enhanced child IQ or development. In other programs, outcomes may be improved interactions between parent and child, decreased levels of family stress, or increased family income.

Having determined the intervention and control groups, the next step in the evaluation requires an assessment of children and/or families using instruments designed to measure the desired outcomes. These measurements are undertaken before beginning the intervention itself, creating a baseline, against which children's subsequent progress can be compared. There should be no difference in children's performance between the intervention and the control groups at baseline.

Intervention is then delivered to the experimental group. The control group continue in their normal manner. After a specified period of intervention, (or at the conclusion of the intervention, whichever is most relevant to the context) the researchers again assess children using the same instruments they used at baseline. This enables them to compare children's levels and rates of change between intervention and control groups. Sometimes, researchers collect information on the original data used for matching and may add additional data they think necessary or relevant. More sophisticated statistical manipulation of data enable the impact of these independent variables to be removed ('controlled for' in statistical terminology) from the outcome data in an attempt to isolate the impact of the intervention from any other factors which might effect outcomes.

There are occasions when it would be unethical to create control groups by refusing to offer service to some children and families (Eayrs & Jones, 1992). In these situations researchers use a variety of quasi-experimental designs to try and create a group which can be used as a control:

- create a baseline, offer intervention, compare progress during the period of intervention with progress during baseline.
- split a group of children into two, then follow both groups to create a baseline. Intervention for group 1, not group 2. Then intervene for group 2 not group1. This may be followed by intervention for both groups.
- all receive intervention, with no control group—most common in the real world of service delivery but least effective.

In addition to assessing the impact of intervention at the end of a programme, there is a need to determine the long-term impact of the intervention. Some researchers have been able to follow subjects over a period of years to determine if advantages arising from intervention are maintained. The most often cited research of this kind is that arising from the High/Scope Perry Preschool Project which has published information tracking subjects up to the age of 27 years (Schweinhart & Weikart, 1993).

Some argue that, unless programme evaluations are carried out using this empirical approach, their results are meaningless (Marshall & Watt, 1999). Others argue that strict adherence to empirical methods results in a distortion of reality through oversimplification (Zimiles, 1993). Lewis (1998) and Hebbeler (2001) point out that randomised control trials are simply not possible or sensible in all cases, particularly in community initiatives, and that alternative evaluation strategies need to be considered.

Family support programs are particularly difficult to evaluate, not only because of these factors, but because desired outcomes are unique to each family served in the programme (Family Support America, 1996). One family may target improvement in family interactions, another may prefer to focus on obtaining employment, whilst a third may want to lower parenting stress by locating appropriate supports for babysitting and childcare. In other words, intervention is not delivered in a systematic manner, and nor is it consistent from family to family. Another problem with using a positivist approach to evaluation in community-based initiatives is the need for large sample sizes in order to demonstrate significant changes (Ghate, 2001). The real-world requirements of family support programs necessitate an evaluation methodology that is do-able within strict budget constraints, yet produces results of sufficient quality to be useful, meaningful and ethical. Diversity in evaluation began emerging in the 1990s (Newburn, 2001). It is now recognised that evaluation can be undertaken in may different ways, and that evaluation strategies must be dependent on the understandings of the various evaluation stakeholders about the purpose of the evaluation (Lewis & Utting, 2000).

Classic evaluations

Despite changes in evaluation approaches and thinking, there remain a number of classic programme evaluations, using a more traditional empirical methodology, that have contributed to both our understanding of early intervention and family support, and to our knowledge of evaluation. It is useful to review these before progressing with a discussion on more practical methods of evaluation for programs whose priority is service delivery rather than research.

High/Scope Perry Preschool Project

This project began with the identification of 123 young (3 to 4 years of age) Africa-American children living in poverty in Ypsilanti, Michagan who were identified at risk for school failure. These children were demonstrating intellectual delays at the time of the project (Schweinhart, Weikart, & Larner, 1986, Schweinhart, Barnes, & Weikart, 1993).

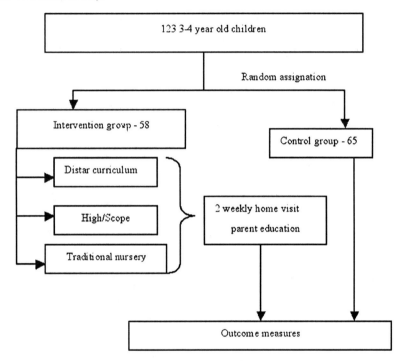

Figure13: Program design

The researchers collected information from the children and their families from ages 3 to 11, then again at 14, 15, 19 and 27 years. Results showed that (Schweinhart et al., 1986):

- All intervention children showed significant gains in IQ until 10 years of age—average IQ rose 27 points (to 105) in year 1, dropped to 98 in year 2, continued to drop during the early years of schooling to 94 by age 10. IQ of the control group remained between 85 to 90
- Differences in IQ scores between the three different curriculum models were small and generally insignificant.

- IQ differences between experimental and control groups by age 15 were insignificant—average IQ of 80.
- 15 years—experimental children had test scores averaging at 15th percentile on the California Achievement Test—control group below the 10th percentile.
- Distar group—5x more acts of property violence, 2x personal violence 2x acts of drug abuse, more likely to be reported as not succeeding by their families (1 in 3 compared to 1 in 36), more likely to experience family disharmony, less likely to contribute towards family expenses, perceived as less socially skilled.
- High/Scope graduates—more likely to participate in sport, read books.
- Nursery—more likely to take on special responsibilities at school.
- 66% nursery school and High/Scope graduates expected to go on to post-secondary education compared to 50% of the Distar graduates.

Whilst different curriculum models in the early years were likely to have similar impacts on cognitive development, they had different impacts on social outcomes (Schweinhart et al., 1986). The Distar children demonstrated insignificant, but telling differences in sociability and co-operation throughout their early years, and these differences became much more pronounced by the time they were 15. However their social behaviour was no worse than that of the children in the control group, and their academic performance was significantly better, so the Distar approach should not be perceived as harmful to children. High quality programs, the researchers' conclude, must be based on child-initiated learning activities.

By age 27 (Schweinhart & Weikart, 1993), of the intervention group:

- 71% graduated from high school compared to 54% of controls.
- 84% of females graduated from High School compared to 35% of controls.
- 1.1 years of their schooling lives in special education programs compared to 2.8 years for the controls.

Success in schooling has flow-on effects to other aspects of children's lives:

- 29% experimental groups had monthly incomes of $2000 or more at age 27 compared to 7% of the control group.

- 42% of the experimental group males and 6% of the controls reported a monthly income of $2000 or more.
- 80% of the experimental group females and 55% of the control group females were employed.
- home ownership: experimental group—36% compared with 13%
- car ownership: experimental group 30% owned two cars compared with 13%
- 80% control group had received welfare or other social service assistance in the past 10 years compared with 59%.
- 26% of males in both groups married, experimental group males married for longer (6.2 years compared with 3.3 years).
- 40% experimental group females married, compared with 8%
- births to unmarried women experimental group 56% compared with 83%.
- experimental group 2.3 arrests compared with 4.6
- 7% experimental group (12% of males) arrested five or more times, compared with 35% (49% of males)
- 25% arrests in the control group for drug dealing, compared with 7%
- 12% experimental group had been placed on probation at some time, compared with 26%.

A cost-benefit analysis of the programme took into account costs to society of providing additional support in schools, special education services, increased taxes paid by those in employment, savings in welfare payments, and savings in the criminal justice system (Schweinhart et al., 1993). The calculation reveals that for every dollar invested in the programme, the savings to the community by age 27 was $7.16. In 1992 dollars, a year in the programme cost $7258 per child. Run as a service programme rather than a research project, the costs per child could be reduced to $5500 per child without compromising intensity that is an essential component of the intervention. Full-day centre-based care would be slightly more expensive. The researchers argue that the programme was successful, not because it made enduring differences in children's intellectual levels, but because it empowered children, families and teachers to make permanent changes in their lives which led to improved opportunities for success (Schweinhart & Weikart, 1993).

Abecedarian Project

This design uses a control group which receives some services, but not full intervention (Campbell & Ramey, 1995, Ramey & Landesman Ramey, 1998, Ramey & Ramey, 2000).

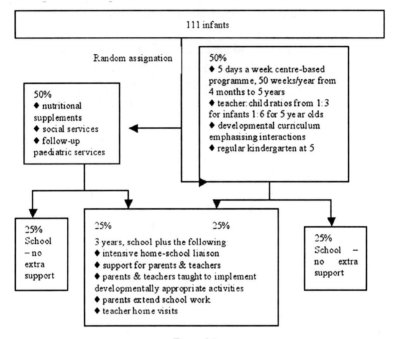

Figure14

In comparison to the High/Scope Perry Preschool project, the children in the Abecedarian Project maintained significantly higher IQs through to fifteen years of age, although the difference between experimental and control group children did decline in that period (Campbell, Pungello, Miller-Johnson, Burchinel, & Ramey, 2001):

- 18 months—experimental children average IQ scores 10 to 15 points higher—differences maintained throughout the preschool years.
- Age 15—experimental group IQ 95 compared to 90.
- Age 21—small IQ differences maintained despite steady ongoing IQ decline in both groups.

The experimental group children showed advantages in other areas of development (Ramey & Ramey, 2000, Campbell et al., 2001). Experimental group children:

- learned new tasks more quickly.
- larger mean length of utterances
- larger vocabularies
- better comprehension
- better use of language
- more task oriented
- more socially responsive
- more likely to achieve at school
- less likely to repeat a grade
- lower rates of placement in special education services
- more likely to attend a 4-year college course (34.5% compared with 13.7%
- better reading scores and maths achievement
- better mother-child interaction
- elicited more frequent and more positive responses from their mothers
- experienced more positive development-enhancing interactions
- mothers rated them as having a better temperament
- Mothers were more likely themselves to undertake post-secondary education and to be employed.

Head Start

The difficulty with Head Start compared to the Perry High/Scope and Abecedarian projects, is that Head Start was always planed as a service delivery programme rather than as an experimental, research programme. The evaluation component of Head Start has been secondary to service delivery, and thus the programme, whilst enormously significant in the lives of millions of families and children, contributes little to the research literature on evaluation. It does, however, illustrate the many difficulties in undertaking evaluation in the day-to-day world of service delivery.

The evaluation of the first Head Start programs was planned the week before the programme began. The researchers given the task of evaluating Head Start were psychologists, thus they focused on the areas of development with which they were most familiar; cognitive/intellectual development, and ignored other components such as health. Tools used were The Preschool Inventory, a parent interview form, a schedule for demographic information, a health form, and a social competence form (Zigler & Muenchow, 1992).

Researchers were swamped with the data taken from half a million children in the first two weeks of attendance, and much of it remained unanalysed. Much of the data was so badly planned and collected that it was useless. Subsequent to this, 14 regional evaluation centres were set up to collect and process decentralised and more intensive evaluation data. These centres were staffed, in the main, by University personnel who combined their University work with part-time employment with Head Start, thus creating over time, a range of longitudinal databases.

Most of the evaluations showed significant IQ gains in Head Start children. These data were used to justify ongoing funding of the various Head Start programs. However, research following school progress of the first Head Start graduates showed that IQ gains demonstrated at the end of the 8 week programme (initially of up to 10 points) soon disappeared once the children were in school.

The future of Head Start began to look doubtful so a national evaluation was undertaken, testing 1980 Head Start children and 1983 control children using well known standardised tests of intellectual abilities (Zigler & Muenchow, 1992). The report showed some positive effects of the full-year Head Start programme continued into first and second grade. Head Start was found to be more effective in certain subgroups, such as African-American children in the Southeast. Head Start parents strongly supported the programme. In contrast, the children who attended the 8 week summer programme demonstrated no positive effects: the control group children actually showed a slight advantage over the Head Start children in Grades 1 to 3.

There were significant flaws in this national evaluation:
- Control children were selected three years after the programme began, rather than at the beginning.
- Instruments used to measure outcomes were focused on cognitive/intellectual achievement, and not other components of development (such as motivation, school performance, health, and nutritional status).
- The study assumed that all Head Start programs were homogeneous.

The result of these evaluations was a reduction in the summer programme component of Head Start, a capping of Head Start funding, and the establishment, by President Nixon, of an Office of Child Development to oversee the programme.

Evaluation research in the seventies began to explore the impact of Head Start on parents. Stories of parents' successes were collected. Most of these stories tell of how individual parents, with minimal schooling and no positive expectations for themselves, gained employment, qualifications and, in some cases, university degrees. Head Start itself provides employment opportunities for parents, and over a third of staff are parents. Head Start offers a Supplementary Training Programme and by 1973, more than 12,000 Head Start staff had been involved in college courses, and 1000 had received Associate or Bachelor level degrees. Head Start mothers felt more in control of their lives, and experienced greater self-satisfaction after being involved (Parker, Piotrkowski, & Peay, 1987). However, as this study did not use a control group, interpretation of the results must remain cautious.

Throughout the seventies, various evaluations of Head Start continued to demonstrate that initial advantages 'faded out' over time (Bronfenbrenner, 1975), and although other research did demonstrate positive impacts, this latter research was generally less convincing. In 1976, in an attempt to provide more definite evaluations, the Consortium of Longitudinal Studies used measures already taken in the past in order to have comparative data, but included a range of other variables such as school achievement. At the same time, an independent review of 150 research studies on Head Start reported positive impacts on cognitive development, child health, families and communities (Mann, Harrell, & Hurt, 1977). Subsequent to this, Head Start received its first significant increase in funds since 1967.

Consortium research showed that Head Start graduates were less likely to repeat grades at school and less likely to be receiving special education services. However, comparison of Head Start graduates with middle-class children (rather than children from equivalent backgrounds of deprivation) showed that Head Start graduates were still significantly disadvantaged. A recent study by the Department of Health and Human Services (United States Congress, 2000) showed that children in Head Start were likely to have larger vocabularies and were able to speak proficiently. Head Start parents were more likely to read to their children at home, set regular bed times and were less likely to smack their children. Programs based in a childcare centre were found to have a greater impact on children's cognitive skills whilst those based in the home had a greater impact on parenting and children's language development.

By 1995, Head Start had a budget of $US3.5 billion and provided a service for 750,000 children (40% of all eligible families) (Lynch, 2000). It is generally agreed that Head Start has less of an impact than more intensive programs such as the Perry High/Scope and Abcedarian Projects. Head Start programs generally offer shorter periods of intervention, part-time centre attendance, lower intensity, limited parental involvement and have less qualified staff (Heckman & Lochner, 2000). It is acknowledged that quality in Head Start varies widely (Ramey & Ramey, 2000). There has been a recent call to design rigorous, empirical evaluation of Head Start (United States Congress, 2000).

Elmira Prenatal/Early Infancy Project (PEIP)

This project worked with first time mothers who were identified at risk because of youth, low socioeconomic status or because they were unmarried. Nearly a quarter of the mothers demonstrated all three risk factors, and 85% demonstrated at least one risk factor (some mothers were included in the project on their request, and in order to avoid labelling target mothers, they were accepted) (Olds, Henderson, & Kitzman, 1994).

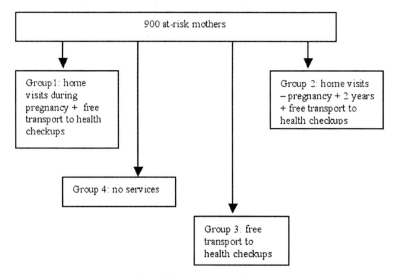

Figure 15: Programme design

Data for the evaluation were collected at the beginning of the programme, at 32 weeks gestation and then 4-6 monthly for 4 years. A follow-up was undertaken when the children were 15 years old. In data analysis a distinction was made between families who were in a high-risk category (from a low socioeconomic background and unmarried) and families who were low-risk (2-parent families, or from a higher socioeconomic background).

Cost-saving analysis showed that savings made 2 years after the end of the project, slightly exceeded the cost of the project (in other words, the project paid for itself within 2 years). Based on the high-risk families only, the government saved 4 times the cost of the project (Olds, Eckenrode, & Henderson, 1997): savings coming from reduced maternal welfare dependency and increased participation in employment compared with the control groups. Other savings came from children's lower probability of being involved in crime (Olds, Hill, & Rumsey, 1998). Because the follow-up study only went to age 15, it is not possible to estimate the savings that might accrue from the children's participation in employment and (estimated) lower dependency on welfare.

For low-risk families mothers demonstrated less welfare dependency and increased employment rates, and children were less involved in criminal activity compared to the control groups but the differences were not sufficiently large to generate substantial savings. However, hidden benefits, such as higher income levels for programme families, and the benefits of those who, without the programme, would have been victims of crime, are as significant and should be considered when evaluating programme success (Karoly et al., 1998).

Healthy Start

The Hawaii Healthy Start programme provided services for 94% of those families who had infants identified as at risk in the first pilot programme. Over the three years of the pilot there were no reports of physical abuse in these families, 4 reports of neglect and 4 of imminent harm. Later evaluations demonstrated the combined rate for abuse and neglect in Healthy Start families was 1.9% compared with 5% for at-risk families not receiving Healthy Start services (Earle, 1995). However, those not receiving Healthy Start, used in this comparison, were not monitored for abuse and neglect, and nor were their medical records reviewed, thus true rates may be higher. As abuse and neglect cases are costed at $US15,000 per year, the reduction in cases between 1987 and 1991 amounted to a savings of over $US1.26 million.

There was a decrease in family stress levels over the duration of the programme. Whilst these positive results were sufficient to elicit funding to expand the programme throughout Hawaii, researchers criticise the evaluation strategies used. There were no control groups, and the follow-up time was limited (Duggan, McFarlane, Windham, Rohde, & al, 1999). A subsequent evaluation of Healthy Start attempted to use a control group, but relied on programme staff to provide assessment information on children and families (whose knowledge of family status as programme or control group, and engagement with programme families had significant potential to bias results). There were also differential drop-out rates between programme and control families over the year of the study, making it difficult to make any meaningful conclusions.

In 1994, a collaboration between several groups created the framework for an ongoing evaluation of Healthy Start which incorporates scientific methods to evaluate not only the outcomes of the programme, but also the extent to which different centres offering Healthy Start comply with the parent model (Duggan et al., 1999). The evaluation used 6 programme centres offering services to 6 geographically different communities on Oahu.

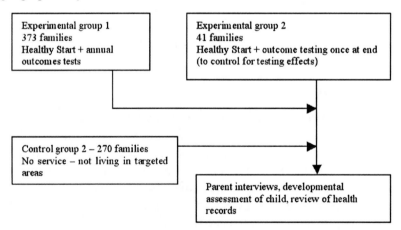

Figure16 : Evaluation design

Comparisons made between the three groups at baseline found experimental groups were more likely to have:

*   worked prior to the birth of the child
*   better health
*   experienced partner violence in the year prior to the child's birth.

At baseline, 75% of the combined samples had fathers who had graduated from high school, 66% were living in families with incomes below the poverty line, 66% were working and 42% had issues around substance abuse.

After 2 years in the programme, families in the experimental groups were more likely to have established a relationship with a health care provider, though immunisation rates were similar between experimental and control groups. There were little differences between the groups in relation to family access to other community services, or in achieving maternal education or work goals.

At the one-year evaluation stage, experimental group mothers were more likely to be mentally healthy but this advantage disappeared at the year 2 evaluation. In the programme delivered by one agency the experimental group mothers were less likely to experience partner violence, but this difference was not reflected in the data from the other areas in the study. Experimental group mothers used more non-violent discipline strategies and this difference increased in the second year. Experimental group mothers reported feeling less stressed and felt more competent. Control group parents were more likely to engage in neglectful parenting behaviours at Year 1 but not so in Year 2.

Going to scale

Evaluations of Head Start and Healthy Start pinpoint the issues associated with effective evaluation in large programs offered from many different sites: issues related to going to scale (Schorr, 1997). Local variations from a standard model is a significant issue which impacts on any attempt at large scale evaluation (Ramey & Ramey, 2000).

Schorr (1997) argues that it is a common belief in the western world that what works in miniature, will work when scaled up. This provided the justification for a proliferation of demonstration and pilot programs in early intervention as researchers and practitioners desperately searched for the 'right' model which, when scaled up and delivered to all children and families, would defeat poverty, disadvantage and inequality. However, none of these programs have successfully been able to 'go to scale'. Schorr argues that this is because they very things that make these programs successful when they are small (such as the ability of people to work together creatively and flexibly) can not be recaptured when large programs are administered by large bureaucracies. She argues that we need a new form of professional practice founded on a new form of collaboration with families and communities.

A new way to evaluate

This requires a new way of thinking about, and practising evaluation.

Old and new evaluations

Old

- standardised intervention offered in the same way at every site
- some get intervention, some do not
- experimental & control groups matched on every variable which might impact on results making it difficult (if not impossible) to obtain samples of appropriate sizes (Eayrs & Jones, 1992)
- outcomes to be specified in advance
- variables outside the programme ignored (Marfo & Dinero, 1991)

New

- unique, local and family interventions
- all receive support - unethical to refuse to deliver services to families because they have been identified in a control group (Kagan, 1999).
- no experimental or control groups–everyone receives a different service depending on needs
- outcomes change through time
- holistic, all-inclusive approach

Hollister and Hill (1995) provide a comprehensive discussion of the problems associated with attempting to evaluate community-wide initiatives (such as family support) using traditional methods of research. All the factors defining successful traditional evaluation are in direct opposition to the principles of effective service delivery discussed in earlier chapters of this book. Despite a growing recognition that traditional evaluation approaches are not possible in real world programs whose focus is on delivering services to children and families, there remains a strong bias in the research world for these approaches. Alternative ways of undertaking evaluation are perceived as flawed, or second class. However, it is these alternative approaches to evaluation which need exploring, as they are the most realistic for evaluating family support programs.

CIPP evaluation

The Context, Input, Process and Product model of evaluation (Stufflebeam, 1968, 1981) was one of the earliest attempts to develop an alternative approach to evaluation able to address issues in the context and process of implementation as well as outcomes. These early attempts at process evaluation:
- defined the context,
- assessed impact of the context on processes of implementation and ongoing measures of effectiveness

At the end of the programme, summative measures examined overall impact, attempting to balance feasibility, economic and productivity factors. Early evaluation efforts using this model tended to continue to use a positivist approach (for example, (Sims & Bridgman, 1984).

In more recent times, the model has been used to develop a framework for the evaluation of parent training programs (Matthews & Hudson, 2001).

Context

- examine the objectives of a programme
- appropriateness, acceptability and technical adequacy of the objectives

Input

- content
- degree of theoretical support, empirical support, appropriateness and acceptability of parenting strategies taught and methods used

Process

- programme implementation
- extent to which the planned programme was actually administered
- participation of parents (attendance and task completion)
- parental satisfaction with the training methods used

Product

Outcomes

- parents' knowledge of principles
- ability to use new skills
- satisfaction with the parenting strategies taught
- parent behaviour change
- child behaviour change
- parents' satisfaction with generalisation outcomes

Utilisation focused evaluation

In 1978 Patton introduced a new model of evaluation that was hailed by many as representing a paradigm change in the way researchers and practitioners thought about evaluation (Alkin et al., 1990). Utilisation evaluation is based on the understanding that evaluation results must be used to improve programme functioning (Patton, 1986). In utilisation based evaluation the first step is to determine who are the people who will be using the evaluation results: these are the key stakeholders. It may be tempting to assume that that managers or senior administrators should be the evaluation audience. However, Patton points out that often evaluation information is used more effectively by people who are enthusiastic about the programme and willing to use the evaluation data to make changes in their day to day work.

These key stakeholders need to be involved in the process of the evaluation. Evaluators and key stakeholders work together in a relationship underpinned by the principle of empowerment. Evaluators should ensure that they do not undertake the evaluation with themselves as the key stakeholders: answering their own questions about issues they think are important. Questions addressed in an evaluation need to be issues identified by the key stakeholders as important. Asking the right questions is the second important step in the process of utilisation based evaluation. When engaging in summative evaluations (those evaluations undertaken at a specific point in service delivery, or at the end of a funded programme) questions might include:

- Did the programme achieve the desired outcomes?
- Is the programme worthwhile?
- Can we justify continuing to fund this programme?

When engaging in formative evaluation (evaluation of ongoing programs) questions might include:

- What are the programme's strengths?
- What are the programme's weaknesses?
- How can the programme be improved?
- What are the perceptions/experiences of those involved in the programme (recipients, staff)?

It is important to also consider how the programme is implemented: to have formative information about how programs operate, even if the main purpose of an evaluation is summative. The extent to which programs follow a model or plan may impact on the outcomes for children and families, and ought to influence decisions about ongoing funding, programme policies and procedures.

There are different ways that the implementation of a programme can be evaluated. The standard (but not necessarily the best) is an evaluation of effort. This evaluation asks questions about programme activity. How many clients are served? Are staff/client ratios appropriate? How many staff and what qualifications do they have? Are appropriate and sufficient resources available?

Another approach is to look at how routine information is managed. Management information systems are developed and used by agencies to monitor information flow. A third approach is to undertake process evaluation. This is an analysis of how the programme operates, rather than what it actually does or achieves (process rather than product). This usually involves working with clients and staff at programme-delivery level as well as other levels of the agency, documenting their day-to-day realities in order to understand both formal and informal processes.

Sometimes complex programs can be broken into components that can then be subject to more traditional forms of evaluation. The more homogeneous the component, the easier it is to undertake empirical methods of evaluation. Finally process can be evaluated by identifying exactly what it is the agency does that is expected to make an impact on the lives of children and families. Once the treatment is clearly identified, the extent to which it is implemented can be measured.

Utilisation focussed evaluation is driven by utility, not by the needs for specific types of evaluation data. Because methods used to collect data depend on the questions asked, they are extremely variable. Evaluators may choose to use standardised tests as in traditional evaluations, but they may instead choose to use any combination of:

- their own checklists,
- interviews,
- observations,
- focus groups,
- questionnaires,
- documentary analysis,
- cost-benefit analyses,
- other techniques.

Questions of validity (that the measure actually measures what it claims to measure) and credibility (do the results actually make sense in the light of what we know about the world) of data are addressed, so that qualitative data can claim to be as valid and rigorous as traditional 'hard' data (Sarantakos, 1998).

The second major contribution made by the utilisation-based approach to evaluation is the involvement of stakeholders. Traditional evaluation tended to be something done by outsiders, and neither workers nor clients were involved in the design or implementation (except as 'subjects'). Utilisation-based evaluation has the potential to empower stakeholders, who share in defining the questions to be asked, the strategies used to get the answers, and the analysis and presentation of the final evaluation report. Through their participation, stakeholders learn the skills to take control of their future evaluations. This links closely with the empowerment underpinning of family support.

Outcomes-based evaluation

The focus of outcome-based evaluation is not the extent to which a programme replicates a model, nor how a programme goes about getting its results, but on the results; does the programme achieve what it set out to do (Peisher, Sewell, & Kirk, 2001)? Outcomes are an indication of change that has occurred through participation in a programme (Jones, 1991). Outcome-based evaluation can be used in contexts where large programs are run in different ways in different communities and encourages a focus on why things are being done.

Effective outcome-based evaluation requires clarity about the goals of a programme. Goals need to balance the long-term desired outcomes with shorter term, measurable steps. Ultimately, outcomes are what the programme will be held accountable for. Outcomes need to be capable of being addressed with the services the programme has to offer. Outcomes need to be defined widely (Danziger & Waldfogel, 2000). Had outcome measures such as attitude towards schooling, and a range of social variables been taken in the early years of Head Start for example, the benefits of early intervention might have been documented from the start.

Although the focus must remain on results, process is important in determining ethical practice occurs in all situations. Monitoring of process ensures that opportunities for fraud, corruption, discrimination and power differentials are minimised. Process information also provides data on the ways in which programs are delivered, so that outcomes can be judged against the processes undertaken to produce them.

Family Support America define outcomes as the desired state for children, families and communities (2001). In many programs, desired outcomes are healthy children able to learn to their potential, economically self sufficient families, and supportive communities. However, outcomes as broad as these can not be measured, thus Family Support America introduce the concept of promotional indicators. These are measures of specific achievements which contribute towards the outcomes. Often each outcome will have several different indicators. Indicators may include (Coulton, 1995):

- infant hospitalisation rates,
- immunisation rates,
- child maltreatment rates,
- delinquency rates,
- child development,

- contextual factors such as age and family structure of the community, residential mobility, substandard housing, fear of crime.

Indicators must address strengths, not deficits: they must measure increased ability to address challenges. Schorr (1997) suggests that when communities and families are involved in the selection of promotional indicators and outcomes, programme workers can be sure that what they are working towards is what the community really wants and needs. This links with the concept of empowerment, one of the fundamental theoretical frameworks of the family support movement.

Family Support America, working in collaboration with a range of professionals involved in family support across the country, have developed a set of core promotional indicators. They claim these truly reflect the theoretical frameworks of the sector, even though by doing so, they are imposing these on programs, rather than developing these from the bottom-up. They argue there are significant benefits in having a core set of promotional indicators because this will increase the numbers of programs being effectively evaluated and thus increasingly demonstrate to governments and other funding bodies, the effectiveness of family support. They are currently developing an evaluation toolkit which they hope will be used widely across the sector.

The proposed core outcomes and promotional indicators that ought to be applied to family support programs, according to Family Support America are shown below (Family Support America, 2001).

Outcome 1: children will be ready to start school by the relevant age

Indicator: percentage of children entering their pre-primary (or the year prior to the first compulsory year in school) will demonstrate developmentally appropriate skill levels in a range of areas including physical-motor, cognitive, language, social, and emotional)

Outcome 2: children will succeed in school

Indicator: percentage of parents engaged in their children's learning and education through in-home and in-school activities

Outcome 3: families remain stable

Indicator: percentage of adults who have a support network/ someone to rely on for support other than themselves

Outcome 4: communities are supportive

Indicator: percentage of people in a community to participate in voluntary activities within their community

Outcome 5: young people are offered appropriate developmental opportunities

Indicator A: percentage of young people who have frequent involvement with their parents, and who receive emotional support from both parents

Indicator B: percentage of young people who report they have a meaningful relationship with an adult

Indicator C: percentage of young people who are involved in sports, Clubs, school organisations and/or the community for 3 or more hours each week

Indicator d: the percentage of young people whose families set them clear expectations, rules and consequences

Outcome 6: children and families are healthy

Indicator A: percentage of children who are fully immunised by the age of 2

Indicator B: percentage of pregnant women who undergo pre-natal care in their first trimester of pregnancy

Indicator C: percentage of children and families who are covered by health insurance (this latter is less relevant in Australia because of universal Medicare)

Schorr (1997) argues that it should not be up to individual family support programme to measure all of these factors themselves. She suggests that governments (national, state and local) have a responsibility to collect relevant data into which family support programs could tap to measure their own progress. In Australia, the first step in achieving this is a set of indicators of social and family functioning recommended for national collection (Zubrick, Williams, Silburn, & Vimpani, 2000). The indicators identified include:

Time available for quality parenting

- maternal and paternal employment and hours at work
- unpaid labour
- time spent interacting with children (activities, routine tasks, week days, weekends etc)

- time children spend watching TV, playing video games, on the internet etc
- time parents spend in home tasks not involving direct interaction with children

Family income (material resources available to the family)

- total family income, and summary measures of this
- source of family income
- disposable income
- family assets
- ratio of debts to assets
- poverty
- welfare receipt (current and historical)
- health insurance
- rent or own home
- receive fringe benefits

Amount of human capital available in the family

- parent/carer education—highest level
- parent/carer physical health including: disciplinary strategies; parenting style—punitiveness, warmth, acceptance, aversive parenting, monitoring behaviour, rules of behaviour; parent/child communication, style and content; extent of positive interactions; modelling of behaviour
- transmission of culturally acquired knowledge, values and practices including participation in religious activities or traditional, cultural practices, knowledge of the world gained through personal experience.

Amount of psychological capital available in the family

- conflict—parent/child, parent-parent
- violence in the family
- family cohesion
- parental mental health
- measures of parental depression

- parents' satisfaction with their parenting
- parents' job satisfaction
- life stressful events and levels of perceived stress including number of job changes, living in crowded conditions, occupational complexity, residential mobility
- perceived levels of social support
- parental self-efficacy
- parents' perceptions work/family tensions

Amount of social capital available to the family and in their community

- levels of trust
- levels of civic involvement and participation (eg participation in community events, school activities etc)
- levels of social engagement
- reciprocity
- participation in the local community (formal—sports, clubs etc as well as informal)
- neighbourhood and work networks
- community violence and crime
- availability of friends and family
- tolerance of diversity
- experiences of discrimination
- feelings about the value of life
- sense of community

Other confounding factors

- family type; different family structures such as step parents, divorce, foster parents, adoption, extended family, non-resident parents 9and extent of non-resident parent involvement with children), family size, teenage parents;
- childcare arrangements: type of childcare, quality of childcare, changes in childcare arrangements over time, hours in alternative care, costs of care, age at which care experienced.

A similar project in New Zealand, designed to develop indicators against which to evaluate the Strengthening Families strategy proposed the following outcome measures (Ministries of Social Policy, 1997):

Deaths

- infant mortality
- under 5 mortality rate
- road traffic death rate 15–19 years
- youth suicide rate 15–24 years

Illness and injury

- hospital injury discharge rate for 0–4 years, 15–19 years

Abuse

- death rate (1–14 years) from injuries inflicted by other persons
- Abuse and neglect
- abuse and neglect re-notification rate 0–6 years, 7–16 years

Care and protection

- out of family care and protection services 0–6 years

Reproductive health

- smoking during pregnancy
- low birthweight (less than 2500 grams)
- teenage fertility rate 13–17 years

Developmental measures

- hearing loss at school entry
- tobacco smoking 18–24 years
- drug and alcohol risk behaviour 15–19 years
- incidence of repeat and serious re-offending cases 10–16 years
- school leavers with a formal qualification
- participation
- immunisation rates at 2 years
- 3 year-olds in early childhood programs

Ife (1995) points out that, as social justice underpins the empowerment approach to working with families and children, one of the most important outcomes must be that of reducing power inequalities. Any evaluation of the effectiveness of family support must therefore include an outcome addressing social justice, with promotional indicators which measure the extent to which the programme has improved people's experiences in their home and communities in relation to discrimination. Whilst the promotional indicators discussed above both allow opportunities to address discrimination, the more direct approach of having a specific outcome relating to social justice would be more appropriate.

Parker (1998) warns that it is necessary to be cautious about identifying outcomes and using these as measures of the success of a programme because of instability in some outcome measures. Interventions may have delayed impacts; for example long term benefits now demonstrated for early intervention programs were not identified in the earlier evaluation studies. Negative impacts may also be delayed: for example children returned home after being in alternative care face a 24% chance of re-abuse in the first two years. Measurements of status after one year usually demonstrate positive outcomes—it is only when measures are continued that re-offending behaviour is detected in significant intensity.

Another issue of concern in using population-wide measures is that change may be small, or occur in a small number of people, so that the population-wide indicators do not detect it (Weiss, 1995). Thus, whilst outcomes-based evaluation is popular because it lends itself to quantitative measurement, there are many who question total reliance on this kind of data (Weiss, 1995). Other forms of evaluation, which lend themselves to different (and qualitative) kinds of data have much to offer our understanding of evaluation.

Participatory Action Research as evaluation

Participatory Action Research (PAR—sometimes called participatory evaluation or action evaluation) is grounded in a challenge to traditional hierarchies of knowledge that legitimise existing structures of inequality and power. PAR arose out of work in developing countries where people wanted to include their own interpretation of reality in the evaluation process, and to have control over the evaluation of programs developed to impact on their lives (Sohng, 1995). PAR is people-centred and involves evaluators, staff and clients in a true partnership. It promotes empowerment through a sharing of individual constructions of reality. Participants are encouraged to question how the dominant power system suppresses and shapes their understanding of the world. It encourages a view of theory and practice as inseparable, and thus an evaluation of practice based on peoples' internalised theory and understandings of the world.

In the real world of service delivery, PAR is often undertaken without the involvement of an outside evaluator. However, within the programme being evaluated there needs to be a person designated as responsible for fulfilling the responsibilities of the PAR evaluation. The evaluator is ideally a person living in the community and involved in the programme. This person acts as a facilitator and a technical resource person.

PAR is linked to reflective practice (Newman, 1998). Quality service delivery requires individual workers to reflect daily on their practice. Quality programme evaluation requires those workers to share their reflections with others. Groups of workers and family members develop a shared understanding about the programme, what it does, what it does well, what it does not do well, and what it could be doing.

The first step in PAR is the creation of a team who will work together on the evaluation. The team must include community/family members, and staff in the programme (including management if the organisation is hierarchical). This team set up meetings with all stakeholders to reflect on the service(s) they are delivering/receiving. This is a dialogic process in which the evaluation team and the groups share information and create a joint understanding of the service environment of the programme (in comparison to an interview approach where staff and participants tell their experiences to the evaluator).

In the process of this reflection, groups may identify they lack particular types of information needed to help them clarify their understanding. They plan together how to collect this information. In PAR, methods of data collection thus arise out of the context, and are shaped by the group's perceptions of what they need to know;

methods are not planned before hand and imposed on the situation (Newman, 1998).

Sharing reflections and understandings involves critical analysis of the assumptions made by each different person, and of how different interpretations of the same situation shape responses and decisions. Once groups feel they have a shared understanding of how and why the programme is operating the way it is, they begin to plan improvements. This planning involves all stakeholders. No decisions are made unless everybody agrees they are the right decisions for the programme at that time. Once agreement is reached, strategies can be developed to implement the new plans. Again, this occurs with the involvement of all participants. The PAR circle (Wadsworth, 1991) of reflect, collect information, plan, implement then back to reflect begins again.

Empowerment evaluation

In some ways, empowerment evaluation is similar to PAR. As well as producing evaluation information, empowerment evaluation focuses on using evaluation as a tool to provide opportunities to foster self-esteem and self determination (Fetterman, 2000). Thus evaluation is a collaborative activity in which people help improve the services which help them. If an outside evaluator is involved, it is only as a coach or facilitator who aims to ultimately ensure that participants run the evaluation. Empowerment evaluation shares with utilisation focused evaluation a commitment to use the results of evaluation to inform service delivery (Schnoes, Murphy-Berman, & Chambers, 2000): the results from evaluation feed into service planning.

Empowerment evaluation consists of a number of steps. All involve all stakeholders from programme recipients through to funders (Fetterman, Kaftarian, & Wandersman, 1996), providing a bridge between all levels of the programme.

- *Step 1:* using participatory techniques, such a focus groups, establish a mission statement. This mission statement is equivalent to a set of outcome statements as it focuses on what the programme is trying to achieve.
- *Step 2:* groups work backwards, identifying what the programme has to achieve in order to work towards the outcomes.

Outcome: increased support networks for parents, improved parenting

Interim aim: parents to develop friendships

Short term aim: parents get together and participate in activities/groups where they share common interests

- *Step 3:* identify the most significant activities offered by the programme working towards these outcomes.
- *Step 4:* participants and staff rate how effective they think the programme is doing in each of these activities (usually on a scale of 1 to 10). Self-study workbooks (Secret, Jordan, & Ford, 1999) may be used. Group meetings are used to come to a consensus about the overall programme strengths and weaknesses. In Australia, the Childcare Accreditation scheme uses an empowerment approach by requiring that centres engage in self study (staff and parents individually first) before meeting and coming to a consensus about the ratings on the various principles which define quality service (National Childcare Accreditation Council, 1993).
- *Step 5:* groups develop a vision for the future. This involves articulation of goals for the programme and the development of strategies to work towards those goals. As part of this process, participants and staff plan the types of evidence needed to continue to evaluate the programme on an ongoing basis.

Theory of change approach to evaluation

Family support programs are based on theories about why the programme ought to work, and how the programme will achieve its results. These theories are held, implicitly or explicitly, all involved in the programme. The theory of change approach requires these theories of change (or assumptions) to be identified and laid out so they can be examined and tracked (Weiss, 1995). The advantages of this is that those involved in the programme need to make clear their assumptions and expectations and attempt to reach agreement with others about what the programme aims to do and why. However, consensus is not necessary, as programs can operate with different people in them holding different theories of change. Expected outcomes for programs can be facilitated by different routes.

In an evaluation guided by the theory of change approach, paths from activities to outcomes are graphically displayed to create a map of the programme theory of change (Kagan, 1999). The first step in this process is to determine (Connell & Kubisch, 1999):

- Programme intended outcomes
- Activities needed to achieve these outcomes
- Contextual factors which will influence the activities and outcomes

These determinations are made in conjunction with programme funders, administrators, staff and participants. Knowledge from the literature and previous experience of those involved will also influence the decisions made at this point.

In determining outcomes and activities, it will be necessary to consider interim outcomes: those steps which need to be achieved along the way before the longer term outcomes can occur. Thinking needs to begin with the long term outcomes; what needs to be achieved before these can occur? Then, working backwards through a chain of interim outcomes, identification of the first interim outcome(s) can be made. Activities associated with each interim outcome can be developed. Consideration needs to be given to the contextual factors at each level of interim outcome, as the impact of contextual factors will vary for different outcomes and activities. In addition, the necessary resources for successful achievement of each level of interim outcome (and the final outcome) need to be identified.

A good theory of change should be sensible and realistic. Research, experience and common sense should indicate that activities are likely to lead to the outcomes. Ultimately a good theory of change should be capable of being evaluated; of demonstrating that changes made in the lives of participants are related to the programme. For example, a commonly held theory of change is illustrated below:

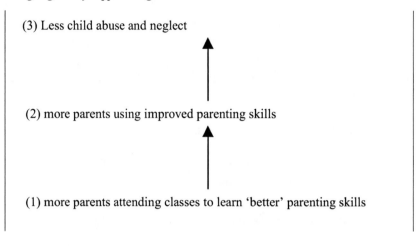

(3) Less child abuse and neglect

(2) more parents using improved parenting skills

(1) more parents attending classes to learn 'better' parenting skills

The activity associated with achieving the early outcome is that of parenting education classes, and the resources will include what ever is necessary to offer classes at various locations in the community, at the times most likely to be acceptable to parents. However, programme-funders would do well to consider contextual factors. Firstly, the incidence of child abuse and neglect may be related to, not only inadequate parenting skills, but other factors such as drug and alcohol abuse, family stress and feelings of powerlessness. Unless the programme is resourced in ways that these can be addressed, the impact of the programme on the long-term outcome may be significantly weakened.

Once the programme's theory (or theories) of change are identified, consideration needs to be given to measurement of outcomes and activities. On occasions, measures may be quantitative, but qualitative measures are also relevant. Measures need to cover multiple levels (Connell & Kubisch, 1999). As measures are taken, the results are compared against the theory of change. In the example above, does increasing the number of parents attending parent education classes result in an increased number of parents in the community using 'good' parenting skills? Does an increased number of parents using 'good' parenting skills lead to a decreased community incidence of child abuse and neglect? If the evidence suggests the answers to these questions is yes, then it is reasonable to assume that the changes observed are attributable to the programme. Although this does not produce the 'hard' evidence of a traditional evaluation, it is considered by most social scientists to be evidence of a suitable standard on which to judge programme efficacy (Connell & Kubisch, 1999).

Most Significant Changes as evaluation

The Most Significant Changes approach to evaluation evolved out of work done by researchers such as Bogdan and Taylor (1990) who focused on identifying programs, and components of programs, which were working well. They undertook site visits and collected as much qualitative data as possible (through interview with key people, participants, staff, documents) in order to create an in-depth case study of what the agency was doing, the contexts in which it was operating, and why things were working well. Innovative approaches were described, problems were discussed and written reports focused on illustrating how the agency impacted on the lives of those receiving its services. These studies of excellence were then made available to others to use as benchmarks against which their own programs could be compared.

The Most Significant Change approach does more than identify and describe cases of excellence. It's focus is not on the everyday experiences of a programme, but on the extremes (Davies, 1998); the unexpected rather than the 'normal' (MostSignificantChanges, 2001). It is a participatory approach, where programme participants, staff and different levels of management are all involved in the identification of the most significant changes occurring as a result of the programme. It uses individuals' stories of these changes as the data (Dart, 1999).

To begin an evaluation using the Most Significant Changes method, it is necessary to identify the domains in which change ought to be taking place, and in which change ought to be monitored. This can be done through consultations and collaboration with all stakeholders. Dart used a postal Delphi technique to involve stakeholders in identifying these domains. In the work done by Davies in Bangladesh, the domains were identified by senior staff in the organisation. Once these are identified, people involved in direct service delivery are questioned:

Most significant changes questions

- what is the most significant change, in your opinion, that has occurred

- in your life

- in the lives of the children and families with whom you work

- as a result of the programme over the past month (or other identified period of time)?

In answering, staff and participants are instructed to describe what happened, who was involved, where and when this happened. In effect, the answer involves telling the story of the selected event. There is also a requirement to reflect on why this event was thought to be the most significant, and what difference it actually made.

In a programme which is offered across several different communities, each local group would collect stories from workers and participants and assign them to each of the predetermined domains of change. They would then select what they considered the best story from each domain and pass these on to the next level within the organisation (perhaps a regional group). This group would then review all the stories passed on to them, select one for each domain and pass this on to the next level (perhaps state level). If the programme was national, then each state would then pass on one story representing the most significant change in each domain on to the national body who would make the final selection of one story for each domain. The national stories would then be circulated throughout the entire organisation to clarify management perspective of the organisations' mission and accomplishments.

Dart (1999) suggests that there may be some value in collecting 'bad' new stories, as well as positive stories. In her evaluation project, the central management body felt that discussion of 'bad' news stories helped them in planning improvements in their organisation.

Conclusion

For those delivering family support services in community-based settings, an appropriate evaluation of their work is essential. In these times of economic rationalism and contracting-out of public services, accountability for public funds is an indispensable component of any programme. For many workers, evaluation sparks thoughts of academic research, statistics, and a process far removed from the realities of day-to-day service delivery. Many agencies think of evaluation as something tacked on in the last month before they are due to submit their application for funding for the next financial year.

Increasing demands for accountability result in such ad hoc evaluations being perceived negatively by funding agencies and may influence the allocation of future funds. It is important that community-based agencies find ways of evaluating the work they do, so they can demonstrate their success not just to funding bodies, but to the communities in which they work, and to their own staff.

Evaluation in the world of community-based service delivery has evolved a long way from the traditional, empirical approaches taken in previous years. There are different methods and strategies available, developed with an understanding of the realities of day-to-day community work. Effective evaluation is something that needs to happen alongside service delivery: not something that is done at a rush towards the end. Staff and service participants can be empowered to develop the skills to evaluate their daily experiences. With appropriate support, these can contribute to a more systematic programme evaluation.

This chapter has covered several traditional, empirical evaluations. These evaluations have been influential in the evolution of the family support movement. There remain many people (in academia, funding bodies and agencies sponsoring programs) who continue to hold to the belief that services can not be evaluated effectively unless these traditional practices are followed. Agency staff may find themselves in a position where they must attempt such evaluations because of the requirements imposed upon them by funders or their own management. Despite this, many are open to exploration of different evaluation strategies: strategies collecting different kinds of data in different ways, and resulting in different types of evaluation reports. Many claim that these approaches are not inferior to the traditional, empirical approaches, just different.

A number of these approaches align particularly well with the theoretical approaches underpinning family support. Evaluation approaches that include those who receive services, as well as staff delivering those services, encourage partnership and equality. Some approaches specifically target empowerment of staff and programme participants and thus address the social justice issues inherent in the family support movement. These new approaches to evaluation are not hindered by different approaches to implementation taken in different communities, nor is diversity in process and outcome at the level of individual families a concern. Evaluation no longer requires a standardised approach to be implemented for all participants, and nor does it require an evaluation of how close each agency comes to delivering that standardised approach. The outcome measures used to identify programme success need no longer be built around problems and deficits; they can be specified in terms of strengths at individual, family and community levels.

New methods of evaluation, whilst not meeting the expectations and requirements of traditionalists in the evaluation field, have the advantage of being realistic and do-able within the constraints of real-world service delivery. Community-based programs must incorporate evaluation into their service delivery. Those working in these programs must have an understanding of evaluation and be able to select the most appropriate evaluation tool for their programme and their purpose.

Chapter 9
Where to from here?

Introduction

The world has changed, and is continuing to change. These changes have brought with them considerable risks which impact on our children and reduce their chances of growing and developing into healthy, self fulfilled adults who can achieve to their highest potential. Our society has become socially toxic for children. Existing human services are struggling to cope with the consequences of all these changes.

Family support is one strategy that has the potential to make a significant impact on the shape of our society. Family support operates on the assumption that children's outcomes will be more positive if parents are supported to make a better job of rearing their children. Improving child rearing requires that parents themselves have their needs met and so have the energy, time and resources to met the needs of their children. Communities need to have the facilities, resources and social environments which will support parents in their child rearing tasks. The leaders of our communities and our society itself must learn to value the importance of children, and allocate priority and resources to addressing the urgent needs of children and families. Without this holistic approach, human service programs simply tinker at the edges of social toxicity without having any major impact.

However, whilst family support may contribute to a long-term decrease in social toxicity, it can not, alone, alter the shape of our society. Irrespective of beliefs about how social change should and does occur (via revolution or incremental changes), family support can only claim to be one tool in the shaping of our future. Appropriate programs can enhance children and family resilience to risk factors, so that they are less damaged by their exposure.

Family support programs develop resilience by taking a new approach to delivering services. The approach has evolved out of a range of different community-based service models and is, in itself, not new. What is new is the unification of these ways of thinking and delivering services targeted at individuals, families and communities in an integrated attack on social toxicity. An understanding of these theoretical underpinnings of family support is crucial if family support is to progress as a respected and viable service type (Pinkerton, Higgins, & Devine, 2000).

Family support programs operate on an ecological framework which identifies the importance of this multi-pronged attack at all levels of the system: individual, microsystems, exosystems, mesosystems and macrosystems. The ecological approach is put into practice using the empowerment and strengths approaches. Working successfully with families requires practitioners to work from families' strengths, acknowledging the equality of each family member in the partnership. Families must be given opportunities at all times to exercise their own skills and expertise in self-determination, so they are able to take control of their own lives and facilitate the changes in their lives and their communities they perceive as necessary.

In an attempt to disrupt the bureaucratic nature of many sponsoring agencies, and to operationalise the theoretical underpinnings of the movement, it is suggested that family support programs follow as flat a management structure as possible. This generally means a co-ordinator is appointed to be responsible for the overall running and supervision of the programme. The co-ordinator works with a team of staff who may all have different backgrounds and/or responsibilities. There is likely to be staff who work with families, and staff who work with children. There may be paraprofessional or volunteer staff who may not only work with families and/or children, but undertake a variety of other tasks (such as driving families to parent education classes). Administrative workers also contribute significantly to the success of family support programs.

As an emerging area, family support does not yet have a clear career path for workers. Certainly, the interdisciplinary and complex nature of family support work supports the notion of teams of workers, all with different training and professional backgrounds, working together. However, ultimately one worker faces a family and plans, with that family, the relevant and appropriate support. That worker may have come into the programme with previous professional training (for example childcare, social work, early childhood teaching, cultural studies) or may have no previous training. There are few recognised training courses available to meet this need, and some programs run their own training to ensure that all workers, irrespective of their background, are thoroughly conversant with the skills and knowledge necessary to offer high quality praxis. Recent moves in developing interdisciplinary courses in children and family studies, and early childhood in general, are promising indicators that relevant and appropriate pre-service training opportunities are becoming available.

Many family support programs operate on short-term funding, and are dependant on demonstrating accountability in order for funding to be renewed. Evaluation is thus a crucial component of family support programs. Effective evaluation is built in at the planning stage of the service, rather than developed after the programme has been in operation for some time. Traditional, positivist methods of evaluation, whilst still immensely popular with researchers and funding bodies, are extremely difficult to implement in a service that is founded on diversity, and locally appropriate actions. Alternative approaches to evaluating programs in the world of service-delivery involve a range of stakeholders, including families and community members (in common with the empowerment focus of family support).

Family support has come a long way in two decades. From its early beginnings as separate and diverse programs with different functions and rationales, it has now become possible to develop a coherent picture of family support. As an emerging field, family support now has a firmer theoretical foundation, and common strategies by which theory is operationalised into informed and consistent praxis. However, there are many issues around which debate must continue for the field to continue to evolve. These issues include the role of fathers and the ongoing absence of fatherhood in many of the discourses, the rights of children and the rights of families, and the ultimate determination of responsibility for children.

Where are fathers?

Caring for others is seen as one of the defining features of womanhood (Turney, 2000). Caring itself can be thought of as consisting of two components: caring for and caring about (Stehlik,

1993). 'Caring for' includes necessary care-giving tasks such as supervising children, ensuring they are fed, clothed, kept warm, healthy and safe. In more recent times 'caring for' has also come to include the need to provide play opportunities and stimulation to ensure children's cognitive, language and academic growth is maximised. 'Caring about' is the emotional dimension of care-giving; loving, attachment and nurturing. Mothers are expected to both care for and care about their children, and these components of caring are generally considered indivisible.

Mothers who do not care for their children (perhaps putting children in childcare in order to return to the workforce) are often perceived as not caring about them. For example, Turner and Zigler (1987) found that caregivers working in childcare settings felt hostile towards parents for perceived parental neglect of their children. Young, less experienced childcare staff tend to be more judgemental towards parents than more experienced, older staff, perceiving parents to fall below the minimum standards of good child rearing (Kontos, 1984). Childcare providers in general were not in favour of women returning to employment when their children were young (Bell, 1988); an inherent contradiction as these workers make their living providing care for children whose parents are in employment.

Mothers who neglect their children (and thus show impairments in their ability to care for) are also presumed to not care about them. Women who fail in the caring role are seen as 'bad women'. Thus when children are neglected, the focus moves inevitably towards 'bad mothers' who have failed to care for (and presumably about) their children. Fathers are often invisible in this process (Turney, 2000). Neglect is still commonly blamed on mothers whose failures become the targets of intervention (Stevenson, 1998).

In addition to the 'feminising' of child neglect (Turney, 2000), fathers are also often absent in the discourses around parenting (Mills, 2001). Discussions on parenting imply that those doing the parenting within a family share concerns, values and interests. However, this is often not the case. Parenting may well involve mothering and fathering from different perspectives, with different values, and different desired outcomes for children.

Fathers are often considered less important in their children's lives than mothers (Tomison, 1998). Attachment research, for example, focused almost entirely on mother-child attachment (Hutchins &

Sims, 1999, Steele, Steele, & Fonagy, 1996), and failed to consider the importance of father-child relationships. However, it is increasingly recognised that fathers are important in the lives of their children (Hoffman & Moon, 1999).

Addressing father involvement requires an understanding not only of men and men's gender roles, but of the involvement of women in excluding men from their feminine territory. Childcare has for so long been an area where women have experienced power and control, that the possibility of opening the area to male intrusion is perceived as threatening by many women. Many women prefer to carry the dual roles of full-time workers and caregivers for their children, rather than equally sharing the caring tasks with their male partners (Newell, 1992). An early study (Pleck, 1983) found that 60 to 80% of women surveyed preferred that their husbands were no more involved in the children than they were currently. Women act as gatekeepers of the father-child relationship and this is particularly obvious when parents divorce. Women with non-traditional gender attitudes tend to be more supportive of father involvement than women with traditional gender role attitudes. Interestingly, women's marital status and the number of children in the family were not associated with women's support for parental involvement with children (Hoffman & Moon, 1999).

The engagement of fathers in family support programs is an issue which has, to date, failed to capture the attention it deserves. Fathers tend not to attend parent education programs, and that many fathers find the idea of trying to change their parenting style and behaviours unpalatable (Tomison, 1998). In addition, many programs are not able to be flexible about the times when services are available. This can significantly impair fathers' ability to participate (Haapala, Pecora, & Fraser, 1991).

There are a number of programs specifically focusing on fathers, and fathering, but these are in the minority. These include parent education programs (Tomison, 1998) and playgroups designed specifically for fathers and children. Programs are becoming available in some areas to support fathers in prison maintain relationships with their children (Adalist-Estrin, 1994). The Male Involvement Project in America aims to support early childhood programs in getting fathers and other men involved in their programs and involved in the lives of their children (Levine, 1993).

The Fathering Indicators Framework Project (National Center of Fathers and Families, 2001) was specifically designed to investigate the role of fathers in families, and particularly in child rearing. The aim of the project was to develop indicators that could be used by family support programs to facilitate the involvement of fathers in families. Desirable aspects of father involvement and behaviour were found to be best described using 6 indicators as follows:

- Father presence: the ability of fathers to be involved and have positive relationships with their children over their life time. Relationships need to be adaptable in order to change according to children's developmental needs, and to the social context (eg maintaining positive relationships after divorce). Components of father presence are quality and quantity of father-child interactions, accessibility of father to children, degree of paternal responsibility taken for child development, and paternal ability to work co-operatively with others who are responsible for childcare.

- Care-giving: this relates to the caring for dimension discussed above, and includes meeting basic physiological, physical, health and developmental needs as well as needs for attachment and emotional security.

- Children's social competence and academic achievement: the ability of fathers to actively engage with their children and others in facilitating children's social and academic development. It involves actual interaction, and the provision of appropriate opportunities to foster development.

- Co-operative parenting: the nature of the sharing of parenting responsibilities between the relevant adults (usually the mother and father). It looks at the ability of these adults to co-operate and work together for the benefit of the children and elements of shared expectations and values.

- Father's healthy living: fathers with a healthy life style are more able to contribute to their children's lives in a positive manner. Limited literacy levels, alcohol and drug abuse problems, mental health problems, incarceration, behaviour problems and family violence are all issues of paternal health that impact on children and families.

- Material and financial contributions: fathers are traditionally expected to provide the necessary finances and resources for their children's welfare. This category reflects an attempt to identify the necessary financial supports for families and it is noted that fathers' financial contributions should no longer be considered in isolation from mothers' (and others, such as the state) contributions.

It is important that family support programs consider ways in which they can make their programs more father-friendly (Mills, 2001). This includes, but is not limited to, having males working in family support. In addition, it is crucial workers consider the impact of their interventions, not only on mothers but on fathers and other members of the family. Policy makers can, for example, consider the impact of longer working hours on fathers and on their children. Fathers are important parts of our families: they have the right to receive appropriate support to enhance their fathering roles and their positive impact on their children.

The rights of children and the rights of families

For centuries, western world children have not been considered as important as adults. Children traditionally belonged to their fathers, who had rights to treat them as they saw fit. Aristotle argued that children were part of an adult's body, and therefore adults should have total control over children. In Roman law, fathers had the ultimate right to sell their children into slavery, or to murder them if they wished. St Augustine's model of original sin postulated that children were born weak, and prone to corruption and sin. Until they were learned to submit to appropriate controls, they were not considered worthy human beings (Gittins, 1998). Parents and teachers were encouraged to be severe with children in order to eradicate their original sin.

Perceptions of children began to change just over a hundred years ago. A landmark court case in America (in 1874) ruled that a young girl (who had been found neglected, beaten and cut) was, as a member of the animal kingdom, entitled to protection under the law (Cloke & Davies, 1995). At the time, there were laws that protected animals, but no laws that protected children. In English law, custody decisions regarding children only began to consider the best interests of the child from the 1870s, although orphaned or deserted children were still being sent from institutions to work as indentured labourers as young as 12 to 14 years of age up until 1925 (Gittins, 1998)

Our view of children has shifted, and they are seen more often now as innocents, at risk for contamination from our society. Thus, they are in need of protection, and in order to protect them, their autonomy is restricted. Childhood is seen as a golden age, where children need freedom to play, learn and develop whilst being sheltered from the realities of the world around them (Joseph, 1995). Children are recognised as having special needs, and it is the role of adults to ensure those needs are met for children. Children are the recipients of adult actions, rather than actors in their own right. Parents are empowered by law to act on behalf their children (Landsdown, 1995).

The United Nations Convention on the Rights of the Child requires that children contribute to decision-making that impacts on their lives. However, current adult protectionist thinking generally restricts children's involvement in decision-making, using the reasoning that children should not be required to participate in difficult and complex issues. In addition, questions are raised about children's ability to process and understand complex information, and their ability to utilise that information in rational decision making (Landsdown, 1995). Protectionist thinking requires that adults (and families) take on this responsibility for children, and should be supported and encouraged to do so in the best interests of children. This creates a vicious cycle, where adults protect children, children do not learn the skills for autonomy, so continue to need protection.

In order to honour the intentions of the Convention, this thinking needs to be questioned. Children will not be capable of making complex decisions if they have never been given opportunities to experience decision-making. Children need to be empowered and supported to participate in making decisions, in order to gain more autonomy and to exercise their rights under the Convention. The role of adults is not to protect children, but to structure opportunities for them to learn how to make decisions, to empower children so they develop the skills and confidence in their decision making capacities.

The Convention identifies that:
- parents are primarily responsible for their children
- children ought to remain with their parents unless separation is absolutely necessary

- children have right to be protected from economic exploitation and harmful work
- children have the right to be protected from drug abuse
- children have the right to services to rehabilitate and facilitate their recovery from maltreatment & neglect
- children have additional needs than adults so have a right to special safeguards beyond those available for adults
- adults and government have responsibility to act in children's interests

Many see a conflict between the rights of children identified under the Convention, and the rights of adults and families. Debates rage around the rights of families to rear their children as they see fit. For example, the implementation of a 'no smacking' policy in Scandanavia is perceived in many other western countries as an unnecessary, inappropriate state intervention in the right of families to discipline their children in the ways they believe necessary and appropriate. Hysterical outbursts in the media often focus on the despair of parents who feel that a 'no smacking' policy gives their children free reign to grow into uncontrollable delinquents, for whom they, as parents, will be blamed.

No one argues that children should not, in general, have the same rights as adults. It is also recognised that children have special needs, and thus may need additional support than that required by adults. In clear cases of abuse and neglect, few would argue that the rights of children to safety and protection should be over-ridden by the rights of their families to rear them as they see fit. However, there are many other inequities in our society. Children growing up in poverty, or in violent families and/or communities are significantly disadvantaged. Does their rights for a 'fair go' over-ride their families' rights to rear their children? Certainly the underpinning motive of family support programs is to make changes in families and communities which expose children to high levels of risk. But who decides what is the right environment (physical, social and psychological) for children, and who has the right to impose those environments on all families? Just who is ultimately responsible for children?

Who is ultimately responsible for the children?

Traditionally, children were the responsibility of their parents. In the western world a cultural tradition of minimal government, and an emphasis on private property and individualism have combined to create an understanding of families as being outside the realm of government (Zimmerman, 1988). Ultimately, a man's home was seen as his castle, and he could behave how he wished behind his own closed doors.

However, the state has always been interested in shaping the citizen's of tomorrow: today's children. Universal education was originally offered to mould lower class children into accepting the status quo, and preparing them to adequately fulfil their adult (lower class) roles in society. In the same way, the state's involvement in child rearing in some families functioned to punish those parents who failed to provide adequately for their children. Inadequate provision was perceived as increasing the risk that children would become potential future threats to the well-being of society (threats through criminal behaviour or welfare dependency). Intervention thus tended to happen in the lower classes and was targeted at removing future challenges to the status quo.

In more recent times the status quo has been constantly under threat. Rising crime rates, levels of poverty, violence, increasing levels of inequity and increasing unemployment are all factors which attest to an uneasy society. Citizens are increasingly demanding the state take responsibility for 'fixing' these social concerns. Children are being made ill through the conditions of the social world in which they live. Hart (2001) draws a parallel between the invisible germs that caused infectious disease outbreaks last century, and the invisible forces responsible for today's social inequities. He argues that we need a co-ordinated state approach in terms of public policy and action in order to address the most significant issue of the twentieth century: the social toxicity of our society.

In Britain and the United States proponents of a new political approach, called *The Third Way* refuse to identify the state as the saviour or as the cause of the problems (Halpern & Mikosz, 2001). Some level of responsibility does rest with the state: in particular, the responsibility to facilitate citizen action and empowerment. Social change will only occur, it is believed, through partnerships between citizens and state that are founded on sustainable economic, social and environmental principles. In the on-line debate about the third way reported by Halpern (2001), Julian Le Grand summarised the principles of the Third Way as community, responsibility, accountability and opportunity. Giddens (1998) summarises Third Way values as:

- the need to protect those who are vulnerable. Whilst the state might operate a safety net for those who are vulnerable, these rights do not come without responsibilities. For example, the right to unemployment benefits is coupled with an obligation to look for work. The welfare system must support people in that search, not hinder them.

- authority assumed only through democracy. People need to be supported and encouraged to participate in decision-making and community action. Citizens need to consider how we, as a society, should live, how we should address ecological problems and how should we create solidarity and social justice within a framework that insists on recognising diversity and respecting equality. This includes debates on how do we cope with change, how do we control growth and development in ways that enhance social justice and are ecologically sound.

Family support, the way it is conceptualised in this book, operates out of Third Way thinking. The institutionalisation of justice, recognition of the dignity and sovereignty of each individual person and the expectation that individuals will take control of their own lives are fundamental principles upon which the Third Way is based, all of which are reflected in family support.

The Third Way, lies between state collectivism and unregulated market economic approaches (Naidoo, 2000). It uses principles of supply and demand to regulate the provision of goods and services, but provides overall control through state regulation and state support for groups who are disadvantaged. The state and civil society act in partnership, using local communities as the practical means to address social problems (Giddens, 1998). This is enacted in the ecological focus of family support, where strengthening families requires attention to be paid to the communities in which families live, as well as to the families and individual family members themselves.

In Australia, there is recognition that existing 'passive welfare' strategies are ineffective and undesirable (Shaver, 2001). Passive welfare is thought to encourage lack of responsibility in welfare recipients and a lack of reciprocity. Marginal groups are managed at minimal cost. There is recognition that emphasis in social policy needs to change, and ongoing debate as to whether that change is best enacted by following the Third Way approaches initiated in Britain and the United States.

So who is responsible for families and children? Third Way politics suggest that, whilst the state must set a certain standard, it is not necessarily the best provider of services. For example, the state does not provide jobs for people who are unemployed, but instead provides subsidies to employers to encourage them to employ more labour (Halpern & Mikosz, 2001). In family support, the state does not operate huge, national programs, but instead provides resources to enable the development of small, localised programs who are able to address their own community needs in their own way, whilst following guidelines to ensure they are accountable, responsible and ethical. Family support programs, aimed at improving outcomes for children and ultimately creating a citizenship of ethical and fulfilled adults, are at the heart of the Third Way.

The Third Way identifies children as the joint responsibility of the State, their community and their families. Whilst the state has an obligation to ensure that children are offered the best start in life, that responsibility does not necessitate the state to take total responsibility for children. The state's role is to provide resources, support and expertise. These enable families and communities to develop systems and programs resulting in the creation of quality local environments for neighbourhood children and families. Family support programs, underpinned by an ecological ideology (which requires service planners to think about not just their own local systems, but the impact of changes in their systems on other systems) and a focus on empowerment and strengths, offers a Third Way approach to social service delivery. We are all responsible for our children. Stress and risk can, and should, be compensated for by our actions. The world's children are our children.

Say yes for children

The UN Convention on the Rights of the Child has resulted in substantial progress in improving outcomes for children, but overall gains have fallen short of national obligations and international commitments (Preparatory Committee for the Special Session of the General Assembly on Children, 2001). The United Nations are calling for individuals and nations to recommit to improving the future for all children of the world through the following principles, identified as the *Say Yes for Children* campaign (UNICEF, 2001):

1. leave no child out: all forms of discrimination (for example gender, racial, religious) and exclusion against children must cease;

2. put children first: children's rights must be respected at all levels of society—individuals, government and non-government organisations, religious groups, and private sector;

3. care for every child: all children deserve the best possible start in life;

4. fight HIV/AIDS: children and families deserve protection;

5. stop exploiting and harming children: violence, abuse, sexual and economic exploitation must stop now;

6. listen to children: the rights of children to express themselves and to participate in decisions affecting them must be respected;

7. educate all children: every child should be given opportunities to learn;

8. protect children from war: children should not be exposed to the horrors of armed conflict;

9. protect the earth for children: the environment must be protected globally, nationally and locally;

10. fight poverty: the well-being of all children must be a priority objective. Services that benefit the poorest children and their families (for example basic health and education) must be available. Child poverty must be eliminated.

In order to implement the *Say Yes for Children* imperatives, the UN recommends that we all participate in the creation of a child-friendly world. Included in these recommendations is a requirement for states to respect and provide protection and assistance to parents and families in order to enable children to grow and develop in safe, stable and supportive environments. This includes the rights of families, caregivers and children to information and services which promote child development, protection and participation; and the promotion of attitudes relating to tolerance, equality and non-violence. Inequities in society, which lead to inequitable opportunities for development, must be addressed so that all children can meet their potential.

In the ten years between 2000 and 2010, the UN calls for states to provide a safe and healthy start to life for all children, and promote a healthy life style for all people. National early childhood programs and child development policies are called for with outcomes to be measured against nationally defined goals and indicators of child physical, psychosocial and intellectual development. Education and information programs for parents are part of this, as is appropriate health, hygiene and nutrition services. Legislation, policies and programs to protect children from violence are called for. This includes a requirement to protect children from torture and other cruel, dehumanising or degrading treatment, including corporal punishment. Juvenile justice systems that safeguard children's rights are required. Discrimination (against indigenous, refugee, minority and migrant children, children with disabilities) is to be eliminated and all children must have equal access to education, health and social services.

States are required to recognise that investments in children need to be medium to long term. It is acknowledged that this may require restructuring of state budgets in some circumstances, and a commitment to prioritise resources towards social rather than military objectives. Business and the corporate sector are expected to take on social responsible roles and become involved in research and programme development.

In short, there is a requirement for collective responsibility to improve outcomes for children. It is not only the government's responsibility, nor is it the responsibility of individual families. It is our joint responsibility. Children need our advocacy and our support. Those of us lucky enough to work in family support may feel that we contribute through our employment. That is not sufficient. We all need to contribute in a more holistic way: the way we live our lives in our communities, the interactions we have with our neighbours, the effort we make to lend a listening ear or a helping hand after work or at the weekend, all contribute towards developing a safe and caring world for children. Can children in your neighbourhood walk home safely from school on their own? Few children feel safe doing so now. In 1971 80% 7-8yr olds were going to school on their own; by 1990, only 9% were doing so (Landsdown, 1995). Where do parents go in your community when they are stressed and need a few minutes break from their kids? Are there neighbours available to provide support or are they all out at work? Is there somewhere safe to run to when violence erupts in a house in your street? Or is it just as dangerous out on the footpath at night? We all live in communities. We all have neighbours. We can all contribute towards helping our neighbours feel safe, secure and supported. For the sake of our community's children, it is time we all took responsibility for doing so.

References

Abbott, L., & G, Pugh. (1998). *Training to work in the early years. Developing the climbing frame*. Philadelphia, PA: Open University Press.

Abelson, A. (1999). Respite care needs of parents of children with developmental disabilities. *Focus on Autism and other Developmental Disabilities, 14*(2), (pp. 96–100, 109).

Adalist-Estrin, A. (1994). Family support and criminal justice. In S. Kagan & B. Weissbourd (Eds.), *Putting families first.* (pp. 161–185). San Francisco: Jossey-Bass.

Adalist-Estrin, A. (1995). Strengthening inmate-family relationships: programs that work. *Corrections Today, 57*(7), (pp. 116–120).

Adams, P., & Nelson, K. (1995). Introduction. In P. Adams & K. Nelson (Eds.), *Reinventing human services. Community and Family-centred practice.* (pp. 1–14). New York: Aldine De Gruyter.

Adler, P., & Kwon, S.-W. (1999). *Social capital: the good, the bad and the ugly.*, [Papers in Progress on Social Capital. paper available at http:www.worldbank.org/poverty/scapital/library/papers.htm. 27 pages.]. World Bank Group social Capital Library [2001, 13 March].

Agosta, J., & Melda, K. (1995). Supporting families who provide care at home for children with disabilities. *Exceptional Children, 62*(3), (pp. 271–283).

Aiken, C. (2000). *Surviving post-natal depression. At home, no-one hears you scream*. London: Kingsley Publishers.

Ainsworth, F. (1999). Social justice for 'at risk' adolescents and their families. *Children Australia., 24*(1), (pp. 14–18).

Aldgate, J. (1998). Measuring outcomes in Family Support Services (a case study using respite care). *Children & Society, 12,* (pp. 185–187).

Aldridge, S. (1993). The children of women prisoners. *Health Issues, 34,* (pp. 32–34).

Alford, W. (2000). Child protection education in NSW Schools. *Australian Domestic & Family Violence Clearinghouse Newsletter, 3*(July), (pp. 5–6).

Ali, T., & Green, C. (2001). Rebuilding foster care. *Family Support, 20*(2), (pp. 31–32).

Alkin, M., Patton, M., Weiss, C., Conner, R., House, E., Kean, M., King, J., Klein, S., Law, A., & McLaughlin, M. (1990). *Debates on evaluation*. Newbury Park, CA: Sage.

Allen, D. (2000, 20 August 2000). *Exploring reflective research of practice for professional development.*, [paper available at http://www.ballarat.edu.au/alarpm/cgi-bin/]. ALARPM/PAR Conference University of Ballarat [2001, 8 May].

Alloway, N. (1995). *The construction of gender in early childhood*. Carlton, Victoria: Curriculum Corporation.

Alpert-Gillis, L., Pedro-Carroll, J., & DCowen, E. (1989). The children of divorce intervention program: development, implementation and evaluation of a program for young urban children. *Journal of Consulting and Clinical Psychology, 57*(5), (pp. 583–589).

Ambler, L., & Kupper, L. (Eds.). (1996). *Respite Care. Briefing paper*. Interim. Washington, DC: National Information Center for Children and Youth with Disabilities.

Anderson, S., & Romanczyk, R. (1999). Early intervention for young children with autism: continuum-based behavioural models. *JASH, 24*(3), (pp. 162–173).

Andrews, K., & Ellis, A. (2001/2002). Strengthening parents through caring, connected communities. Developing practice. *The child, youth and family work journal, 2*(Summer), (pp. 14–19).

ARCA National Resource Centre for Respite and Crisis Care Services. (1994a). *Crisis Nursery Services: Responding to Ongoing Family Crises.* (Fact Sheet Number 26), [paper available at http://www.chtop.com/archfs26.htm]. ARCA National Resource Centre for Respite and Crisis Care Services [2001, 25 May].

ARCA National Resource Centre for Respite and Crisis Care Services. (1994b). *Developing and implementing rural respite and crisis nursery programs.* (Fact Sheet Number 35), [paper available at http://www.chtop.com/archfs35.htm]. ARCA National Resource Centre for Respite and Crisis Care Services, [2001, 27 March].

ARCA National Resource Centre for Respite and Crisis Care Services. (1994c). *Respite for children with Disabilities and Chronic or terminal Illnesses.* (Fact Sheet Number 02), [paper available at http://www.chtop.com/archfs02.htm]. ARCA National Resource Centre for Respite and Crisis Care Services [2001, 25 May].

ARCA National Resource Centre for Respite and Crisis Care Services. (1994d). *Respite for foster parents.* (Fact Sheet Number 32), [paper available at http://www.chtop.com/archfs32.htm]. ARCA National Resource Centre for Respite and Crisis Care Services, [2001, 25 May].

ARCA National Resource Centre for Respite and Crisis Care Services. (1996). *Recruiting and retaining respite providers.* (Fact Sheet Number 44), [paper available at http://www.chtop.com/archfs44.htm]. ARCA National Resource Centre for Respite and Crisis Care Services [2001, 25 May].

Arias, O. (2000/2001). 2000 Conference Keynote Address: Dr Oscar Arias. *TASH Newsletter, 26/27*(12/1), (pp. 13–16).

Armstrong, D., & Armstrong, s. (no date). *Building on strengths. A systems focused training resource for community-based family workers.* Concord West, NSW: Family Support Services Association of NSW.

Arnette, J., & Walsleben, M. (1998). Combating fear and restoring safety in schools. *Juvenile Justice Bulletin, April,* 14 pages downloaded.

Ashby, G., Boorsboom, E., & Rosser, S. (1976). *SPAN playgroups for geographically isolated pre-school children: theoretical basis and strategies.* Brisbane, QLD: Department of Education.

Australian Bureau of Statistics. (1996a). *3301.0 Births, Australia, 1996.* Canberra, ACT: Australian Bureau of Statistics.

Australian Bureau of Statistics. (1996b). *4128.0 Women's safety Australia.* Canberra: Australian Bureau of Statistics.

Australian Bureau of Statistics. (1997). *41543.0 How Australians use their time.* Canberra: Australian Bureau of Statistics.

Australian Bureau of Statistics. (1998a). *2034.5 1996 Census of population and housing: Aboriginal and Torres Strait Islander people, Western Australia.* Canberra: Australian Bureau of Statistics.

Australian Bureau of Statistics. (1998b). *4153.0 How Australians use their time, 1997.* Canberra, ACT: Australian Bureau of Statistics.

Australian Bureau of Statistics. (1998c). *4442.0 Family Characteristics, Australia, 1997.* Canberra, ACT: Australian Bureau of Statistics.

Australian Bureau of Statistics. (1999). *Australian Social Trends, 1999.* Canberra, ACT: Australian Bureau of Statistics.

Australian Bureau of Statistics. (1999a). 3236.0 Household and family projections, Australia, 1996 to 2021. Canberra, ACT: Australian Bureau of Statistics.

Australian Bureau of Statistics. (1999b). *Australian Social Trends 1999. Family - family functioning: looking after the children.* Canberra, ACT: Australian Bureau of Statistics.

Australian Bureau of Statistics. (2000a). *3310.0 Marriages and Divorces, Australia, 1999.* Canberra, ACT: Australian Bureau of Statistics.

Australian Bureau of Statistics. (2000b). *6224.0 Labour Force Statistics and other characteristics of Families, Australia.* Canberra, ACT: Australian Bureau of Statistics.

Australian Bureau of Statistics. (2001). *6302.0 Average Weekly Earnings.* Canberra, ACT: Australian Bureau of Statistics.

Australian Infant Child Adolescent and Family Mental Health Association. (2001). *Children of parents affected by a mental illness. Scoping project report.* Canberra, ACT: Mental Health and Special Programs Branch, Department of Health and Aged Care. Commonwealth of Australia.

Australian National Training Authority. (1999). *Australian Recognition Framework Arrangements.* Melbourne, Vic: Australian National Training Authority.

Ayre, E. (1996). *They won't take no for an answer: the Relais Enfants-Parents.* The Hague: Bernard Van Leer Foundation.

Baez, T. (2000). The effects of stress on emotional well-being and resiliency through mediating mechanisms of active coping skills and family hardiness. *Dissertation Abstracts International, 60*(7-A), 2382.

Bagley, C., & LaChance, M. (2000). Intensive family preservation services; an examination of critical service components. *Child & Family Social Work, 5*(3), (pp. 205–213).

Bandura, A. (1977). Self efficacy: toward a unifying theory of behavioural change. *Psychological Review, 84,* (pp. 191–215).

Bandura, A. (1982). Self-efficacy mechanisms in human agency. *American Psychologist, 37* (pp. 122–147).

Bardon, V., & Walk, N. (2000). Mirrung Ngu Wanjarri (Aboriginal Women making changes). *Australian Domestic & Family Violence Clearinghouse Newsletter, 4*(September), (p. 8).

Barnardos Staff. (1996). *The exclusion of vulnerable children from Australian childcare.* (Monograph 28). Ultimo, NSW: Barnardos.

Barnardos Staff. (no date-a). *Barbardos policy on permanency planning.* (Monograph 17). Ultima, NSW: Barnardos.

Barnardos Staff. (no date-b). *Moving from residential care to foster care.* (Monograph 23). Ultima, NSW: Barnardos.

Barr, D., & Cochrane, M. (1992). Understanding and supporting empowerment: redefining the professional role. Empowerment and *Family Support Networking Bulletin, 2*(3), (pp. 1–8).

Barth, R., Courtney, M., Berrick, J., & Albert, V. (1994). From child abuse to permanency planning. Child welfare service pathways and placements. New York: Aldine de Gruyter.

Bath, H. (2001/2002). Is there a future for residential care in Australia? Developing practice. *The child, youth and family work journal., 2*(Summer), (pp. 41–49).

Baxter, J. (2001). Marital status and the division of household labour. *Family Matters, 58*(Autumn), (pp. 16–21).

Bell, J. (1988). *Attitudes of childcare providers.* (Eric Document ED 299 017).

Benjamin, C. (1991). Prisons, parents and problems. Proceedings of the Australian Institute of Criminology Conference, March 1990. In S. McKillop (Ed.), *Keeping people out of prison* (pp. 165–175). Canberra, ACT: Australian Institute of Criminology.

Bergman, A., & Singer, G. (1996). The thinking behind New Public Policy. In G. Singer & L. Powers & A. Olson (Eds.), *Redefining family support. Innovations in public-private partnerships.* (pp. 435–463). Baltimore: Paul H Brookes.

Berk, L. (1999). *Infants, children and adolescents.* (3 ed.). Needham Heights, MA: Allyn and Bacon.

Berry, M. (1994). *Keeping families together.* New York: Garland Publishing.

Berry, M., Cash, S., & Brook, J. (2000). Intensive family preservation services: an examination of critical service components. Child & Family Social Work, 5(3), (pp. 191–203).

Besharov, D. (1990). *Recognising child abuse. A guide for the concerned.* New York: The Free Press.

Bierman, K. (1997). Implementing a comprehensive program for the prevention of conduct problems in rural communities: the Fast Track experience. The Conduct Problems Prevention Research Group. *American Journal of Community Psychology, 25*(4), (pp. 493–514).

Birnbrauer, J., & Leach, D. (1993). The Murdoch Early Intervention Program after 2 years. *Behaviour Change, 10*(2), (pp. 63–74).

Bittman, M., Craig, L., & Folbre, N. (2000). Non-parental childcare arrangements and parents' time spent with children. Social Policy *Research Centre Newsletter, 77*(October), (pp. 13–15).

Bloom, J. (1990). The relationships between social support and health. *Social Science and Medicine, 30*, (pp. 635–637).

Bloom, S. L. (1995). Creating Sanctuary in the School. *Journal for a Just and Caring Education, 1*(No. 4), (pp. 403–433).

Bogdan, R., & Taylor, S. (1990). Looking at the bright side: a positive approach to qualitative policy and evaluation research. *Qualitative Sociology, 13*(2), (pp.183–192).

Boss, P. (1995). Physical punishment in child rearing. *Children Australia., 20*(3), (pp. 27–32).

Bowlby, J. (1969). *Attachment and loss.* (Vol. 1). New York: Basic Books.

Bownes, D., & Ingersoll, S. (1997). Mobilizing communities to prevent juvenile crime. *Juvenile Justice Bulletin, July*, 8 pages downloaded.

Bracken, P., & Thomas, P. (2001). Postpsychiatry: a new direction for mental health. *British Medical Journal, 322*, (pp. 724–727).

Braddock, J. (2000). *Inequality worsens in New Zealand ... but Labour rushes to appease big business.*, [paper available at http://www.wsws.org/articles/2000/jun2000/nz-j16_prn.shtml. 3 pages.]. World Socialist Web Site. [2001, 7 March].

Bradley, V., & Blaney, B. (1996). Decentralising services in three Scandanavian Countries. In G. Singer & L. Powers & A. Olsen (Eds.), *Redefining family support. Innovations in public-private partnerships.* (pp. 333–355). Baltimore, MA: Paul H Brookes.

Bradshaw, J. (2000). Poverty: the outcomes for children. *Children 5–16 Research Briefing, 18* (July), 4 downloaded.

Brandon, P. (2000). An analysis of kin-provided childcare in the context of intrafamily exchanges: linking components of family support for parents raising young children. *The American Journal of Economics and Sociology, 59*(2), 191: 117 pages downloaded.

Braziel, D. (Ed.). (1996). *Family-focused practice in out-of-home care. A handbook and Resource Directory.* Washington, DC: CWLA Press.

Bremner, J., & Narayan, M. (1998). The effects of stress on memory and the hippocampus throughout the life cycle: implications for childhood development and aging. *Development and Psychology, 10*, (pp. 871–885).

Breslau, N., Brown, G., DelDotto, J., Kumar, S., Ezhuthachan, S., Andreski, P., & Hufnagle, K. (1996). Psychiatric sequelae of low birth weight at 6 years of age. *Journal of Abnormal Child Psychology, 24*(3), (pp. 385–400).

Breslau, N., Klein, N., & Allen, L. (1988). Very low birth weight: behavioural sequelae at nine years of age. *Journal of the American Academy of Child and Adolescent Psychiatry, 27*, (pp. 605–612).

Brody, G., & Flor, D. (1997). Maternal psychological functioning, family processes, and child adjustment in rural, single-parent African American families. *Developmental Psychology, 33*, (pp. 1000–1011).

Bronfenbrenner, U. (1975). Is early intervention effective? In B. Friedlander & G. Kirk & G. Sterritt (Eds.), *Exceptional Infants. Assessment and Intervention.* (Vol. 3) (pp. 449–475). New York: Brunner/Mazel.

Bronfenbrenner, U. (1979). *The ecology of human development. Experiments by nature and design.* Cambridge, Mass: Harvard University Press.

Bronfenbrenner, U., & Neville, P. (1994). America's children and families; an international perspective. In S. Kagan & B. Weissbourd (Eds.), *Putting families first.* San Francisco: Jossey-Bass.

Brown, F., & Bambara, L. (1999). Introduction to the special series on interventions for young children with autism: an evolving integrated knowledge-base. *JASH, 24*(3), (pp. 131–132).

Brown, M. (2000). *Recommended practices Parent Education and Support.,* [paper available at http://bluehen.ags.udel.edu/strength/best/crp-part1.html and crp-part2.html 37 pages]. University of Delaware Cooperative Extension [2000, 27 March].

Brown, M., Yando, R., & Rainforth, M. (2000). Effects of an At-Home video course on maternal learning, infant care and infant health. *Early Child Development and Care, 160*, (pp. 47–65).

Bruer, J. (1999). *The Myth of the First Three Years. A new understanding of early brain development and Life Long Learning.* New York: The Free Press.

Brugha, T., Wheatley, S., Taub, N., Culverwell, A., Friedman, T., Kirwan, P., Jones, D., & Shapiro, D. (2000). Pragmatic randomised trial of antenatal intervention to prevent postnatal depression by reducing psychosocial risk factors. *Psychological Medicine, 30*(6), (pp. 1273–1281).

Bruner, J. (Ed.). (1996). *The Culture of Education.* Cambridge, MA: Harvard University Press.

Bryce, H., Ellison, L., Corning, A., & Curtis, S. (2000). *Northern Lakes home visiting. A pilot project by uniting care Burnside evaluated by the University of Newcastle.* (Unpublished Report available from Uniting Care Burnside.). Paramatta: Uniting Care Burnside.

Bullen, P. (1998). *Neighbourhood and Community Centres in NSW, Building Communities, Providing Services.* Sydney, NSW: Local Community Services Association of NSW.

Butler, I., Douglas, G., Fincham, F., Murch, M., Robinson, M., & Scanlan, L. (2000). Children's perspectives and experiences of divorce. *Children 5-16 Research Briefing, 21*(December), 4 downloaded.

Butterfield, P. (1996). The Partners in Parenting Education program: a new option in parent education. *Zero to Three, August/September,* (pp. 3–10).

Butts, D. (2001). Generations United helps share resources. America's *Family Support Magasine, 20*(1), (p. 31).

Campbell, F., & Ramey, C. (1995). Cognitive and school outcomes for high risk African American students at Middle Adolescence: positive effects of early intervention. *American Educational Research Journal, 32*(4), (pp. 743–772).

Campbell, F., Pungello, E., Miller-Johnson, S., Burchinel, M., & Ramey, C. (2001). The development of cognitive and academic abilities: growth curves from an early childhood educational experiment. *Developmental Psychology, 37*(2), (pp. 231–242).

Carcach, C., & Mukherjee, S. (1999). *Women's fear of violence in the community.* (Trends and Issues in Crime and Criminal Justice, No 135), [paper available at http://www.aic.gov.au/publications/tandi/tandi135.html.]. Australian Institute of Criminology [1999, 2 December].

Cardamone, L. (1999). Family predictors of elementary social skills among former Head Start students. *Dissertation Abstracts international, 59*(8-A), 2848.

Carnegie Corporation of New York. (1994). *Starting points: meeting the needs of our youngest children.* New York: Carnegie Corporation of New York.

Carter, N., & Harvey, C. (1996). Gaining perspective on parenting groups. *Zero to Three, 16*(6), (pp. 2–8).

Catan, L. (1989). The development of young children in prison mother and baby units. *Research Bulletin, 26*, (pp. 9–12).

Cavadino, P., & Allen, R. (2000). Children who kill: trends, reasons and procedures. In G. Boswell (Ed.), *Violent children and adolescents. Asking the question why.* (pp. 1–18). London: Whurr Publishers.

Chaiken, M. (2000). *Violent neighbourhoods, violent kids.* (NCJ 178248). Washington, DC: Office of Juvenile Justice and Delinquency Prevention.

Chamberlain, R. (1996). Primary Prevention and the Family Resource Movement. In G. Singer & L. Powers & A. Olson (Eds.), *Redefining family support. innovations in public-private partnerships.* (pp. 115–133). Baltimore, Mass: Paul. H. Brookes.

Chambers, A. (2000, 10/06/00*). Capacity Inventory.,* [paper available at http://www.northwestern.edu/IPR/abcd/abcdciforeward.html 6 pages]. Asset-Based Community Development Institute [2001, 1 March].

Childcare Law Center. (1995). *Childcare as Welfare Prevention* (ED 385385). San Francisco: ERIC Document.

Clarke, C., Harnett, P., Atkinson, J., & Shochet, I. (1999). Enhancing resilience in indigenous people: the integration of individual, family and community interventions. *Aboriginal and Islander Health Worker Journal, 23*(4), (pp. 6–10).

Cloke, C., & Davies, M. (1995). Introduction. In C. Cloke & M. Davies (Eds.), *Participation and empowerment in child protection.We have a say. We have rights.* (pp. xiii–xxiv). London: Pitman Publishing.

Cochran, M. (1992). Parent empowerment: developing a conceptual framework. *Family Science Review, 5*(1 & 2), (pp. 3–21).

Cochran, M., & Brassard, J. (1979). Child development and personal social networks. *Child Development, 50*, (pp. 601–616).

Cochrane, M. (1991). Childcare and the empowerment process. *Empowerment and Family Support Networking Bulletin, 2*(1), (pp. 1–3).

Cohen, N. (1996). Unsuspected language impairments in psychiatrically disturbed children:developmental issues and associated conditions. In J. Beitchman & N. Cohen & M. Konstantareas & R. Tannock (Eds.), *Language, learning, and behaviour disorders: developmental, biological and clinical perspectives.* (pp. 105–127). New York: Cambridge University Press.

Coie, J., & Cillessen, A. (1993). Peer rejection: origins and effects on children's development. *Current Directions in Psychological Service, 2*(3), (pp. 89–92).

Coleman, P., & Karraker, K. (1998). Self-efficacy and parenting quality: findings and future applications. *Developmental Review, 18*(1), (pp. 47–85).

Collier, P. (1998). Social Capital and Poverty. Social Capital Initiative Working Paper No 4. The World Bank Social Development Family Environmentally and Socially Sustainable Development Network., Washington D.C.

Comer, E., & Fraser, M. (1998). Evaluation of sex family-support programs: are they effective? Families in Society: *The Journal of Contemporary Human Services., 79*(2), 134: 114 pages downloaded.

Comer, J. (1993). *School power.* (Revised ed.). New York: Free Press.

Commonwealth Department of Health and Aged Care. (2000*). Promotion, Prevention and Early intervention for Mental Health—A Monograph.* Canberra, ACT: Mental Health and Special Programs Branch, Commonwealth Department of Health and Aged Care.

Community Drug Summit. (2001a). *Addressing illicit drug use among Aboriginal people, including the provision of treatment programs for drug dependent Aboriginal people.* (Issues Paper Number 3). Perth: Community Drug Summit Office.

Community Drug Summit. (2001b). *Prevention and early intervention strategies, including school, parent and public education and action in local communities.* (Issues Paper Number 4). Perth: Community Drug Summit Office.

Community Drug Summit. (2001c). *Drugs and law enforcement, including consideration of the most appropriate legal framework for illicit drugs, diverting drug users into treatment and treating the most serious offenders in prisons.* (Issues Paper Number 7). Perth: Community Drug Summit Office.

Community Drug Summit. (2001d). *Reducing harm to the community and individuals caused by continued drug use.* (Issues Paper Number 8). Perth: Community Drug Summit Office.

Community Drug Summit. (2001e). *Illicit Drug use in WA: Facts and figures.* (Issues Paper). Perth: Community Drug Summit Office.

Community Drug Summit. (2001f). *Supporting families to deal with illicit drug issues, particularly regarding issues for children of drug users and parents and siblings of drug users.* (Issues Paper Number 2). Perth: Community Drug Summit Office.

Community Drug Summit. (2001g). *Reducing harm to the community and individuals caused by continued drug use.* (Issues Paper Number 8). Perth: Community Drug Summit Office.

Community Drug Summit. (2001h). *Treatment for drug users and reintegration of drug dependent people into the community.* (Issues Paper Number 5). Perth: Community Drug Summit Office.

Community Drug Summit. (2001i). *Young people and illicit drug use.* (Issues Paper Number 1). Perth: Community Drug Summit Office.

Connell, J., & Kubisch, A. (1999). Applying a theory of change approach to evaluation of comprehensive community initiatives: progress, prospects and problems. In K. Fulbright-Anderson & A. Kubisch & J. Connell (Eds.), *New approaches to evaluating community issues.* (Vol. 2 Theory, Measurement and Analysis, (16 pages downloaded). Washington D.C.: The Aspen Institute.

Contreras, J., Mangelsdorf, S., Rhodes, J., Diener, M., & Brunson, L. (1999). parent-child interaction among Latina Adolescent mothers: the role of family and social support. *Journal of Research on Adolescence, 9*(4), (pp. 417–439).

Cornell Empowerment Group. (1989). Empowerment through family support. *Empowerment and Family Support Networking Bulletin, 1*(1), (pp. 2–12).

Corter, C. (2001). Integrating early childhood services and communities. A role for schools. *Every Child, 7*(3), (pp. 10–11).

Coulton, C. (1995). Using community-level indicators of children's well-being in comprehensive community initiatives. In J. Connell & A. Kubisch & L. Schorr & C. Weiss (Eds.), *New approaches to evaluating community initiatives.* (Vol. 1 Concepts, Methods, and Contexts., pp. 18 pages downloaded.). Washington D.C.: The Aspen Institute.

Cowger, C. (1992). Assessment of client strengths. In D. Saleebey (Ed.), *The strengths perspective in social work practice.* (pp. 139–147). White Plains, NY: Longman.

Cox, C. (Ed.). (2000). *To Grandmother's house we go. Perspectives on custodial grandparents.* New York: Springer Publishing Company Inc.

Cox, E., & Caldwell, P. (2000). Making policy social. In I. Winter (Ed.), *Social capital and public policy in Australia.* (pp. 43–73). Melbourne: Australian Institute of Family Studies.

Crane, B., & Dean, C. (1999). *Empowerment Skills for Family Workers. The comprehensive curriculum of the New York State Family Development Credential. Trainer's Manual.* Ithaca, NY: Cornell Empowering Families Project.

Crittenden, P. (1988). Relationships at risk. In J. Belsky & T. Nezworski (Eds.), *The Clinical Implications of Attachment* (pp. 136–174). Hillsdale, NJ: Lawrence Erlbaum.

Crnic, K., & Booth, C. (1991). Mothers' and fathers' perceptions of daily hassles of parenting across early childhood. *Journal of Marriage and the Family, 53*(4), (pp. 1042–1050).

Cuff, R., & Pietsch, J. (1997). *Final Report: What are the best forms of intervention for children who have a parent with a mental illness?* Parkville: Mental Health Research Institute.

Dahl, R. (1961). *Who governs?* New Haven: Yale University Press.

Dai, Y. (1999). Relationships among parenting styles, parental expectations and attitudes, and adolescents' school functioning: a cross-cultural study. *Dissertation Abstracts International, 59*(12-A), 4356.

Dalton, K., & Holton, W. (1996). *Depression after childbirth—How to recognise, treat and prevent postnatal depression.* (3 ed.). Oxford: Oxford University Press.

Danziger, S. (2000). *Approaching the limit: early national lessons from welfare reform.* Ann Arbor, MI: University of Michigan, Poverty Research and Training Center.

Danziger, S., & Waldfogel, J. (2000). Investing in children: what do we know? what should we do? In S. Danziger & J. Waldfogel (Eds.), *Securing the future. Investing in children from birth to college.* (pp. 1–15). New York: Russell Sage Foundation.

Dart, J. (1999). *A story approach for monitoring change in an agricultural extension project.,* [paper available at http://www.latrobe.edu.au/www/aqr/offer/papers/JDart.htm 8 pages]. Conference of the Association for Qualitative Research, Melbourne, July [2001, 3 May].

Davies, R. (1998). An evolutionary approach to facilitating organisational learning: an experiment by the Christian Commission for Development in Bangladesh. *Impact Assessment and Project Appraisal, 16*(3), (pp. 243–250).

Davis, C., Martin, G., Kosky, R., & O'Hanlon, A. (1999). *The National Stocktake of Prevention and Early Intervention Programs.* Bedford Park, SA: The Australian Early Intervention Network for Mental health in Young People.

de Vries, M. (1984). Temperament and infant mortality among the Masai of East Africa. *American Journal of Psychiatry, 141*, (pp. 1189–1194).

Dean, C. (2000). *Empowerment skills for family workers. The comprehensive curriculum of the New York State Family Development Credential. A Worker handbook.* Ithica, NY: Cornell Empowering Families Project.

Dean, C., & Macmillan, C. (2001). *Serving the children of parents with a mental illness: barriers, break-throughs and benefits.* Paper presented at the Building

Bridges: Promoting Mental Health for Families and Communities. 4th National Conference., Brisbane.

Deater-Deckard, K., Dodge, K., Bates, J., & Petit, G. (1996). Physical discipline among African American and European American mothers: links to children's externalising behaviours. *Developmental Psychology, 32*, (pp. 1065–1072).

Debord, K., Heath, H., McDermott, D., Wolfe, R., & Team, w. N. M. (1999). *Parenting Education Fact Sheet.* (Fact Sheet Number 10). Chicago, Ill: Family Support America.

DeFrain, J. (1999). Strong families around the world. *Family Matters, 53*, (pp. 6–13).

Denham, S. (1995). Family routines: a construct for considering family health. *Holistic Nursing Practice, 9*(4), (pp. 11–23).

Department for Education and Employment. (1999). *The role of Development workers.* (available online at www.dfee.gov.uk/eyd_c/index.htm ed. Vol. Ref: EYDCP Rep 3). Annesley, Nottingham: Department for Education and Training.

Department of Family and Community Services. (2000). *Parenting and early childhood intervention.,* [paper available at http://www.facs.gov.au]. Department of Family and Community Services [2000, 14 November].

Dinkmeyer, D., & McKay, G. (1983). *The parent's handbook : systematic training for effective parenting (STEP).* Circle Pines, Minn: American Guidance Service.

Dinkmeyer, D., McKay, G., & Dinkmeyer, J. (1989). *Early childhood STEP : systematic training for effective parenting of children under six. Leader's manual.* Circle Pines, Minn: American Guidance Service.

Donahoe, D., & Tienda, M. (2000). The transition from school to work: is there a crisis? What can be done? In S. Danziger & J. Waldfogel (Eds.), *Securing the future. Investing in children from birth to college.* (pp. 231–263). New York: Russell Sage Foundation.

Donham, K. (2001). Cutting the red tape. A model of co-location and collaboration. *Family Support, 20*(2), (p. 46).

Duggan, A., McFarlane, E., Windham, A., Rohde, C., & al, e. (1999). Evaluation of Hawaii's Healthy Start Program. *The Future of Children, 9*(1), 66; 21 pages downloaded.

Duigan, B., & Felus, J. (2000). The Central Violence Intervention program – 'A model of collaboration.'. *Australian Domestic & Family Violence Clearinghouse Newsletter, 5*(December), (pp. 4–6).

Duke, R. (1995). Children's and adults' attitudes towards parents smacking their children. *Children Australia., 20*(2), (pp. 24–27).

Dunlap, G. (1999). Consensus, engagement and family involvement for young children with autism. *JASH, 24*(3), (pp. 222–225).

Dunst, C. (1995). *Key characteristics and features of community-based family support programs.* Chicago, Ill: Family Resource Coalition.

Dunst, C., Trivette, C., & Mott, D. (1994). Strengths-based family-centred intervention practices. In C. Dunst & C. Trivette & A. Deal (Eds.), *Supporting and strengthening families. Methods, strategies and practices.* (Vol. 1, pp. 115–131). Cambridge, MA: Brookline Books.

Earle, R. (1995). *Helping to prevent child abuse and future criminal consequences. Hawai'i Healthy Start.,* [paper available at http:www.ncjrs.org/txtfiles/hawaiihs.txt/ 19 pages]. National Institute of Justice [2001, 3 May].

Early Childhood Development Unit. (2001). *Awhina Maatua,* [information available at http://www.wcdu.govt.nz]. Early Childhood Development Unit [2001, 24 August].

Early Childhood Development Unit. (2001b). *Parents as First Teachers (PAFT),* [information available at http://eee.ecdu.govt.nz]. Early Childhood Development Unit [2001, 24 August].

Easterbrooks, M., & Biringen, Z. (2000). Guest editors' introduction to the special issue: Mapping the terrain of emotional availability and attachment. *Attachment and Human Development, 2*(2), (pp. 123–129).

Eayrs, C., & Jones, R. (1992). Methodological issues and future directions in the evaluation of early intervention programs. *Child: care, health and development, 18*, (pp. 15–28).

Eccles, J., & Wigfield, A. (2000). Schooling's influences on motivation and achievement. In S. Danziger & J. Waldfogel (Eds.), *Securing the future. Investing in children from birth to college.* (pp. 153–181). New York: Russell Sage Foundation.

Elliot, B. (2000). *Promoting family change.* St Leonards, NSW: Allen & Unwin.

Else, A. (1999). *Hidden Hunger—Food and low income in New Zealand. A report of the National Nutrition survey.* Wellington: New Zealand Network Against Food Poverty.

Emde, R. (2000). Next steps in emotional availability research. *Attachment and Human Development, 2*(2), (pp. 242–248).

Erikson, E. (1950). *Childhood and society.* New York: Norton.

Evans, J., & Stansbery, P. (1998). *Parenting in the early years: a review of programs for parents of children from birth of three years of age.* Washington D.C.: The World Bank.

Evanston, J., Duggan, A., Windham, A., McFarlane, E.,& Fuddy, L. (2000). Hawaii's healthy start program of home visiting for at risk families: evaluation of family identification, family engagement and service delivery. *Pediatrics, 105*(1 pt 3), (pp. 250–259).

Family Resource Coalition of America. (no date). *The History of the Family Support Movement. Some highlights.* Chicago, Ill: The Family Resource Coalition of America.

Family Support America. (1996). *Making the case for Family support.* Chicago, Ill: Family Support America.

Family Support America. (2001). *Evaluation and Family Support.,* [paper available at http://www.familysupportamerica.org/content/projects/eval.htm 3 pages]. Family Support America [2001, 20 April].

Farquhar, S.-E. (1990). *Yet to make the grade: New Zealand National Government's Early Education Policy.* (ED329342): Eric Document.

Farrell, A. (1994). The experience of young children and their incarcerated mothers: a call for humanly-responsive policy. *International Journal of Early Childhood, 26*(2), (pp. 6–12).

Farrington, D., & Welsh, B. (1999). Delinquency prevention using family-based interventions. *Children & Society, 13*, (pp. 287–303).

Farrington, D., & West, D. (1990). The Cambridge Study in delinquent development: a long term follow up of 411 London males. In H. Kerner & G. Kaiser (Eds.), *Criminality: personality, behaviour, life history.* (pp. 115–138). Berlin: Springer Verlag.

Fawcett, M., & Calder, P. (1998). Early childhood Studies degrees. In L. Abbott & G. Pugh (Eds.), *Training to work in the early years. Developing the climbing frame.* (pp. 99–108). Philadelphia, PA: Open University Press.

Feldman, M., Ducharme, J., & Case, L. (1999). Using self instructional pictorial manuals to teach child-care skills to mothers with intellectual disabilities. *Behaviour Modification, 23*(3), (pp. 480–497).

Felton, B., & Berry, C. (1992). Groups as social network members: overlooked sources of social support. *American Journal of Community Psychology, 20*(2), (pp. 253–261).

Fergusson, D., & Lynskey, M. (1993). Maternal age and cognitive and behavioural outcomes in middle childhood. *Paediatric and Perinatal Epidemiology, 7*, (pp. 77–91).

Fetterman, D. (2000). *Foundations of empowerment evaluation.* Thousand Oaks, CA: Sage.

Fetterman, D., Kaftarian, S., & Wandersman, A. (1996). *Empowerment evaluation: knowledge and tools for self-assessment and accountability.* Thousand Oaks, CA: Sage.

Fick, A., Osofsky, J., & Lewis, M. (1997). Perceptions of violence: children, parents and police officers. In J. Osofsky (Ed.), *Children in a violent society.* (pp. 261–276). new York: The Guilford Press.

Fight Crime: Invest in Kids. (2001). *California's Childcare Crisis: A Crime Prevention Tragedy.* (paper available at http://www.fightcrime.org). Oakland, CA: Fight Crime: Invest in Kids.

Finch, J. (1984). A first-class environment? Working-class playgroups as pre-school experience. *British Educational Research Journal, 10*(1), (pp. 3–17).

Fine, M. (1989). *The second handbook on parent education: contemporary perspectives.* San Diego, CA: Academic Press.

Finn-Stevenson, M., & Stern, B. (1997). Integrating early-childhood and family-support services with a school improvement process. *The Elementary School Journal, 98*(1), 51 (16 pages downloaded).

Fisher, L. (2001). Putting it under one roof. School, after school and family support. *America's Family Support Magazine, 20*(1), (pp. 17–20).

Fitzpatrick, P., Molloy, B., & Johnson, Z. (1997). Community mothers' programme: extension to the travelling community in Ireland. *Journal of Epidemiology and Community Health, 51*, (pp. 299–303).

Flese, B. (1992). Dimensions of family rituals across two generations: relation to adolescent identity. *Family Process, 31*, (pp. 151–162).

Flora, J. (2000). *Social capital and communities of place.,* [Papers in Progress on Social Capital. paper available at http:www.worldbank.org/poverty/scapital/library/papers.htm. 36 pages.]. The World Bank Group Social Capital Library [2001, 13 March].

Follett, C., Dayton, C., Simonds, J., & Rosenblaum, K. (1999). *The importance of context and social support in moderating depression in mothers of young infants. Michigan Family Study.* (Eric Document ED438 890). Bethesda, MD: National Institute of Mental Health (DHHS).

Forrest, D. (1999). Education and empowerment: towards untested feasibility. *Community Development Journal, 34*(2), (pp. 93–107).

Foucault, M. (1980). *Power/knowledge.* New York: Pantheon.

Franklin, C., Corcoran, J., & Ayers-Lopez, S. (1997). Adolescent pregnancy: multisystemic risk and protective factors. In M. Fraser (Ed.), *Risk and resilience in childhood.* (pp. 195–219). Washington D.C.: National Association of Social Workers.

Frankrijker, H. (1998). Cross-cultural learning from incidents, the critical incident method: some applications concerning the practice of teacher education and parent support. *European Journal of Intercultural Studies, 9*, S55–S70.

Freedman, L., & Stark, L. (1993). When the white system does not fit. *Australian Social Work, 46*(1), (pp. 29–36).

Freire, P. (1973). *Pedagogy of the oppressed.* New York: Seabury.

Friedman, M. (1970). The social responsibility of business to increase its profits. *New York Times Magasine, September 13*, 32–33, (pp. 122–126).

Frost, N., Johnson, L., Stein, M., & Wallis, L. (2000). Home-Start and the delivery of family support. *Children & Society, 14,* (pp. 328–343).

Furstenberg, F., Brooks-Gunn, J., & Morgan, S. (1987). *Adolescent mothers in later life.* Cambridge, UK: Cambridge University Press.

Garbarino, J. (1992). *Children & Families in the Social Environment.* New York: Aldine De Gruyter.

Garbarino, J., & Abramowitz, R. (1992). Sociocultural risk and opportunity. In J. Garbarino (Ed.), *Children and families in the social environment.* (pp. 38–63). New York: Aldine de Gruyter.

Garbarino, J., & Benn, J. (1992). The ecology of childbearing and child rearing. In J. Garbarino (Ed.), Children & Families in the Social Environment (pp. 133–177). New York: Aldine De Gruyter.

Garbarino, J., & Garbarino, A. (1992). In conclusion: the issue is human quality. In J. Garbarino (Ed.), *Children and families in the social environment.* (2 ed., pp. 303–327). New York: Aldine de Gruyter.

Garbarino, J., & Kostelny, K. (1994). Family support and community development. In S. Kagan & B. Weissbourd (Eds.), *Putting families first.* (pp. 297–320). San Francisco: Jossey-Bass.

Garbarino, J., & Kostelny, K. (1997). What Children Can Tell Us about Living in a War Zone. In J. Osofsky (Ed.), *Children Living in a Violent Society.* (pp. 32–41). New York: Guilford Press.

Garbarino, J., Dubrow, N., Kostelny, K., & Pardo, C. (1992). *Children in danger. Coping with the consequences of community violence.* San Francisco, CA: Jossey-Bass.

Gattai, F., & Musatti, T. (1999). Grandmothers' involvement in grandchildren's care: attitudes, feelings and emotions. *Family Relations, 48*(1), (pp. 35–42).

Gaventa, J. (1980). *Power and powerlessness.* Urbana, Ill: University of Illinois Press.

Gayla, M., & Gordis, E. (2000). The effects of family and community violence on children. *Annual Review of Psychology, 51,* (pp. 445–479).

Ghate, D. (2000). Family violence and violence against children. *Children & Society, 14*, (pp. 395–403).

Ghate, D. (2001). Community-based evaluations in the UK: scientific concerns and practical considerations. *Children & Society, 15*, (pp. 23–32).

Gibbs, C. (1991). Being hospitalised as a child - is it healthy? *Australian Journal of Early Childhood, 16*(2), (pp. 9–14).

Giddens, A. (1998). *The Third Way. The renewal of social democracy.* Cambridge, UK: Polity Press.

Gill, A. (1998). *What makes parent training groups effective. Promoting positive parenting through collaboration.* Unpublished PhD, University of Leicester, Leicester.

Gilligan, J. (1996). *Violence: our deadly epidemic and its causes.* New York: G.P. Putnam.

Gilligan, R. (1998). The importance of schools and teachers in child welfare. *Child and Family Social Work, 3*(1), (pp. 13–25).

Gilligan, R. (2000). Adversity, resilience and young people: the protective value of positive school and spare time experiences. *Children & Society, 14*, (pp. 37–47).

Gittens, D. (1993). *The family in question. Changing households and familiar ideologies.* Houndmills: Macmillan.

Gittins, D. (1998). *The child in question.* Houndsmills, UK: Macmillan Press.

Glass, N. (1999). Sure Start: the development of an early intervention programme for young children in the United Kingdom. *Children & Society, 13*, (pp. 257–264).

Gledhill, M. (1994). Community support services for families fro prevention to promotion of family strengths. In J. Inglis & L. Rogan (Eds.), *Flexible families. New directions on Australian communities.* (pp. 93–111). Leichhardt, NSW: Pluto Press LTD.

Glisson, C., & Hemmelgarn, A. (1998). The effects of organisational climate and interorganisational co-ordination on the quality and outcomes of Children's Services systems. *Child Abuse & Neglect, 22*(5), (pp. 401–421).

Goddard, H., & adapted by Rodgers, K. (2001). *Principles of parenting. Building family strengths.,* [paper available at http://nnfr.org/curriculum/topics/famstr.html 4 pages]. University of Tennessee Agricultural Extension Service [2001, 1 March].

Goldsmith, M. (1992). Parents as Teachers. *The Australian Journal of Forensic Sciences, 24*(1/2), (pp. 35–37).

Goldstein, H. (1992). Victors or victims: contrasting views of clients in social work practice. In D. Saleebey (Ed.), *The strengths perspective in social work practice.* (pp. 27–38). White Plains, NY: Longman.

Gonzalez, R.-A. (1998). The challenge of parenting education: new demands for schools in Spain. *Childhood Education, 74*(6), (pp. 351–354).

Gordon, M. (1999). *The roots of empathy.* Ottawa: Caledon Institute of Social Policy.

Gordon, T. (2000). *Parent Effectiveness Training: the proven program for raising responsible children.* (Revised ed.). New York: Three Rivers Press.

Gorman, J., & Balter, L. (1997). Culturally sensitive parent education. *Review of Educational Research, 67*(3), (pp. 339–369).

Graycar, A. (2001). *Crime and Justice,* [paper available at http://www.abs.gov.au/Ausstats/html. 21 pages.]. Australian Bureau of Statistics [2001, 6 March].

Graycar, A., & Nelson, D. (1999). *Crime and social capital.* Paper presented at the Australian Crime Prevention Council 19th Biennial International Conference on Preventing Crime., Melbourne.

Greene, B., Renee, N., Searle, M., Daniels, M., & Lubeck, R. (1995). Child abuse and neglect by parents with disabilities; a tale of two families. *Journal of Applied Behaviour Analysis, 28*(4), (pp. 417–434).

Greenwood, P., Model, K., Rydell, C., & Chiesa, J. (1998). *Diverting children from a life of crime: measuring costs and benefits.* (MR-699-1-UCB/RC/IF). Santa Monica, CA: Rand Corporation Report.

Grotberg, E. (1997). The international resilience project. In M. John (Ed.), *A charge against society. The child's right to protection.* (pp. 19–32). London: Jessica Kingsley Publishers.

Guba, E., & Lincoln, Y. (1994). Competing paradigms in qualitative research. In N. Denzin & Y. Lincoln (Eds.), *Handbook of Qualitative Research.* (pp. 643). Thousand Oaks, CA: Sage.

Haapala, D., Pecora, P., & Fraser, M. (1991). Implications for practice, policy, research and the future. In M. Fraser & P. Pecora & D. Haapala (Eds.), *Families in crisis. The impact of intensive family preservation services.* (pp. 289–312). New York: Aldine De Gruyter.

Hall, C. (1999). Integrating services for children and families: the way forward? *Children & Society, 13*, (pp. 216–222).

Hallam, H., Malmud, E., Braitman, L., Betancourt, L., Brodsky, N., & Giannetta, J. (1998). Inner-city achievers: who are they? *Archives of Pediatrics and Adolescent Medicine, 152*(10), (pp. 993–997).

Halpern, D., & Mikosz, D. (2001). *The Third Way: summary of the NEXUS on-line discussion.,* [paper available at http://www.nexus.org/library/papers/3way.html 25 pages]. NEXUS [2001, 26 June].

Ham, D., & Schocet, I. (2001). *A controlled trial of the RAP-P Parent program to foster adolescent well-being.* Paper presented at the Building Bridges; Promoting mental health for families and communities. 4th National Child and Adolescent Mental Health Conference., Brisbane.

Hampson, J., Rahman, M., Brown, B., Taylor, M., & Donaldson, C. (1998). Project Self. Beyond resilience. *Urban Education, 33*(1), (pp. 6–33).

Hanley, J. (2998). Postnatal depression. *Nursing Management, 4*(8), (pp. 12–13).

Harding, A., & Szukalska, A. (1998). *A portrait of Child Poverty in Australia in 1995–96.* Paper presented at the 6th Australian Institute of Family Studies Conference, Melbourne.

Harker, R. (1990). Schooling and cultural reproduction. In J. Codd & R. Harker & R. Nash (Eds.), *Political issues in New Zealand Education.* (2 ed.). Palmerston North: Dunmore Press.

Harnish, J., Dodge, K., & Valente, E. (1995). Mother-child interaction quality as a partial mediator of the roles of maternal depressive symptomatology and socioeconomic status in the development of child behaviour problems. Conduct problems Prevention research Group. *Child Development, 66*(3), (pp. 739–753).

Harris, P. (2000). Participation and the new welfare. *Australian Journal of Social Issues, 35*(4), (p. 279).

Harrison, L., & Ungerer, J. (1997). Infant-mother attachment relationships and the experience of childcare. *Every Child, 3*(2), (pp. 8–9).

Harrison, R., Boyle, S., & Farley, O. (1999). Evaluating the outcomes of family-based intervention for troubled children: a pretest-posttest study. *Research on Social Work Practice, 9*(6), (pp. 640–655).

Hart, B. (2001). *The third millenium miasma—a challenge for and saviour of public health.,* [NIFTeY electronic mailing list headed by gvvimpani@bigpond.com]. NIFTeY-list [2001, 12 June].

Hartz-Karp, J. (1983). The impact of infants in prison on institutional life: a study of the mother/infant prison programme in Western Australia. *Australia & New Zealand Journal of Criminology, 16*, (pp. 172–188).

Harvey, E. (1999). Short-term and long-term effects of early parental employment on children of the National Longitudinal Survey of Youth. Developmental Psychology, 35(2), (pp. 445–459).

Hasazl, S., Johnston, A., Liggett, A., & Schattman, R. (1994). A qualitative policy study of the Least Restrictive Environment provision of the Individuals with Disabilities Education Act. *Exceptional Children, 60*, (pp. 491–507).

Hawkins, J., Herrenkohl, T., Farrington, D., Brewer, D., Catalano, R., Harachi, T., & Cothern, L. (2000*). Predictors of youth violence.* (NCJ 179065). Washington, DC: Office of Juvenile Justice and Delinquency Prevention.

Head, M. (1998). *Poverty and inequality worsen in Australia.,* [paper available at http://www.wsws.org/news/1998/apr1998/pov-a8.shtml. 5 pages.]. World Socialist Web Site [2001, 6 March].

Health Department of Western Australia. (1993). *Mental Health Occasional Paper Number 1.* Perth, WA: Health Department of Western Australia.

Hebbeler, K. (2001). Supporting effective after school programs: the contribution of developmental research. *The Evaluation Exchange, VII*(2), (pp. 3–6).

Hechtman, L. (1989). Teenage mothers and their children: risks and problems: a review. *Canadian Journal of Psychiatry, 34*, (pp. 569–575).

Heckman, J. (1996). What should our human capital investment policy be? *Milken Institute for Job and Capital Formation, Spring*, (pp. 3–10).

Heckman, J., & Lochner, L. (2000). Rethinking education and training policy: understanding the sources of skill formation in a modern economy. In S. Danziger & J. Waldfogel (Eds.), *Securing the future. Investing in children from birth to college*. (pp. 47–83). New York: Russell Sage Foundation.

Heller, T. (1998). Current trends in providing support for families of adults with mental retardation. *TASH Newsletter, 24*(5), (pp. 21–24).

Hernandez, L. (2000). *Families and Schools Together. Building organisational capacity for family-school partnerships*. Boston, Mass: Harvard Family Research Project.

Hetherington, E. (1992). Coping with family transitions: winners, losers and survivors. *Child Development, 60*, (pp. 1–14).

Hill, M. (1999). Towards effective ways of working with children and their families. In M. Hill (Ed.), *Effective ways of working with children and their families*. (pp. 270–286). London: Jessica Kingsley Publishers.

Hillman, S., Silburn, S., Green, A., & Zubrick, S. (2000). *Youth suicide in Western Australia involving cannabis and other drugs. a literature Review and research report*. Perth: TVW Telethon Institute for Child Health Research, WA Youth Suicide Committee.

Hoffman, C., & Moon, M. (1999). Women's characteristics and gender role attitudes: support for father involvement. *The Journal of Genetic Psychology, 160*(4), (pp. 411–418).

Hollister, R., & Hill, J. (1995). Problems in the evaluation of community-wide initiatives. In J. Connell & A. Kubisch & L. Schorr & C. Weiss (Eds.), *New approaches to evaluating community initiatives. (Vol. 1 Concepts, Methods, and Contexts.*, (pp. 34 pages downloaded). Washington D.C.: The Aspen Institute.

Honikman, J. (2001). Treating and preventing postpartum depression. *Family Support, 20*(3), (pp. 23–26).

Houston, S., & Griffiths, H. (2000). Reflections on risk in child protection: is it time for a shift in paradigms? *Child & Family Social Work, 5*(1), (pp. 1–10).

Howden-Chapman, P., Wilson, N., & Blakely, T. (2000). Summary and Conclusions. In P. Howden-Chapman & M. Tobias (Eds.), *Social inequalities in Health*: New Zealand 1999. (document available at http://www.moh/govt/nz 219 pages ed., (pp. 147–167). Wellington: Ministry of Health.

Howell, J., & Bilchik, S. (Eds.). (1995). *Guide for implementing the comprehensive strategy for serious, violent and chronic juvenile offenders*. Washington, DC: Office of Juvenile Justice and Delinquency Prevention.

Howes, C., Rodning, C., Galluzzo, D., & Myers, L. (1988). Attachment and childcare. *Early Childhood Research Quarterly, 3*, (pp. 401–416).

Hughes, P., Bellamy, J., & Black, A. (2000). Building social trust through education. In I. Winter (Ed.), *Social capital and public policy in Australia*. (pp. 225–249). Melbourne: Australian Institute of Family Studies.

Hutchins, T., & Sims, M. (1999). *Program planning for Infants and Toddlers. An ecological approach*. Sydney: Prentice Hall.

Huttenlocher, J. (1998). Language input and language growth. *Preventive Medicine, 27*(2), 195–199.

Hvinden, B. (1994). *Divided against itself*. Oslo: Scandanavian University Press.

Ife, J. (1995). *Community development: creating community alternatives—vision, analysis and practice*. Melbourne: Longman.

Ife, J. (1997). *Rethinking social work. Iowards critical practice*. South Melbourne: Longman.

Institute of Medicine. (2001). *Health and behaviour: the interplay of biological, behavioural and social influences.* Washington DC: National Academy Press.

Jackiewicz, S. (1998). *The lived experience of a group of mothers, geographically isolated from their extended families, in establishing their social support networks.* Unpublished Master of Social Science (Human Services), Edith Cowan University, Perth.

Jackson, J. (1993). Multiple caregiving among African Americans and infant attachment: the need for an emic approach. *Human Development, 36*(2), (pp. 87–102).

Jacobsen, G. (2001). Matching Mothers. Parents 'swapping' care. *Every Child, 7*(2), (p.14).

Jamrozik, A. (1994). Social Class and community services. The paths to privilege. In M. Wearing & R. Berreen (Eds.), *Welfare and Social Policy in Australia.* (pp. 99–120). Sydney: Harcourt Brace.

Jenkins, E., & Bell, C. (1997). Exposure and response to community violence among children and adolescents. In J. Osofsky (Ed.), *Children in a violent society* (pp. 9–31). New York: The Guilford Press.

Jenkins, J., & Keating, D. (1999). *Risk and resilience in Six- and Ten-Year-Old Children.* (paper available at http://www.hrdc-drhc.gc.ca/dgra/ W-98-23E). Hull, Quebec: Applied research Branch, Strategic Policy, Human Resources Development Canada.

Johnston, J. (2001). Evaluating national initiatives: the case of "On Track". *Children & Society, 15*, 33–36.

Jones, M. A. (1991). Measuring outcomes. In K. Wells & D. Biegel (Eds.), *Family preservation services. research and evaluation.* (pp. 159–186). Newbury Park, CA: Sage.

Jones, P. (1999). Parenting education and support: issues in multi-agency collaboration. In S. Wolfendale & H. Einzig (Eds.), *Parenting education and support: new opportunities.* (pp. 137–149). London: David Fulton.

Jonson-Reid, M. (2000). Evaluating empowerment in a community-based child abuse prevention program: lessons learned. *Journal of Community Practice, 7*(4), (pp. 57–76).

Joseph, Y. (1995). Child protection rights: can an international declaration be an effective instrument for protecting children? In C. Cloke & M. Davies (Eds.), *Participation and empowerment in child protection. We have a say. We have rights.* (pp. 1–18). London: Pitman Publishing.

Joshi, H., Wiggins, D., & Clarke, L. (2000). The changing home: outcomes for children. *Children 5–16 Research Briefing, 6*(January), 4 pages downloaded.

Julian, T., McKenry, P., & McKelvey, M. (1994). Cultural variations on parenting. Perceptions of Caucasian, African-American, Hispanic and Asian-American parents. *Family Relations, 43*(1), (pp. 30–37).

Kagan, S. (1999). Using a theory of change approach in a national evaluation of family support programs: practitioner reflections. In K. Fulbright-Anderson & A. Kubisch & J. Connell (Eds.), *New approaches to evaluating community issues. (Vol. 2 Theory, Measurement and Analysis,* pp. 6 pages downloaded.). Washington DC: The Aspen Institute.

Kagan, S., & Weissbourd, B. (1994). Toward a new normative system of family support. In S. Kagan & B. Weissbourd (Eds.), *Putting families first* (pp. 473–490). San Francisco: Jossey-Bass.

Kapi'olani Health. (1998, 1998). *Hawaii Family support Centre, HFSC—Healthy Start,* [paper available at http://www.kapiolani.org/home.html 2 pages]. Kapi'olani Health [2001, 3 May].

Karoly, L., Greenwood, P., Everingham, S., Hoube, J., Kilburn, M., Rydell, C., Sanders, M., & Chiesa, J. (1998*). Investing in our children. What we know and don't know about the costs and benefits of early childhood interventions.* Santa Monica, CA: RAND.

Karr-Morse, R., & Wiley, M. (1997). *Ghosts from the nursery.* New York: Atlantic Monthly Press.

Keating, D., & Hertzman, C. (1999). Modernity's Paradox. In D. Keating & C. Hertxman (Eds.), *Developmental health and the wealth of nations.* (pp. 1–17). New York: The Guilford Press.

Kellehear, A. (1992). Beliefs about death throughout the lifespan. In P. Heaven (Ed.), *Life span development.* (pp. 329–345). Marrickville, NSW: Harcourt Brace Jovanovich.

Kelley, S. (1993). Caregiver stress in grandparents raising grandchildren. Image: *Journal of Nursing Scholarship, 25,* (pp. 331–337).

Kelley, S., Sikka, A., & Venkatesan, S. (1997). A review of research on parental disability: implications for research and counselling practice. *Rehabilitation Counselling Bulletin, 41*(2), (pp. 105–121).

Keltner, B. (1990). Family characteristics of preschool social competence among Black children in a Head Start program. *Child Psychiatry and Human Development, 21*(2), (pp. 95–108).

Keltner, B. (1992). Family influences on child health. *Pediatric Nursing, 18,* (pp. 128–131).

Kenny, S. (1999). *Developing communities for the future. Community development in Australia.* South Melbourne: Nelson.

Kilgore, K., Synder, J., & Lentz, C. (2000). The contribution of parental discipline, parental monitoring and school risk to the early-onset conduct problems in African American boys and girls. *Developmental Psychology, 36*(6), (pp. 835–845).

Kilmartin, C. (1997). Children, divorce and one-parent families. *Family Matters, 48*(Spring/Summer), (pp. 34–35).

Kirby, L., & Fraser, M. (1998). *Risk and resilience in childhood.* Washington D.C.: National Association of Social Workers.

Kirk, R. (2000). *Tailoring intensive Family Preservation Services for family reunification cases: research, evaluation and assessment.* (White paper prepared for the National Family Preservation Network and the Packard Foundation). Chapel Hill, Carolina: School of Social Work, University of North Carolina.

Klemm, D., & Santelli, B. (1999). The match: everyone benefits when parents find a connection through Parent to Parent. *The Exceptional Parent, 29*(11), (pp. 80–81).

Kontos, S. (1984). Congruence of parent and early childhood staff perceptions of parenting. *Parenting Studies, 1*(1), (pp. 5–10).

Koser, G. (2001). Two ends of the rainbow. Intergenerational family support bridges the gap. *America's Family Support Magasine, 20*(1), (pp. 28–30).

Kretzmann, J., & McKnight, J. (1993a). *Capacity Inventory,* [paper available at http://northwestern.edu/IPR/abcd/abcdci.html 7 pages]. Asset-based Community Development Institute [2001, 1 March].

Kretzmann, J., & McKnight, J. (1993b). Introduction. In K. J & J. McKnight (Eds.), *Building communities from the inside out: a path toward finding and mobilising a community's assets.* (pp. 1–11). Evanston, Ill: Institute for Policy Research.

Kumpfer, K., & Alvarado, R. (1998). Effective family strengthening interventions. *Juvenile Justice Bulletin, November,* 16 pages downloaded.

Kumpfer, K., & Tait, C. (2000). Family skills training for parents and children. *Juvenile Justice Bulletin, April,* 11 pages downloaded.

269

Laing, L. (2000). *Children, young people and domestic violence.* (Issues Paper 2). Sydney, NSW: Australian Domestic and Family Violence Clearinghouse.

Laing, L. (2000). *Progress, trends and challenges in Australian responses to domestic violence.* (Issues Paper 1). Sydney, NSW: Australian Domestic and Family Violence Clearinghouse.

Landsdown, G. (1995). Children's rights to participation and protection: a critique. In C. Cloke & M. Davies (Eds.), *Participation and empowerment in child protection. We have a say. We have rights.* (pp. 20–38). London: Pitman Publishing.

Latham, M. (1998). *Civilising global capital. New thinking for Australian labour.* Sydney: Allen and Unwin.

Laucht, M., Esser, G., & Schmidt, M. (1997). Developmental outcome of infants born with biological and psychosocial risks. *Journal of Child Psychology and Psychiatry, 38*(7), 843–853.

Lawrence, B., Dull, J., Crane, B., & Dean, C. (1999*). Empowerment skills for family workers: The comprehensive curriculum of the New York State Family Development Credential. Field Advisor's Manua*l. Ithaca, NY: Cornell Empowering Families Project.

Lawrence, M. (1990). *Recommendations for a Child Abuse prevention Programme at Middlemore Hospital.* (Report presented to Middlemore Hospital.). Manakau, Ak: Lawrence Consulting.

Leach, R. (1993). *Political ideologies. An Australian introduction.* (2 ed.). South Melbourne: Macmillan Education.

Lein, J. (2000). The relations among attachment style, perceived parental weight expectations and weight concerns in preadolescent girls. *Dissertation Abstracts International, 60*(10-B), 5228.

Lennon, L., Maloney, C., Miller, J., Underwood, M., Walker, J., Wright, C., & Chambliss, C. (1997). *An evaluation of informal parent support groups.* (Eric Document ED 408 078): Ursinus College.

Leon, A. (1999). Family Support Model: integrating service delivery in the twenty-first century. Families in Society: *The Journal of Contemporary Human Services., 80*(1), 14 (19 pages downloaded).

Levine, J. (1993). *Getting men involved: strategies for early childhood programs.* New York: Families and Work Institute.

Levine, J., Pollack, H., & Comfort, M. (2000). *Academic and behavioural outcomes among the children of young mothers* (paper presented at the 2000 annual meeting of the Population Association of America.). Chicago, Ill: University of Chicago, School of Social Service Administration.

Lewis, J. (1998). Evaluating community initiatives. *Children & Society, 12,* 188–189.

Lewis, J., & Utting, D. (2000). Made to measure? Evaluating community initiatives for children: introduction. *Children & Society, 15*, 1–4.

Lewis, R., Walton, E., & Fraser, M. (1995). Examining family reunification services: a process analysis of a successful experiment. *Research on Social Work Practice, 5*(3), 259–282.

Li, X., Stanton, B., & Feigelman, S. (2000). Impact of perceived parental monitoring on adolescent risk behaviour over 4 years. *Journal of Adolescent health, 27*(1), 49–56.

Linke, P. (1998*). Let's stop bullying.* Watson, ACT: Australian Early Childhood Association.

Little, M. (1999). New research on residential care. *Children & Society, 13,* 61–66.

Little, M. (1999). Prevention and early intervention with children in need: definitions, principles and examples of good practice. *Children & Society, 13*, 304–316.

Lloyd, E. (Ed.). (1999). *Parenting matters. What works in parenting Education.* Ilford, Essex: Barnardos.

Lobato, D. (1990). *Brothers, sisters and special needs*. Baltimore: Paul H Brookes.

Lowenthal, B., & Lowenthal, R. (1997). Teenage parenting: challenges, interventions and programs. *Childhood Education, 74*, 29–32.

Lupton, C., & Sheppard, C. (1999). Lost lessons? the experience of a time-limited home-school support project. *Children & Society, 13*, 20–31.

Lynch, L. (2000). Trends and consequences of investments in children. In S. Danziger & J. Waldfogel (Eds.), *Securing the future. Investing in children from birth to college.* (pp. 19–46). New York: Russell Sage Foundation.

Lyons, M. (2000). Non-profit organisations, social capital and social policy in Australia. In I. Winter (Ed.), *Social capital and public policy in Australia.* (pp. 165–191). Melbourne: Australian Institute of Family Studies.

Lyons-Ruth, K., Alpern, L., & Prepacholi, B. (1993). Disorganised infant attachment classification and maternal psychosocial problems as predictors of hostile-aggressive behaviour in the preschool classroom. *Child Development, 64*(2), (pp. 572–585).

Lyons-Ruth, K., Easterbrooks, M., & Cibelli, C. (1997). Infant attachment strategies: infant mental lag, and maternal depressive symptoms: predictors of internalizing and externalizing problems at age 7. *Developmental Psychology, 33*(4), (pp. 681–692).

Mackerras, D. (2001). Birthweight changes in the pilot phase of the Strong Women Strong Babies Strong Culture Program. Australian and New Zealand *Journal of Public Health, 25*(1), (pp. 34–40).

Maluccio, A. (1998). Assessing Child Welfare Outcomes: the American perspective. *Children & Society, 12*, (pp. 161–168).

Mann, A., Harrell, A., & Hurt, M. (1977). *A review of Head Start research since 1969 and an annotated bibliography.* Washington D.C.: Social Research Group, The George Washington University.

Maori Health Committee. (1998). *Rangahau Hauora Maori. Maori Health Research Themes.*, [paper available at http://www.hrc.govt.nz/themes.htm. 19 pages]. Health Research Council of New Zealand [2001, 7 March].

Mardell, B. (1992). A practitioner's perspective on the implications of attachment theory for daycare professionals. *Child Study Journal, 22*(3), (pp. 201–229).

Marion, M. (1999). *Guidance of young children* (5 ed.). Upper Saddle River, NJ: Merrill.

Marshall, J., & Watt, P. (1999). *Child behaviour problems. a literature review of its size and nature and prevention interventions.* East Perth: Interagency Committee on Children's Futures.

Maslow, A. (1970). *Motivation and personality.* New York: Harper and Row.

Mason, V. (2001). *Mapping and certifying. Certification of Family Support programs.* Unpublished manuscript, Chicago, Illinois.

Matthews, J., & Hudson, A. (2001). Guidelines for evaluating parent training programs. *Family Relations, 50*(1), (pp. 77–86).

Matthews, S., & Sprey, J. (1984). The impact of divorce on grandparenthood: an exploratory study. *Gerontologist, 24*(1), (pp. 41–47).

Mattingly, J. (1998). Family to family: reconstructing foster care in the US. *Children & Society, 12*, (pp. 180–184).

Maxwell, G. (1995). Physical punishment in the home in New Zealand. *Australian Journal of Social Issues, 30*(3), (pp. 291–309).

McCain, M., & Mustard, J. (1999). *Reversing the real brain drain. Early Years Study. Final Report. Report presented to the Hon. Michael Harris, Premier of Ontario, Canada, February 16 1999.*, [Paper available at:

http://www.childsec.gov.on.ca/newsrel/apr2099.html.]. Ontario Children's Secretariat [2000, 1 July].

McCubbin, H., & Figley, C. (1983*). Coping with normative transitions*. (Vol. 1). New York: Brunner-Mazel.

McCubbin, H., McCubbin, M., Thompson, A., Han, S.-Y., & Allen, C. (1997). *Families under stress: what makes them resilient. 1997 American Association of Family and Consumer Sciences Commemorative Lecture.*, [paper available at http://www.cyfernet.org/research/resilient.html 13 pages]. Institute for the Study of Resiliency in Families [2001, 1 March].

McDonald, L., & Frey, H. (1999). Families and schools together: building relationships. *Juvenile Justice Bulletin, November,* 19 page downloaded.

McEachin, J., Smith, T., & Lovaas, O. (1993). Long-term outcome for children with autism who received early intensive behavioural treatment. *American Journal on Mental retardation, 97*, (pp. 359–372).

McGee, G., Morrier, M., & Daly, T. (1999). An incidental teaching approach to early intervention for toddlers with autism. *JASH, 24*(3), (pp. 133–146).

McGee, R., Partridge, F., Williams, S., & Silva, P. (1991). A twelve-year follow-up of preschool hyperactive children. *Journal of the American Academy of Child and Adolescent Psychiatry, 20*, (pp. 224–232).

McGrath, P. (2001). Trained volunteers for families coping with a child with a life-limiting condition. *Child & Family Social Work, 6*(1), (pp. 23–29).

McGurk, H. (1996). *Childcare in a caring society*. Opening address. Paper presented at the 5th Australian Family Research Conference, Brisbane.

McIntyre, J. (1995). *Achieving social rights and responsibility: towards a critical humanist approach to Community Development.* Melbourne: Community Quarterly.

McVeigh, P. (2000). RAGE project - Berry Street, Melbourne. Australian *Domestic & Family Violence Clearinghouse Newsletter, 5*(December), (pp. 2–3).

Meadow-Orlans, K. (1995). Parenting with a sensory or physical disability. In M. Bornstein (Ed.), *Handbook of parenting. Applied and practical parenting.* (Vol. 4, pp. 57–84). Mahwah, NJ: Lawrence Erlbaum Associates.

Meager, I., & Milgrom, J. (1996). Group treatment for postpartum depression: a pilot study. *Australian and New Zealand Journal of psychiatry, 30*(6), (pp. 852–860).

Meisels, S., & Shonkoff, J. (Eds.). (1990). *Handbook of early childhood intervention.* New York: Cambridge University Press.

Mertensmeyer, C., & Fine, M. (2000). ParentLink: a model of integration and support for parents. *Family Relations, 49*(3), (pp. 257–265).

Metcalfe, J., & Jacobs, W. (1998). Emotional memory. The effects of stress on 'cool' and 'hot' memory systems. *The Psychology of Learning and Motivation, 38*, (pp. 187–222).

Miller, D., & Jang, M. (1997). Children of alcoholics: a 20-year longitudinal study. *Social Work Research and Abstracts, 13*, (pp. 23–29).

Mills, S. (2001). What about fathers? *America's Family Support Magazine, 20*(1), (p. 7).

Ministries of Social Policy, Education and Health. (1997). *Strengthening Families Strategy. Report on outcome measures and Targets 1997.* (paper available at http:www//strengtheningfamilies.govt.nz). Wellington: Strengthening Families: Whakakahe Whanau.

Ministry of Social Policy. (1999). *Strengthening Families. Report on Cross-Sectoral Outcome Measures and Targets.* (paper available at http://www.dsw.govt.nz/). Wellington: Ministry of Social Policy.

Molgaard, V., Spoth, R., & Redmond, C. (2000). Competency training. The Strengthening Families Program: For parents and Youth 10-14. *Juvenile Justice Bulletin, August*, 12 downloaded.

Moon, L., Rahman, N., & Bhatia, K. (1998). *Australia's children: their health and well-being 1998*. Canberra: Australian Institute of Health and Welfare and the Commonwealth of Australia.

Moore, K. (1998). Oh brother! siblings need support. *TASH Newsletter, 24*(5), (pp. 25–27).

Morris, B. (1997). Is your family wrecking your career? (and vice versa). *Fortune, 135*(5), 7 pages downloaded.

Moss, P., Brophy, J., & Statham, J. (1992a). Parental involvement in playgroups. *Children & Society, 6*(4), (pp. 297–316).

Moss, P., Brophy, J., & Statham, J. (1992b). Poor relations in the preschool family: the funding of playgroups. *Journal of Education Policy, 7*(5), (pp. 471–491).

MostSignificantChanges. (2001). *The "Most significant changes" approach to participatory monitoring and evaluation.* A file repository and discussion forum. MostSignificantChanges [2001, 3 May].

Mukherjee, S. (1999*). Ethnicity and Crime.*, [paper available at http://www.aic.gov.au/publications/tandi/tandi117.html.]. Australian Institute of Criminology. Trends and issues in Crime and Criminal Justice Series, Number 117. [1999, 12 February].

Murphy, J., & Thomas, B. (2000). Developing social capital; a new role for business. In I. Winter (Ed.), *Social capital and public policy in Australia.* (pp. 136–164). Melbourne: Australian Institute of Family Studies.

Musil, C. (1998). Health, stress, coping and social support in grandmother caregivers. *Health Care for Women International, 19*, (pp. 441–455).

Myers, R. (1993). *Toward a fair start for children: programming for early childhood care and development in the developing world.*, [paper available at http://www.unesco.org/education/educprog/ecf/html/twfc/twfs.htm]. UNESCO [2001, 19 March].

Nahom, D., Richardson, M., Romer, L., & Porter, A. (2000). Family support and community guiding. Families in Society: *The Journal of Contemporary Human Services., 81*(6), 629 (006 pages downloaded).

Naidoo, R. (2000). The 'Third Way' to widening participation and maintaining quality in higher education: lessons from the United Kingdom. *Journal of Educational Enquiry, 1*(2), (pp. 24–38).

National Center of Fathers and Families. (2001). *The fathering indicators study. A tool for quantitative and qualitative analysis*. Philadelphia, PA: Graduate School of Education, University of Pennsylvania.

National Childcare Accreditation Council. (1993). *Putting children first. Quality improvement and accreditation system handbook*. Sydney: Commonwealth of Australia.

National Council for the International Year of the Family. (1994*). The Heart of the Matter. Families at the Centre of Public Policy*. Canberra, ACT: Australian Government Publishing Service.

National Crime Prevention. (1999). *Pathways to Prevention*. Canberra: National Crime Prevention, Commonwealth Attorney-General's Department.

National Crime Prevention. (2001a). Family Violence. *Crime Prevention Bulletin, Summer*, 1.

National Crime Prevention. (2001b). *Violence in indigenous communities*. Full report. Barton, ACT: Commonwealth of Australia.

National Family Caregivers Association. (1997*). Survey of members: A profile of Caregivers*, [paper available at http://nfcacares.org/survey.html]. National Family Caregivers Association [2001, 25 May].

National Inquiry into the Separation of Aboriginal and Torres Strait Islander Children from their Families. (1997). *Bringing them Home.* Sydney: Human Rights and Equal Opportunity Commission, Commonwealth of Australia.

National Research Council and Institute of Medicine. (2000). *From Neurons to neighbourhoods: the Science of Early Childhood Development.* Washington D.C.: National Academy Press.

National Respite Coalition. (1998). *Respite: Key component of a comprehensive, inclusive childcare strategy.*, [paper available at http://www.chtop.com/key.htm]. National Respite Coalition [2001, 25 May].

New Zealand Government. (1998). *Towards a Code of Social and Family Responsibility. He Kaupapa Kawenga Whanau, Kawenga Hapori.* Public Discussion Document. Wellington: Department of Social Welfare.

Newburn, T. (2001). What do we mean by evaluation? *Children & Society, 15,* (pp. 5–13).

Newell, S. (1992). The myth and destructiveness of equal opportunities: the con. *Personnel Review, 21*(4), (pp. 37–48).

Newman, J. (1987). Learning to teach by uncovering our assumptions. *Language Arts, 64*(7), (pp. 727–737).

Newman, J. (1998). Action Research: exploring the tensions of teaching. In J. Newman (Ed.), *Tensions of teaching: beyond tips to critical reflection.* (pp. 1–24). Toronto/New York: Canadian Scholars' press/Teachers College Press.

Newman, J. (2000). Action research: a brief overview. Forum: Qualitative *Social Research, 1*(1), 5 pages downloaded.

NICHD Early Childcare Research Network. (1998). Early childcare and self control. Compliance and problem behaviour at twenty-four and thirty-six months. *Child Development, 69*(4), (pp. 1145–1170).

Nicholson, P. (1998). *Post-natal depression: psychology, science and the transition to motherhood.* London: Routledge.

Norton, D. (1994). Education for professionals in family support. In S. Kagan & B. Weissbourd (Eds.), *Putting Families first.* (pp. 401–440). San Francisco: Jossey-Bass.

Oberhuemer, P. (1998). A European perspective on early years training. In L. Abbott & G. Pugh (Eds.), *Training to work in the early years. Developing the climbing frame.* (pp. 136–146). Buckingham: Open University Press.

O'Brien, J. (2001). Planned respite care: hope for families under pressure. *Australian Journal of social issues, 36*(1), (p. 51).

O'Connor, P. (1999). *Parents supporting parents: an evaluative report on the National Parent Support Programme Mid-West.* Limerick: Mid-Western Health Board, Centre for Governance and Public Management.

Olds, D., Eckenrode, J., & Henderson, C. (1997). Long-term effects of home visitation on maternal life course, child abuse and neglect, and children's arrests: fifteen year follow-up of a randomised trial. *Journal of the American Medical Association, 278*(8), (pp. 637–643).

Olds, D., Henderson, C., & Kitzman, H. (1994). Does prenatal and infancy nurse home visitation have enduring effects on qualities of parental caregiving and child health at 25 to 50 months of life? *Pediatrics, 93*(1), (pp. 89–98).

Olds, D., Hill, P., & Rumsey, E. (1998). Prenatal and early childhood nurse home visitation. *Juvenile Justice Bulletin, November,* 7 page downloaded.

O'Loughlin, M. (1989). *The influence of teachers' beliefs about knowledge, teaching and learning on their pedagogy: a constructivist reconceptualisation and research agenda for teacher education.*: ERIC Document Number ED339679.

Olweus, D. (1994). Bullying at school. Basic facts and an effective intervention programme. *Promotion and Education, 1*(4), (pp. 27–31, 48).

Organisation for Economic Co-operation and Development. (2001). *The well-being of nations: the role of human and social capital.* Paris: Organisation for Economic Co-operation and Development.

Ortega, D. (2001). Parenting efficacy, aggressive parenting and cultural connections. *Child & Family Social Work, 6*(1), (pp. 47–57).

Osbourne, B. (2001). An overview of research. Informing teaching students from different cultural backgrounds. In B. Osbourne (Ed.), *Teaching, diversity and democracy* (pp. 1–50). Altona, Vic: Common Ground.

Osofsky, J. (1997). Children and youth violence: an overview of the issues. In J. Osofsky (Ed.), *Children in a violent society* (pp. 3–8). New York: The Guilford Press.

Parker, F., Piotrkowski, C., & Peay, L. (1987). Head Start as a social support for mothers: the psychological benefits of involvement. *American Journal of Orthopsychiatry, 57*(2), (pp. 220–233).

Parker, L., & Ireland, L. (2000). The 'Savvy Schools' Project, Queensland. *Australian Domestic & Family Violence Clearinghouse Newsletter, 3*(July), 6.

Parker, R. (1998). Reflections on the assessment of outcomes in childcare. *Children & Society, 12*, (pp. 192–201).

Parker, R. (1999). Re-partnering following relationship breakdown. *Family Matters, 53*(Winter), (pp. 39–43).

Patterson, G., Reid, J., & Dishion, T. (1992). *Antisocial boys.* Eugene, OR: Castalia Publishing.

Patton, M. (1986). *Utilization-focused evaluation.* Newbury Park, CA: Sage.

Patton, M., & Jones, E. (1997). CHILD-PACs make for happy families. *Teaching Exceptional Children, 29*(4), (pp. 62–63).

Pecora, P. (1991). Family-based and intensive family preservation services: a select literature review. In M. Fraser & P. Pecora & D. Haapala (Eds.), *Families in crisis. The impact of intensive family preservation services.* (pp. 17–47). New York: Aldine De Gruyter.

Pedro-Carroll, J., & Cowen, E. (1985). The children of divorce intervention program: an investigation of the efficacy of a school-based prevention programme. *Journal of Consulting and Clinical Psychology, 53*(5), (pp. 603–611).

Peisher, A., Sewell, M., & Kirk, R. (2001). Understanding and carrying out outcome accountability. *Family Support, 20*(3), (pp. 49–52).

Peisner-Feinberg, E., Burchinal, M., Clifford, R., Culkin, A., Howes, C., Kagan, S., Yazejian, N., Byler, P., Rustici, J., & Zelazo, J. (2000). *The children of the cost, quality and outcomes study go to school: Technical Report.* Chapel Hill: University of North Carolina, Frank Porter Graham Child Development Center.

Pence, A. (2001). Through the looking glass. Cross-cultural early childhood education. *Every Child, 7*(3), (pp. 8–9).

Pence, E., & Paymor, M. (1993). The Duluth Domestic Abuse Intervention Project. In Women's Issues and Social Empowerment (Ed.), *Domestic Violence Information Manual.* (pp. 9 pages downloaded.). Melbourne, Vic: Women's Issues and Social Empowerment and Springer Publishing Company.

Perry, B. (1997). Incubated in terror: neurodevelopmental factors in the "Cycle of violence". In J. Osofsky (Ed.), *Children in a violent society* (pp. 124–149). New York: The Guilford Press.

Petr, C. (1998). *Social work with children and their families. Pragmatic foundations.* New York: Oxford University Press.

Pew Charitable Trusts. (2001). *Making the Grade: The influence of religion upon the academic performance of youth in disadvantaged communities.* (Grantee Publication). Philadelphia, PA: Pew Charitable Trusts.

Pfannenstiel, J., & Seltzer, D. (1989). New Parents as Teachers: evaluation of an early parent education program. *Early Childhood Research Quarterly, 4,* (pp. 1–18).

Pinderhughes, E., Dodge, K., Bates, J., Pettit, G., & Zelli, A. (2000). Discipline responses: influence of parents' socioeconomic status, ethnicity, beliefs about parenting, stress, and cognitive-emotional processes. *Journal of Family Psychology, 14*(3), (pp. 380–400).

Pinkerton, J., Higgins, K., & Devine, P. (2000). *Family support - linking evaluation to policy analysis.* Aldershot: Ashgate.

Pithouse, A., & Holland, S. (1999). Open access family centres and their users; positive results, some doubts and new departures. *Children & Society, 13,* (pp. 167–178).

Pithouse, A., & Tasiran, A. (2000). Local authority family centre intervention: a statistical exploration of services as family support or family control. *Child & Family Social Work, 5*(2), (pp. 129–141).

Pithouse, A., Lindsell, S., & Cheung. (1998*). Family support and family centres services.* Aldershot: Ashgate.

Pleck, J. (1983). Husband's paid work and family roles: current research issues. In H. Lopata & J. Pleck (Eds.), *Families and jobs: a research annual: Research in the interweave of social roles.* (Vol. 3, pp. 231–333). Greenwich, CT: JAI Press.

Pomerantz, P., Pomerantz, D., & Colca, L. (1990). A case study: service delivery and parents with disabilities. *Child Welfare, 69*(1), 65–73.

Pouncy, H. (2000). Directions in job training strategies for the disadvantaged. In S. Danziger & J. Waldfogel (Eds.), *Securing the future. Investing in children from birth to college.* (pp. 254–282). New York: Russell Sage Foundation.

Powell, J. (1998). The pathways to professionalism project: making an Early Childhood Studies degree accessible. In L. Abbott & G. Pugh (Eds.), *Training to work in the early years. Developing the climbing frame.* (pp. 109–119). Philadelphia, PA: Open University Press.

Preparatory Committee for the Special Session of the General Assembly on Children. (2001). *A world fit for children. Revised draft outcome document.* (Report prepared for the Third Substantive session 11–15 June 2001 A/AC.256/CRP.6/Rev1 0129359). New York: United Nations.

Press, F., & Hayes, A. (2001). *OECD Thematic Review of Early Childhood Education and Care Policy. Australian Background Report.* Canberra, ACT: Department of Education, Training and Youth Affairs.

Prilleltensky, I., & Nelson, G. (2000). Promoting child and family wellness: priorities for psychological and social interventions. *Journal of Community and Applied Social Psychology, 10,* (pp. 85–105).

Prior, M. (1992). Development of temperament. In P. Heaven (Ed.), *Lifespan Development* (pp. 94–118). Sydney: Harcourt Brace Jovanovich.

Prior, M., Smart, D., Sanson, A., & Oberklaid, F. (1993). Sex differences in psychological adjustment from infancy to eight years. *Journal of the American Academy of Child and Adolescent Psychiatry, 32,* (pp. 291–305).

Public Policy Research Centre. (1988). *Attitudes towards domestic violence in Australia.* Canberra: Australian Government Office of the Status of Women.

Pugh, G., De'Ath, E., & Smith, C. (1994). *Confident parents, confident children.* London: National Children's Bureau.

Putnam, R. (1996). The strange disappearance of Civic America. *Policy, Autumn,* (pp. 3–15).

Raine, A., Reynolds, C., Venables, P., Mednick, S., & Farrington, D. (1998). Fearlessness, stimulation-seeking, and large body size at age 3 years, as early predispositions to childhood aggression at age 11 years. *Archives of General Psychiatry, 55*(8), (pp. 745–751).

Raine, A., Venables, P., & Williams, M. (1995). High autonomic arousal and electrodermaal orienting at age 15 years as oritective factors against criminal behaviour at age 29 years. *American Journal of Psychiatry, 152*(11), (pp. 1595–1600).

Ramey, C., & Landesman Ramey, S. (1998). Prevention of intellectual disabilities: early intervention to improve cognitive development. *Preventive Medicine, 27*(2), (pp. 224–232).

Ramey, C., Campbell, F., Burchinel, M., Skinner, M., Gardner, D., & Ramey, S. (2000). Persistent effects of early childhood on high-risk children and their mothers. *Applied Developmental Science Education, 4*(1), (pp. 2–14).

Ramey, S., & Ramey, C. (2000). Early childhood experiences and developmental competence. In S. Danziger & J. Waldfogel (Eds.), *Securing the future. Investing in children from birth to college* (pp. 122–150). New York: Russell Sage Foundation.

Ramey, S., & Ramey, C. (2000). Early childhood experiences and developmental competence. In S. Danziger & J. Waldfogel (Eds.), *Securing the future. Investing in children from birth to college* (pp. 122–150). New York: Russell Sage Foundation.

Ramirez Barranti, C. (1985). The grandparent/grandchild relationship: family resource in an era of voluntary bonds. Family Relations: *Journal of Applied Family and Child Studies, 34*(3), (pp. 343–352).

Rapp, C. (1998). *The strengths model.* New York: Oxford University Press.

Redmond, G. (2000). *Children in large families: disadvantaged or just different?* Unpublished manuscript, Syracuse, NY: Luxembourg Income Study Working Paper No 225, Maxwell School of Citizenship and Public Affairs, Syracuse University.

Resiliency in Action. (2001, 03/26/2001). *Resiliency in Action. Bouncing back from Adversity: ideas for youth, families and communities.,* [paper available at http://www.resiliency.com 2 pages]. Resiliency in Action [2001, 3 March].

Reynolds, A. (1994). Effects of a preschool plus follow-on intervention for children at risk. *Developmental Psychology, 30*(6), (pp. 787–804).

Rice, J. (2001). Poverty, welfare and patriarchy: how macro-level changes in social policy can help low-income women. *Journal of Social Issues, 57*(2), (pp. 355–374).

Rigby, K. (1996). *Bullying in schools and what to do about it.* Melbourne: Australian Council for Educational Research.

Ritchie, I. (1996). *A new approach. the need for a new approach to our society which includes a universal basic Income.* Paper presented at the 3rd national Conference on Unemployment, Queensland University of Technology, Brisbane, 13–15 June.

Robbins, M., & Szaporcznik, J. (2000). Brief Strategic Family Therapy. *Juvenile Justice Bulletin, April,* 11 pages downloaded.

Roberts, R., Wasik, B., Casto, G., & Ramey, C. (1991). Family support in the home. Programs, policy and social change. *American Psychologist, 46*(2), (pp. 121–137).

Roe, K., Minkler, M., Saunders, F., & Thomson, G. (1996). Health of grandmothers raising grandchildren of the crack cocaine epidemic. *Medical Care, 34,* (pp. 1072–1084).

Rosenau, P. (1992). *Post-modernism and the Social Sciences: insights, inroads and intrusions*. Princeton: Princeton University Press.

Rosenau, V. (1990). *A child's birthright; to live in a family. A vicarious visit to Maccomb-Oakland Regional Centre. Mt Clemens, Michigan*. Syracuse: Center on Human Policy.

Saleebey, D. (1992). Introduction: Power in the people. In D. Saleebey (Ed.), *The strengths perspective in social work practice*. (pp. 3–17). White Plains, NY: Longman.

Salmond, C., & Crampton, P. (2000). Deprivation and Health. In P. Howden-Chapman & M. Tobias (Eds.), *Social inequalities in Health: New Zealand 1999*. (pp. 9–64). Wellington: Ministry of Health.

Sanson, A., & Wise, S. (2001). Children and parenting. The past one hundred years. *Family Matters, 60*(Spring/Summer), (pp. 36–45).

Sarantakos, S. (1996). *Modern Families. An Australian text*. South Melbourne: Macmillan Education Australia PTY LTD.

Sarantakos, S. (1998). *Social research* (2 ed.). South Melbourne: MacMillan Education Australia PTY LTD.

Scarpa, A., & Raine, A. (1997). Psychophysiology of anger and violent behaviour. *Psychiatric Clinics of North America, 20*(2), (pp. 375–394).

Schnoes, C., Murphy-Berman, V., & Chambers, J. (2000). Empowerment evaluation applied: experiences, analysis and recommendations from a case study. *American Journal of Evaluation, 21*(1), (pp. 53–64).

Schorr, E. (1995). Developing communality: family-centered programs to improve children's health and well-being. *Bulletin of the New York Academy of Medicine, 72*(2), (pp. 413–442).

Schorr, L. (1997). *Common Purpose. Strengthening families and neighbourhoods to rebuild America*. New York: Anchor Books.

Schweinhart, L., & Weikart, D. (1993). Success by empowerment: the High/Scope Perry Preschool Study through Age 27. *Young Children, 49*(1), (pp. 54–58).

Schweinhart, L., Barnes, H., & Weikart, D. (1993). *Significant benefits: the High/Scope Perry preschool Study through age twenty-seven*. Ypsilanti, Mich: High Scope Press.

Schweinhart, L., Weikart, D., & Larner, M. (1986). Consequences of three preschool curriculum models through age 15. *Early Childhood Research Quarterly, 1*, (pp. 15–45).

Scott, D. (2001). Building communities that strengthen families. *Family Matters, 58*(Autumn), (pp.76–79).

Scott, E. (2001/2001). Up to standard. Developing practice. *The child, youth and family work journal, 2* (Summer), (pp. 34–38).

Scott, S., Jackson, S., & Backett-Milburn, K. (2000). The impact of risk and parental risk anxiety on the everyday worlds of children. *Children 5–16 Research Briefing, 19* (December), 4 downloaded.

Scott, S., Knapp, M., Henderson, J., & Maughan, B. (2001). Financial cost of social exclusion: follow up study of antisocial children into adulthood. *British Medical Journal, 323* (28 July), (pp. 1–5).

Scott, S., Spender, Q., Dolan, M., Jacobs, B., & Aspland, H. (2001). Multicentre controlled trial of parenting groups for childhood antisocial behaviour in clinical practice. *British Medical Journal, 323* (28 July), (pp. 1–7).

Secret, M., Jordan, A., & Ford, J. (1999). Empowerment evaluation as a social work strategy. *Health and Social Work, 24*(2), (pp. 120–128).

Seligman, M., & Darling, R. (1989). *Ordinary families, special children. A systems approach to childhood disability*. New York: The Guilford Press.

Sexon, S., & Madan-Swain, A. (1988). School re-entry for the child with chronic illness. *Journal of Learning Disabilities, 26*(2), (pp. 115–125, 137).

Seyler, D., Monroe, P., & Garand, J. (1995). Balancing work and family: the role of employer-supported childcare benefits. *Journal of Family Issues, 16*(2), (pp. 170–193).

Shaver, S. (2001). From the Director. Social Policy Research Centre Newsletter, 79, (pp. 3–5).

Shore, R. (1997). *Rethinking the Brain: New Insights into Early Development. New Frontiers for Research. Policy and Practice*, University of Chicago: Families & Work Institute.

Showell, W., & White, J. (1990). In-home and in-office intensive family services. *Prevention Report, 6*, (pp. 10).

Sidey, M. (2001). *Creating New Choices: a violence prevention project for schools in Australia.* (Innodata Monographs Number 9). Geneva: International Bureau of Education, UNESCO.

Silberberg, S. (2001). Searching for family resilience. *Family Matters, 58*(Autumn), (pp. 52–57).

Silburn, S., Zubrick, S., Garton, A., Gurrin, L., Burton, P., Dalby, R., Carlton, J., Shepherd, C., & Lawrence, D. (1996). *Western Australian Child Health Survey: family and community health.* Perth, WA: Australian Bureau of Statistics, Catalogue No 4304.5 and the TVW Telethon Institute for Child Health Research.

Silliman, B. (2001). 1994 *Resiliency Research Review: conceptual and research foundations.*, [paper available at http://www.cyfernet.org/research/resilreview.html 10 pages]. University of Wyoming [2001, 1 March].

Silva, P., McGee, R., & Williams, S. (1983). Developmental language delay from three to seven years and its significance for low intelligence and reading difficulties at age seven. *Developmental Medicine and Child Neurology, 29*, (pp. 630–640).

Sims, M. (1997). *Including all children and families. A practical guide to using inclusion for meeting diverse and different care and development needs in Children's Service settings.* Perth: Praxis Education.

Sims, M. (in review). *Employment outcomes for children's services graduates.* paper submitted to the Journal of Australian Research into Early Childhood Education.

Sims, M. (in review-a). *Making Values Matter: training in difference and diversity.* paper submitted to the Journal of Australian Research in Early Childhood Education.

Sims, M. (in review-b). *Value-based education for pre-service students in Children and Family Studies.* paper submitted to the Journal of Further and Higher Education.

Sims, M., & Bridgman, G. (1984). Evaluation of progress using the context input process and product model. *Child: care, health and development., 10*, (pp. 359–379).

Sims, M., & Hutchins, T. (1996). The many faces of childcare: roles and functions. *Australian Journal of Early Childhood, 21*(1), (pp. 21–26).

Sims, M., & Hutchins, T. (1999). Positive transitions. *Australian Journal of Early Childhood, 24*(3), (pp. 12–16).

Sims, M., & Hutchins, T. (2001). Transition to childcare for children from culturally and linguistically diverse backgrounds. *Australian Journal of Early Childhood, 26*(3), (pp. 7–11).

Sims, M., & Omaji, A. (1999). Migration and Parenting. *Journal of Family Studies, 5*(1), (pp. 84–96).

Sims, M., Hayden, J., Palmer, G., & Hutchins, T. (2000). Working in early childhood settings with children who have experienced refugee or war-related trauma. *Australian Journal of Early Childhood, 25*(4), (pp. 41–46).

Sims, M., Omaji, P., O'Connor, M., & Omaji, M. (in review). *Bridging two worlds: young African migrants' settlement experiences.* Australian Journal of Social Issues.

Sinclair, I., & Gibbs, I. (1998). *Children's homes. A study in diversity.* Chichester: Wiley.

Smale, G. (1995). Integrating community and individual practice: a new paradigm for practice. In P. Adams & K. Nelson (Eds.), *Reinventing Human Services. Community and family-based practice.* (pp. 59–85). New York: Aldine de Gruyter.

Smith, C. (1997). *Developing parenting programs.* London: National Children's Bureau.

Smith, E., Lowrie, T., Hill, D., Bush, A., & Lobegeier, J. (1997). *Making a difference? How competency-based training has changed teaching and learning.* Wagga Wagga, NSW: Charles Sturt University.

Smith, T. (1999). Neighbourhood and preventive strategies with children and families: what works? *Children & Society, 13,* (pp. 265–277).

Sohng, S. (1995). *Participatory Research and community organising.,* [paper available at http://www.interweb-tech.com/nsmnet/docs/sohng.htm 13 pages]. New Social Movement Network [2001, 7 May].

Stacey, J. (1996). *In the name of the family. rethinking family values in the Postmodern age.* Boston: Beacon Press.

Stamp, G., Williams, A., & Crowther, C. (1995). Evaluation of antenatal and postnatal support to overcome postnatal depression: a randomised, controlled trial. *Birth, 22*(3), (pp. 138–143).

Stanley, F. (2001). Towards a national partnership for developmental health and wellbeing. *Family Matters, 58*(Autumn), (pp. 65–69).

Starr, E. (2001). *Schools as Communities.,* [paper available at http://communitybuilders.nsw.gov.au/building_stronger/safer/schooly.html]. Communitybuilders.nsw [2001, 20 June].

Statham, J., & Brophy, J. (1991). The role of playgroups as a service for preschool children. *Early Child Development and Care, 74,* (pp. 39–60).

Statistics New Zealand. Te Tari Tatau. (1996a). *Highlights of Households from the 1996 Census,* [paper available from http://www.stats.gov.nz]. Statistics New Zealand. Te Tari Tatau [2001, 12 March].

Statistics New Zealand. Te Tari Tatau. (1996b). *Income highlights from the 1996 Census.,* [paper available from http://www.stats.gov.nz]. Statistics New Zealand. Te Tari Tatau [2001, 12 March].

Statistics New Zealand. Te Tari Tatau. (1998). *Highlights from the New Zealand Childcare survey 1998.,* [paper available at http://www.stats.gov.nz. 2 pages.]. Statistics New Zealand. Te Tari Tatau. [2001, 12 March].

Statistics New Zealand: Te Tari Tatua. (1999*). Vital Statistics June 1999 quarter.,* [paper available at http://www.stats.gov.nz]. Statistics New Zealand: Te Tari Tatua [2001, 12 March].

Statten, H., & Klackenberg-Larsson, I. (1993). Early language and intelligence development and their relationship with future criminal behaviour. *Journal of Abnormal Psychology, 102,* (pp. 369–378).

Stattin, H., & Kerr, M. (2000). Parental monitoring: a reinterpretation. *Child Development, 71*(4), (pp. 1072–1085).

Steele, H., Steele, M., & Fonagy, P. (1996). Associations among attachment classifications of mothers, fathers, and their infants. *Child Development, 67,* (pp. 541–555).

Steele, L. (2000). The day fostering scheme: a service for children in need and their parents. *Child & Family Social Work, 5*(4), (pp. 317–325).

Stehlik, D. (1993). *Untying the knot. A socialist-feminist analysis of the social construction of care*. Perth, WA: Centre for the Development of Human Resources.

Stein, A., Gath, D., Bucher, J., & Bond, A. (1991). The relationship between post-natal depression and mother-child interaction. British *Journal of Psychiatry, 158*, (pp. 46–52).

Sterpini, D. (1993). *Playgroups as an extended family network*. Paper presented at the Forth Australian Family Research Conference, Manly, NSW.

Stevenson, O. (1998). *Neglected children: issues and dilemmas*. Oxford: Blackwell.

Stewart-Weeks, M. (2000). Trick or treat? Social capital, leadership and the new public policy. In I. Winter (Ed.), *Social capital and public policy in Australia*. (pp. 276–309). Melbourne: Australian Institute of Family Studies.

Stott, F., & Musick, J. (1994). Supporting the family support worker. In S. Kagan & B. Weissbourd (Eds.), *Putting families first*. (pp. 189–215). San Francisco: Jossey-Bass.

Strauss, J. (2001). Hard data shows family support works. Long term study brings long awaited results. *Family Support, 20*(2), (pp. 9–13).

Stufflebeam, D. (1968). Towards a science of educational evaluation. *Educational Technology, 8,* (pp. 5–12).

Stufflebeam, D. (1981). *Standards for evaluation of educational programs, projects and materials*. New York: McGraw-Hill.

Sullivan, W. (1992). Reconsidering the environment as a helping resource. In D. Saleebey (Ed.), *The strengths perspective in social work practice* (pp. 148–157). White Plains, NY: Longman.

Swan, W. (1999). Is the Australian family becoming an endangered species? *Family Matters, 54*(Spring/Summer), (pp. 42–51).

Sylva, K., & Evans, E. (1999). Preventing failure at school. *Children & Society, 13*, (pp. 278–286).

Szikla, C. (1995). Evaluation of the "surviving Together" support group for women and children (women's group). In Women's Issues and Social Empowerment (Ed.), *Domestic Violence Information Manual*. (pp. 11 pages downloaded). Melbourne: Women's Issues and Social Empowerment.

Taskforce on Families in Western Australia. (1995). *W.A. families. Our future*. Perth, WA: Department of Community Development.

Tasman Enterprises. (2001). *Enhancing Australia's capacity to deliver developmentally appropriate children's services*. Carlton South, Vic: Health Employees Superannuation Trust Australia.

Taylor, S., Knoll, J., Lehr, S., & Walker, P. (1989). Families for all children: value-based services for children with disabilities and their families. In G. Singer & L. Irvin (Eds.), *Support for caregiving families. Enabling positive adaptation to disability*. (pp. 41–54). Baltimore: Paul H Brookes.

Teather, S., Evans, L., & Sims, M. (1997). Maintenance of mother-child relationship by incarcerated women. *Early Child Development and Care, 131*, (pp. 65–75).

Temple, J., Reynolds, A., & Miedel, W. (2000). Can early intervention prevent high school dropout?: Evidence from the Chicago Child-Parent Centres. *Urban Education, 35*(1), (pp. 31–56).

The NICHD Early Childcare Research Network. (2001). *Early Childcare and Children's Development Prior to School Entry*. Paper presented at the Society for Research on Child Development Biennial Meeting April, Tampa, Florida.

The Response Analysis Team. (1998). *Towards a code of social and family responsibility. The response report*. Wellington: Ministry of Social Policy.

Thomas, A., & Chess, S. (1977). Temperament and development. New York: Brunner/Mazel.

Thomas, J., Sperry, L., & Yarbrough, M. (2000). Grandparents as parents: research findings and policy recommendations. *Child Psychiatry and Human Development, 31*(1), (pp. 3–22).

Thomas, R. (1988). *Care of dying children and their families*. Birmingham: National Association of Health Authorities.

Thompson, C., Beauvais, L., & Lyness, K. (1999). When work-family benefits are not enough: the influence of work-family culture on benefit utilisation, organisational attachment and work-family conflict. *Journal of Vocational Behaviour, 54*(3), (pp. 392–415).

Thompson, L., Lobb, C., Elling, R., Herman, S., Jurkiewicz, T., & Hulleza, C. (1997). Pathways to family empowerment: effects of family-centred delivery of early intervention services. *Exceptional Children, 64*(1), (pp. 99–113).

Thompson, R. (1998). Early sociopersonality development. In N. Eisenberg (Ed.), *Handbook of child psychology: Social, emotional and personality development* (5 ed., Vol. 3, (pp. 25–104). New York: Wiley.

Thompson, R., Ruma, P., Schuchmann, L., & Burke, R. (1996). A cost-effectiveness evaluation of parent training. *Journal of Child and Family Studies, 5*(4), (pp. 415–429).

Thurtle, V. (1995). Post-natal depression: the relevance of sociological approaches. *Journal of Advanced Nursing, 22*(3), (pp. 416–424).

Tinsley, B., & Parke, R. (1987). Grandparents as interactive and social support agents for families with young infants. *International Journal of Aging and Human Development, 25*(4), (pp. 259–277).

Tomison, A. (1998). *Valuing parent education. A cornerstone of child abuse prevention.* (Child Abuse Prevention Issues Paper). Melbourne: National Child Protection Clearinghouse, Australian Institute of Family Studies.

Tomison, A. (2001). A history of child protection. *Family Matters, 60*(Spring/Summer), (pp. 46–57).

Tronick, E. (1989). Emotions and emotional communication in infants. *American Psychologist, 44,* (pp. 112–119).

Tsey, K., & Every, A. (2000). Evaluating Aboriginal empowerment programme: the case of family wellbeing. *Australian and New Zealand Journal of Public Health, 24*(5), (pp. 509–514).

Turnell, A., & Edwards, S. (1999). *Signs of Safety. A solution and safety oriented approach to child protection.* New York: W. W. Norton and Company.

Turner, L. (2001). Skip: a grandmother's solution is a community solution. *America's Family Support Magasine, 20*(1), (pp. 32–33).

Turner, P., & Zigler, E. (1987). *Parents and day care: the search for an alliance.* (ERIC Document ED 300 123).

Turney, D. (2000). The feminizing of neglect. *Child & Family Social Work, 5*(1), (pp. 47–56).

Twenge, J. (2000). The Age of Anxiety? Birth cohort change in anxiety and neuroticism, 1953–1993. *Journal of Personality and Social Psychology, 79*(6), (pp. 1007–1021).

UNICEF. (2001). *Say Yes for Children.*, [electronic resource available at http://www.unicef.org/say_yes/imperitives.htm]. UNICEF [2001, 20 June].

United Nations. (1959). *Declaration of the Rights of the Child. Proclaimed by General Assembly resolution 1386(XIV) of 20 November 1959.*, [paper available at http://unhchr.ch/html/menu3/b/25.htm 3 pages.]. Office of the United Nations high Commissioner for Human Rights, Geneva, Switzerland. [2001, 20 March].

United Nations. (1989). *Convention on the Rights of the Child. Adopted and opened for signature, ratification and accession by General Assembly resolution 44/25 of 20 November 1989, entry into force 2 September 1990, in accordance with article 49.,* [paper available at http://www.ungchr.ch/html/menu3/b/k2crc.htm 16 pages.]. Office of the United Nations High Commissioner for Human Rights, Geneva, Switzerland. [2001, 20 March].

United States Congress. (2000). *Early childhood programs for low-income families : availability and impact.* (Hearing before the Subcommittee on Children and Families of the Committee on Health, Education, Labor, and Pensions, United States Senate, One Hundred Sixth Congress, second session). Washington, D.C.: Senate. Committee on Health, Education, Labor, and Pensions. Subcommittee on Children and Families.

Valentine, G., & Holloway, S. (1999). Cyberkids: children's social networks, 'virtual communities' and on-line spaces. *Children 5–16 Research briefing, 2*(October), 4 pages downloaded.

van den Boom, D. (1994). The influence of temperament and mothering on attachment and exploration: an experimental manipulation of sensitive responsiveness among lower class mothers with irritable infants. *Child Development, 65,* (pp. 1457–1477).

Vandell, D. (2001). *Early childcare and children's development prior to school entry. NICHD Early Childcare Research Network.* Paper presented at the Biennial Meeting, Tampa, FL.

Venkatraman, R. (2000). Building safer communities—a pilot project on early intervention in primary schools. *Australian Domestic & Family Violence Clearninghouse Newsletter, 4*(September), (pp. 5–6).

Viruru, R. (2001). Colonised through language; the case of early childhood education. *Contemporary Issues in Early Childhood, 2*(1), (pp. 31–47).

Voight, J., Hans, S., & Bernstein, V. (1996). Support networks of adolescent mothers: effects on parenting experience and behaviour. *Infant Mental Health Journal, 17*(1), (pp. 58–73).

Voigt, L., & Tregeagle, S. (1996). Buy Australian: a local family preservation success. *Children Australia., 21*(1), (pp. 27–30).

Vygotsky, L. (1962). *Thought and knowledge* (E. V. Hanfmann, G, Trans.). Cambridge, Mass: MIT Press.

WACOSS. (2001). More Australians living in poverty. *WACOSS E-News, Thursday 13 December,* 2 pages downloaded.

Wadsworth, Y. (1991). *Everyday evaluation on the run.* Melbourne: Action Research Issues Association Inc.

Waldegrave, C., Frater, P., & Stephens, B. (1997). An overview of research on poverty in New Zealand. *New Zealand Sociology, 12*(2), (pp. 213–259).

Waldegrave, C., Stephens, B., & Frater, P. (1996). Most recent findings on the New Zealand Poverty Measurement Project. *Social Work Review, 8*(3), (pp. 22–24).

Walker, J. (1997*). Estimates of the cost of crime in Australia in 1996. Trends and issues in crime and criminal justice paper number 72.,* [paper available at http://www.aic.gov.au/publications/tandi/tandi72.html.]. Australian Institute of Criminology [1999, 12 February].

Wamboldt, M., & Wamboldt, F. (2000). Role of the family in the onset and outcome of childhood disorders: selected research findings. *Journal of the American Academy of Child and Adolescent Psychiatry, 30*(10), (pp. 1212–1219).

Wasik, B., Bryant, D., & Lyons, C. (1990*). Home visiting. Procedures for helping families.* Newbury Park, CA: Sage.

Weatherburn, D., & Lind, B. (1998). *Poverty, parenting, peers and crime-prone neighbourhoods.*, [paper available at http://www.aic.gov.au/publications/tandi/tandi85.html. 8 pages]. Australian Institute of Criminology. Trends and Issues in Criminal Justice Series Number 85. [2001, 3 March].

Weiler, K. (1988). *Women teaching for change: gender, class and power.* Massachusetts: Bergin and Garvey.

Weiss, C. (1995). Nothing as practical as good theory: exploring theory-based evaluation for comprehensive community initiatives for children and families. In J. Connell & A. Kubisch & L. Schorr & C. Weiss (Eds.), *New approaches to evaluating community initiatives.* (Vol. 1 Concepts, Methods, and Contexts., pp. 19 pages downloaded.). Washington D.C.: The Aspen Institute.

Wellman, B. (1979). The community question: the intimate networks of East Yonkers. *American Journal of Sociology, 84*, (pp. 1201–1231).

Westman, J. (1994). *Licensing parents. Can we prevent child abuse and neglect?* New York: Insight Books, Plenum Press.

Weston, R., & Hughes, J. (1999). Family forms—family wellbeing. *Family Matters, 53*(Winter), (pp. 14–20).

Weston, R., & Smyth, B. (2000). Financial living standards after divorce. *Family Matters, 55*(Autumn), (pp. 10–15).

Whitehead, B. (1998). Parent support, not childcare. *New Perspectives Quarterly, 15*(3), (pp. 73–78).

Wigfall, V., & Moss, P. (2000). *"One-stop shopping": meeting diverse family needs in the inner city?* (paper presented at the 10th European Early Childhood Education Research Association Conference, London. August 29–September 1, 2000 ED 445 826). London: Eric Document.

Wilkinson, R. (1999a). Health, hierarchy and social anxiety. In N. Adler & M. Marmot & B. McEwen & J. Stewart (Eds.), *Socioeconomic status and health in industrialised nations: social, psychological and biological pathways.* (Vol. 896), (pp. 48–63): Annals of the New York Academy of Science.

Wilkinson, R. (1999b). Income inequality, social cohesion and health: clarifying the theory. A reply to Muntaner and Lynch. *International Journal of Health Services, 29*(3), (pp. 525–543).

Williams, A., Silburn, S., & Zubrick, S. (1998). *The Perth Positive Parenting Demonstration Project: preparing families for challenging futures.* Paper presented at the 6th Australian Institute of Family Studies Conference, Melbourne, Vic.

Williamson, L. (1997). Parents as teachers of children program (PATCH). *Professional School Counselling, 1*(2), (pp. 7–12).

Wilson, J. (2000). *Children as victims.* (NCJ 180753). Washington DC: Office of Juvenile Justice and Delinquency Prevention.

Winter, I. (2000). Major themes and debates in the social capital literature: the Australian connection. In I. Winter (Ed.), *Social capital and public policy in Australia.* (pp. 17–42). Melbourne: Australian Institute of Family Studies.

Winter, M. (1985). Parents as first teachers: when parents are taught to teach, the first three years of a child's life become an invaluable learning time. *Principal, 64*(5), (pp. 22–24).

Withers, G., & Russell, J. (2001). *Educating for Resilience. Prevention and intervention strategies for young people at risk.* Melbourne, Vic: Australian Council for Educational Research.

Wolfensberger, W. (1983). Social role valorisation: A proposed new term for the principle of normalisation. *Mental Retardation, 216*, (pp. 234–239).

Work and Family Unit. (1992). *Commonwealth Strategy for implementing International Labour Organisation (ILO) Convention No 156, Workers with Family Responsibilities*. (Brochure). Canberra, ACT: Department of Industrial relations.

World Socialist Web Site. (1998). *Poverty in Australia: some indicators,* [paper available at http://wsws.org/news/1998/po2-a8.shtml . 2 pages]. World Socialist Web Site [2001, 6 March].

Worthington, A., & Dollery, B. (2000). Can Australian local government play a meaningful role in the development of social capital in disadvantaged rural communities? *Australian Journal of social Issues, 35*(4), (p. 349).

Yoos, H., Kitzman, H., & Cole, R. (1999). Family routines and the feeding process. In D. Kessler & P. Dawson (Eds.), *Failure to thrive and pediatric undernutrition: a transdisciplinary approach* (pp. 375–384). Baltimore, MD: Paul H Brookes.

Young, M. (1995*). Investing in young children*. World Bank Discussion Paper Number 275. Washington DC: The World Bank.

Zeitlin, S., & Williamson, G. (1994). *Coping in young children*. Baltimore, MA: Paul H Brookes.

Zigler, E., & Muenchow, S. (1992). *Head Start: the inside story of America's most successful educational experiment*. New York: Basic Books.

Zimiles, H. (1993). The adoration of "Hard Data": a case study of data fetishism in the evaluation of infant day care. *Early Childhood Research Quarterly, 8*(3), (pp. 369–385).

Zimmerman, S. (1988). *Understanding family policy. Theoretical approaches*. Newbury Park, CA: Sage.

Zubrick, S., Silburn, S., Garton, A., Burton, P., Dalby, R., Carlton, J., shepherd, C., & Lawrence, D. (1995). *Western Australian Child Health Survey: developing health and well-being in the nineties*. Perth, WA: Australian Bureau of Statistics and the Institute for Child Health Research.

Zubrick, S., Silburn, S., Gurrin, L., Teoh, H., Shepherd, C., Carlton, J., & Lawrence, D. (1997). *Western Australian Child Health Survey: education, health and competence*. Perth, WA: Australian Bureau of Statistics and the TVW Institute for Child Health Research.

Zubrick, S., Williams, A., Silburn, S., & Vimpani, G. (2000). *Indicators of social and family functioning*. Canberra, ACT: Department of Family and Community Services

Zuckerman, B., & Brazelton, B. (1994). Strategies for a family-supportive child health care system. In S. Kagan & B. Weissbourd (Eds.), *Putting families first. America's family support movement and the challenge of change*. (pp. 73–92). San Francisco: Jossey-Bass Publishers.

234672LV00002B/3/P

9 781863 351058